Plato and Sex

For Ilya and Felix, because some of us do prefer our human children

Plato and Sex

Stella Sandford

polity

First published in 2010 by Polity Press

Polity Press
65 Bridge Street
Cambridge CB2 1UR, UK

Polity Press
350 Main Street
Malden, MA 02148, USA

ISBN-13: 978-0-7456-2640-6 (hardback)
ISBN-13: 978-0-7456-2641-3 (paperback)

A catalogue record for this book is available from the British Library.

Typeset in 10.5 on 12 pt Palatino
by Toppan Best-set Premedia Limited
Printed and bound in Great Britain by MPG Books Group Limited, Bodmin, Cornwall

The publisher has used its best endeavours to ensure that the URLs for external websites referred to in this book are correct and active at the time of going to press. However, the publisher has no responsibility for the websites and can make no guarantee that a site will remain live or that the content is or will remain appropriate.

For further information on Polity, visit our website: www.politybooks.com

Contents

Acknowledgements

In the long gestation of this book I have benefited from the comments, criticisms and suggestions of colleagues (especially Éric Alliez, Christian Kerslake, Stewart Martin and Peter Osborne) at the Centre for Research in Modern European Philosophy staff seminar at Middlesex University, and of participants at the research seminars and philosophy societies at various universities, notably the Center for Psychoanalysis and Philosophical Anthropology at Radboud University, Nijmegen, and the Philosophy Departments at Middlesex University, the universities of Dundee, Reading, Sussex, Lancaster, Hertfordshire and South Stockholm University College. For productive conversations (in person and in print), inspiring ideas and critical debates I would like to thank, in particular, Kathleen Lennon, Peter Osborne and Alison Stone, as well as the two anonymous readers of the manuscript.

An earlier and shorter version of Chapter 1, 'Thinking Sex Politically: Rethinking "Sex" in Plato's *Republic*', was published in *South Atlantic Quarterly*, Vol. 104, No. 4, Fall 2005 (special edition on Thinking Politically, edited by Alberto Moreiras). Material from Chapter 2 was published, with a different emphasis, as 'The Origins and Ends of "Sex" ', in Ray Brassier and Christian Kerslake, eds., *Origins and Ends of the Mind: Philosophical Essays on Psychoanalysis*, University of Leuven Press, Leuven, 2007. Chapter 3 was developed out of 'Sexually Ambiguous: Erōs and Sexuality in Plato and Freud', *Angelaki* Special Issue, 'Encounters with Ancient Thought', ed. John Sellars, Vol. 11, No. 3, 2006, and Chapter 4 from ' "All Human Beings are Pregnant" ': The Bisexual Imaginary in Plato's *Sympo-*

sium', *Radical Philosophy* 150, July/August 2008. The chapters of the present book will, I hope, be read as the final and overriding versions of these earlier attempts.

The advantage of taking a long time to complete a book (this one twice very happily interrupted by the birth of a child) is the opportunity afforded for thought to develop, against the precipitate demands of intellectual industrial production. Even so, I am grateful to a series of editors at the Polity Press, but especially the last, Emma Hutchinson, for their patience and continued support over several years.

Finally, for everything, I thank Peter.

Stella Sandford
London, May 2010

Introduction

Plato *and* sex? What is the nature of this relation? As this book aims to show, it is neither obvious nor simple, despite the brevity and apparently descriptive form of my title. This is not a book about Plato's views on sex or sex 'in' Plato. The 'and' in the title – *Plato and Sex* – is as much disjunctive as conjunctive. Rather, the book stages what I hope is a productive confrontation between aspects of Plato's philosophy and issues in the contemporary philosophy of sex and gender, via discussions of the modern reception of the relevant aspects of Plato's dialogues in philosophy (especially feminist philosophy) and feminist and psychoanalytical theory, and the conceptual presuppositions in that reception. The result, I hope, is new interpretations of particular passages in the dialogues and, simultaneously, a contribution to the contemporary philosophical debate on sex.

Here 'sex' means sex difference – the difference between the sexes (male and female) – in distinction from 'gender' (a category describing historical, cultural and institutional demands or norms), from 'sexual difference' (a specifically psychoanalytical concept, referring to subject positions within the symbolic order), from 'sexuality' (sexual desire and/or its orientation) and from sexual intercourse. It is important to make these *conceptual* distinctions, even if, ultimately, we do not hold that the different concepts name discrete things or phenomena, and even if it is obvious that they form a conceptual constellation in which they depend on each other. For it is important to be able to say what is specific to the *concept* of sex even if, ultimately, we are not able to identify any decisive empirical referent for it. Of course making these conceptual distinctions has its consequences. In particular, distinguishing sex from gender predisposes us to think of sex as a biological phenomenon, a natural given, in opposition to the cultural construction of gender norms. The analytical priority of the category of gender in Anglophone feminist theory from the late 1960s left sex, understood in that way, temporarily untheorized, and the critique of the sex/gender distinction, which put sex back in the spotlight, was perhaps the most important development in late twentieth-century feminist theory.

Although the category of sex was the object of certain French feminist discourses from the 1970s – notably in the work of Christine Delphy and Monique Wittig – it was not until the 1990s, subsequent to the publication of Judith Butler's *Gender Trouble* (1990) that Anglophone feminist theory really sat up and took notice of *sex*, although the question of *sexual difference*, inspired largely by the work of Luce Irigaray, was prominent, especially in 'continental' feminist philosophy. This is a description of the dominant trajectories in feminist theory, and of course there are exceptions to them. Simone de Beauvoir, the most influential figure in the history of feminist theory, did not work with a sex/gender distinction and may easily be read as the first critical theorist of sex.[1] Sex was the central analytical category of Shulamith Firestone's *The Dialectic of Sex: The Case for Feminist Revolution*, which was more influential in the 1970s than its current status in feminist theory might suggest; one of its main aims was to 'attack sex distinctions themselves'.[2] And of course some Anglophone feminists were already focusing on sex before Butler's intervention, especially those influenced by Wittig and Delphy. However, since the 1990s, the far-reaching influence of Butler's work means that the question of the ontological status of sex has become one of the most fundamental issues in contemporary feminist theory. Is there such a thing as 'sex'? If so, what kind of a thing is sex? Are sexes natural-biological kinds, or political categories or medico-legal or cultural constructions?[3]

As will become obvious to readers of this book, my own theoretical sympathies are with those for whom 'sex' is a problematic object, not a natural given. But this does not mean, as it does for some, that 'sex' is subsumed under the category of 'gender'. The now classic argument to this effect in Butler's *Gender Trouble* is that categories such as 'sex' and 'gender' are productions of specific formations of power that 'create the effect of the natural, the original, and the inevitable'.[4] More specifically, the production of 'sex' as the idea of a 'natural', prediscursive origin is an effect of the cultural apparatus of gender, such that 'sex' is, effectively, to be thought under the sign of gender: 'If the immutable character of sex is contested, perhaps this construct called "sex" is as culturally constructed as gender; indeed, perhaps it was always already gender, with the consequence that the distinction between sex and gender turns out to be no distinction at all.'[5] Some years prior to this Suzanne Kessler and Wendy McKenna argued, in Kessler's words, 'that "gender" should be used exclusively to refer to anything related to the categories "female" and "male", replacing the term "sex", which would be restricted to reproductive and "love-making" activities'. The rationale for this was that it 'would emphasize the socially constructed, overlapping nature of all category distinctions, even the biological ones'.[6] Kessler and McKenna's and Butler's position would seem to be that to continue to speak of sex is to collude in what Butler called 'the fictive construction of "sex" ' as the natural foundation of gender and of the stable identity of the sexed subject itself. Gender, on the other hand, in many ways a more complicated category, could be understood, at least for Butler, as the site of possible resistance to or transformation of the 'gendered norms of cultural intelligibility by which persons are defined'.[7]

If I continue to speak of sex and to insist in this context on the *conceptual* distinction between sex and gender (amongst other things), this is not for the purposes of distinguishing between any allegedly empirically determined entities or actually existing phenomena that are the referents of the concepts. It is because it is necessary to make the distinction in order to specify the peculiarity of the concept of sex – of the way in which this concept has functioned and continues to function in various texts and in the everyday worlds of men, women and children. This is not an anti-Butlerian point; far from it. It has Butler's argument in *Gender Trouble* as its condition of existence.

So what is the specificity of the concept of sex? This is not, first of all, a question about the ontology of sex – it does not ask what sex is, or whether it is, or what kind of a thing it is. It asks how 'sex' actually functions as a meaningful element in discourses of many different kinds, what 'sex' actually *means* when it is employed, as if unproblematically, in everyday speech and more formal contexts. Of course 'sex', like any other concept, has a history, and that history is complicated in being multi-lingual; so much so that significant issues arise in translation. The history of the concept of sex is as yet unwritten, but this book works with the presumption that we might speak very broadly of the 'modern' concept of sex to characterize the popular, hegemonic view that operates today, as a way of acknowledging that the presumptions of, say, the past 200 years may not have been shared by the ancient world.[8]

One might expect that 'sex' would function differently in different discourses, but the peculiar thing is that by and large it does not. The peculiar functioning of the concept of sex is such that it tends to figure in the same form in both popular discourses and – the relevant arena here – philosophical texts. I refer to the modern, popular, hegemonic concept of sex as the modern 'natural-biological' concept of sex because of the presumptions that constitute it, not to commit it to a particular disciplinary-scientific origin or ontological status. According to the presumptions that constitute the modern natural-biological concept of sex there simply *is* sex duality (the exclusive division between male and female) and that duality is naturally determined.[9] As such, its referent is presumed to be a natural and not a historical object, and the possibility that the concept is, precisely, modern, is hidden. I contend that this concept has no purely descriptive function in relation to human being, although the presumption in its use is, precisely, that it does. The main reason for thinking this is that the constitutive and exclusive duality of its terms – 'male' and 'female' – is empirically inadequate to the phenomena that it would allegedly encompass without remainder, meaning that its duality is in fact normative and prescriptive. This is as true of the uncontentiously sexed infant who allegedly embodies one term of the sex duality as it is of the intersexed infant who will be made to conform to one. Further, the modern natural-biological concept of sex functions in relation to human being to refer to a natural foundation for existence, such that it offers itself as a naturalistic explanation for some aspects – sometimes even *all* aspects – of human psycho-social existence and behaviour, from the choice of children's play objects, to the choice of sexual objects; from the colours and clothes that toddlers prefer to the life choices and professional capabilities of adults. Thus the modern natural-biological concept of sex functions as something both naturally determined and naturally determining and it is effectively impossible to separate these two aspects. In allegedly describing a natural foundation for human existence the modern natural-biological concept of sex prescribes a duality, the nature of which is taken to be more or less determining of aspects of that existence. This is its specificity in distinction from the concepts of gender and sexuality, for example, which are often conceived as determined by sex.

It is because sex is conceived in this way that it tends to appear as an unproblematized and untheorized referent in philosophical discourse in general, including much feminist philosophical discourse, and in discussions of Plato's dialogues, in particular. This determines the interpretation of certain passages and arguments in Plato's dialogues where the issue of sex seems to arise. What could be less surprising? Not just in the case of the mainstream literature on Plato, which is hardly concerned with sex or gender, but also in the feminist literature, defined by its interest in the latter. What could be less surprising than that feminist philosophers, battling against the presumptive determinism of sex difference, should interpret Book V of the *Republic* in these terms; that, battling against the denegation of all things female or feminine in the history of philosophy, they should read the *Symposium* through the lens of sex?

But this book began with the curious suspicion that, surprisingly, Plato's texts did not yield or support the presumption of the modern, natural-biological concept of sex in their interpretation, precisely where one would most expect them to. It developed into the thesis that certain passages and arguments in Plato's dialogues may be interpreted in such a way, indeed, as to *contest* this conception of sex. This is not the claim that an alternative, perhaps ancient Greek, concept of sex animates Plato's dialogues, nor that the dialogues reveal or even support, speculatively, a theory of sex or of sexual reproduction. (It is not, then, like Thomas Laqueur's claims about the alternative model of sex in the ancient period, which he opposes to the modern account of sex.[10]) It also does not involve the claim that the relevant passages of the dialogues *aim* to do anything that can now be interpreted in terms of the contestation of the modern natural-biological concept of sex – it has nothing to do with Plato's intentions, whatever they may have been. Rather the claim is that certain important passages in these texts do, from the standpoint of the present, nevertheless contest the modern natural-biological concept of sex, understood in the way outlined above, in being recalcitrant to its imposition upon them.

The approach to Plato through which this book attempts to make good this claim needs to be specified in order to understand the nature of the claims in each chapter, and to distinguish it from other approaches. It is perhaps too early to write the history of feminist interpretations of Plato, but it is possible to characterise the broad trends in the literature to this point, some of which parallel the broad trends in the history of feminist philosophy more generally.

First, interpretations from the liberal feminist tradition, with its central concepts of equality and rights, read Plato – principally the *Republic* and, to a lesser extent, the *Laws* – and judge him according to the requirements associated with these concepts. This work – often from political philosophers and theorists in its earliest instances – tends to focus on Plato's explicit mention of women (women's nature, women's defining characteristics, women's capacities and proper role) and those aspects of the dialogues that might reasonably be judged to be of most concern to women (for example, arrangements for the care of the children of the Guardian class in the *Republic*). The title of Gregory Vlastos' famous essay – 'Was Plato a Feminist?' – might seem to sum up the guiding question of this tradition of criticism, but feminist work (notably that of Julia Annas) very quickly went beyond this.[11] Foregoing anachronistic questions about Plato's sexual politics or personal intentions, much of the feminist literature in this tradition focused on the place and nature of the female Guardians in the *Republic* and (what seemingly contradicts this) the instances of sexism or misogyny in his work and attempted to show either how the latter is related to his philosophy as a whole – even to Western philosophy as a whole – or how it is fundamentally unrelated.[12]

This dovetails with the literature from what is sometimes called the 'sexual difference' tradition.[13] This is most famously associated with Luce Irigaray, whose own work on Plato offers interpretations of aspects of the dialogues which span both extremes of the critical feminist compass of this tradition – from the archaeological reconstruction of the suppressed feminine or female in Western thought out of moments in Plato's dialogues, to the coruscating criticism of Plato as the founding philosopher of the (masculine) metaphysics of the same, covering over sexual difference and man's maternal origins.[14] But this tradition also contains an extremely broad range of other positions and theoretical commitments, from Arlene W. Saxonhouse's feminist essentialism to David Halperin's Foucaultianism.

If these are the two most articulated traditions, there are, of course, contributions to the feminist literature that do not fit into either: for example, the more recent, often Derridean, readings claiming to discover theoretical resources for feminism in concepts reappropriated from the dialogues. Mine is also a feminist approach that does not fit into either tradition, but neither is it an attempt to appropriate concepts from Plato. In confronting particular passages in Plato's dialogues from the standpoint of a particular position in the contemporary philosophy of sex and gender the aim is not to read the former through the latter but to create a short circuit without a protective fuse. The aim is not to establish the relation between Plato and 'sex' but to prise it apart, even break it – to relieve the texts of the imposition or presupposition of 'sex' in their modern reception. In this I make no claim to discover their 'original' meaning. It is 'sex', not Plato's philosophy, which has to answer for itself today.

Four of the five chapters in this book focus on a few passages from Plato's *Republic, Symposium* or *Timaeus* where the question of sex seems to arise. After expounding these passages in some detail, each attempts to show how the modern reception of these passages – in both mainstream and feminist philosophical literature and in feminist and psychoanalytical theory – presupposes the modern natural-biological concept of sex in their interpretation, before suggesting alternative interpretations.

Chapter 1 focuses on Socrates' arguments, in Book V of the *Republic*, for the equal education of women in the Guardian class and for their participation in the rule of the polis. In the main interpretations of these passages hitherto, despite their often significantly different conclusions, there is a common presumption that what Socrates must oppose with his arguments is his interlocutors' assumption that sex difference – one's being male or female – determines for which function or job (*ergon*) one is naturally fitted. However, through an analysis of, and a comparison between the functions of, the classical Greek concept of '*genos*' and the modern English concept of 'sex' – the latter often used to translate *genos* in these passages – this chapter argues that, *strictly speaking*, the modern natural-biological concept of sex, understood in the way outlined above, is absent from these passages. It argues that what Socrates must oppose is not the idea that sex difference is determining, but a conception of men and women as different in every aspect of their physical, social and psychical existences, where 'men' and 'women' are constituted ontologically by a set of manly and womanish characteristics, respectively, rather than by their being-male or being-female. Beyond Socrates' arguments in Book V of the *Republic*, the idea that men and women are constituted in this way sheds an interesting light on the prohibition of womanish behaviour for men in ancient Athens, and thus on the arguments to that effect in the *Republic* and *Laws*. In demonstrating the possibility of distinguishing between the conceptual pairs male/female and man/woman in Plato's *Republic*, Chapter 1 endorses the possibility of an alternative ontology of 'men' and 'women' as primarily social and political categories, one that sits uneasily with the professed modern faith in the natural determining role of sex.

Chapter 2 concerns the account of the origin of human beings in Aristophanes' speech in the *Symposium*. That account seems to offer a mythical explanation for the non-mythical fact of sex duality – the derivation of the two sexes from a race of humans originally divided into three – and indeed that is how it is usually interpreted in the philosophical literature, where the question of the status of sex itself is not at issue. This chapter argues, however, that Aristophanes' story is more complicated than this interpretation suggests. Its implicit postulation of the cosmic principle of the division of all things into male and female and its thematization of originary hermaphroditism suggest an interpretation that problematizes, rather than explains, the origin of male and female. The chapter then examines the reception of Aristophanes' myth in the psychoanalytical theories of Freud and Lacan, where sex *is* a central and contested category, to show how they seemed to take on this problematization in their own 'mythic' accounts of sex. In relation to Freud this involves a discussion of his enduring commitment to the theory of anatomical bisexuality and his speculative biological account of the origin of sex inspired by Aristophanes' tale. An interpretation of Lacan's brief references to Aristophanes' speech in the *Symposium* then lead, via a discussion of the conceptual distinction between 'sex' and 'sexual difference' in psychoanalytical theory, to an interpretation of the mythic role of 'sex' in Lacan's theory of sexuation. Finally this chapter asks, in the light of the difficulties posed by even the most 'scientific' use of the concept, whether the modern natural-biological concept of sex can ever escape a mythic function.

Chapter 3 centrally concerns not the modern natural-biological concept of sex but the modern popular conception of *sexuality*, such as it was identified by Freud. It aims to demonstrate the same kind of conceptual imposition in the interpretation of Plato's concept of eros via the modern popular conception of sexuality as in the interpretation of aspects of the *Republic* and *Symposium* via the modern natural-biological concept of sex discussed in the previous two chapters. It begins with Freud's claim that the enlarged concept of sexuality in psychoanalysis coincides with Plato's concept of eros, and with the difficulties inherent in the translation of the Greek '*erōs*' with the vocabulary of 'the sexual' and of 'love'. These difficulties bear directly on a central issue in the interpretation of Socrates' speech in the *Symposium*: is *erōs* a specifically sexual passion or a metaphor for some more general desire or existential force? This chapter investigates both Socrates' account of eros and Freud's psychoanalytical concept of the sexual drive, the latter forged in opposition to what Freud called the (restricted) popular conception of sexuality. Freud's enlarged conception of sexuality, along with the related concept of sublimation, is often mooted, even if only to be dismissed, as a possible interpretative key to Socrates' account of eros in the *Symposium*. However, this chapter tries to show the way in which the persistence of the presumption of the restricted popular concept of sexuality in discussions of Socrates' account continues to determine one particular debate concerning eros in such a way as to prevent an appreciation of what may be its conceptual specificity – namely, its constitutive ambiguity.

Chapter 4 focuses on another intriguing aspect of Socrates' speech in the *Symposium* – the metaphors of pregnancy (specifically male pregnancy) and birth. A survey of the literature, feminist and otherwise, on this topic identifies a common interpretative strategy across widely different and even opposing interpretations of these metaphors in their attempts to separate out what properly belongs to the male from what properly belongs to the female. The chapter argues that this interpretative strategy fails to do justice to the literary specificity and complexity of these images in the *Symposium*, images that work and are constituted precisely by refusing this separation. Instead of presuming sex and the distribution of what is proper to the male and what is proper to the female as the literal ground of the images in the *Symposium*, this chapter investigates instead the possibility that the images can be interpreted as saying something about 'sex' and the distribution of masculine and feminine identifications. Rather than distinguishing between the metaphorical image (the illusion of male pregnancy) and its presumed literal basis (the reality of sex difference), the chapter suggests a reading of the images of pregnancy and birth as aspects of a complex structure of fantasy, in the interpretation of which the opposition reality–illusion is inadequate. In this way the images of pregnancy and birth are interpreted not as the metaphors or fantasies of a man, but in terms of the fantasmatic structure of sexed subjectivization – 'being man' – itself.

The final chapter, Chapter 5, focuses on three passages in the *Timaeus*. In the last of these, almost at the very end of the dialogue, there seems to be an account of the origin of sex difference. This account refers back to two previous passages in which the origin of women and men and the origin of women from men are mentioned. These passages have tended to be dismissed, in modern commentaries on the *Timaeus*, as jest or embarrassing non-philosophical incursions. But to the extent that they have been taken seriously, discussion has focused on two particular issues: according to Timaeus, were men created before women or were men and women created simultaneously? And were there originally sexless human beings? This chapter looks at the difficulties faced by commentators (principally Proclus and the main modern commentators in English) trying to extract a coherent position on sex difference from Timaeus' comments, and shows how this has only been achieved through extremely selective and partial readings. Referring back to the argument of Chapter 1, this chapter then attempts to show how, distinguishing between the conceptual pairs man/woman and male/female, a more complete and coherent reading is possible, a reading in which 'man' and 'woman' are primarily moral categories.

However, much like Timaeus' discourse itself, this chapter then begins again, placing the three passages on men and women in the context of the dialogue as a whole, and in particular in the context of Timaeus' principled insistence that, in every subject, we must begin at the natural beginning and – what sometimes contradicts this demand – his limiting claim that accounts of things must be of the same nature as those things themselves. The remainder of the chapter then shows the impossibility of locating the 'natural beginning' of sex in the *Timaeus*, an impossibility that conforms to the demand that the account of sex reflects the nature of sex itself, and suggests that it is here that the metaphysical meaning and contemporary significance of this aspect of the *Timaeus* is to be found.

Four of the five chapters described above end with a brief indication of the consequences of their arguments for our understanding of the modern natural-biological concept of sex – for what 'sex' might mean for us today. *Plato and Sex* concludes with a Coda in which I attempt (with help from Immanuel Kant) to draw these indications together and to give a philosophical account of the nature of this concept.

1

Sex and Genos (Republic)

When Socrates said, well over 2,000 years ago, in Book V of the *Republic*, that he and his interlocutors were about to rouse 'a swarm of arguments' (450b), he was certainly not mistaken, although the angry buzzing did not reach its height until the second half of the twentieth century. The provocation comes in the form of three well-known proposals concerning the Guardian class of the *Republic*: the holding of wives and children in common, the equal education of men and women, and the participation of women in all aspects of governance. Although the history of written responses to these proposals begins with Aristotle, it is the debates within the context of second-wave feminism, from the 1970s onwards, that will be the focus here. This chapter critically investigates what I identify as a basic shared assumption in the different positions within these debates and – moving away from this assumption – offers a new interpretation of the relevant sections of the *Republic*, an interpretation that suggests why these already heavily commented passages claim our attention today.

Although there has been some sympathy for Socrates' first proposal, to the extent that it prefigures proposals for the abolition of the bourgeois family,[1] the idea that women should be awarded as sexual prizes to men, denied the freedom of choice of sexual partner, mated like animals and then denied access to their off-spring has, not surprisingly, found little support among feminists. Disagreements in the feminist literature have therefore largely centred on the second and third proposals. As the second (a radical transformation of education in its broadest sense of upbringing and acculturation) is the condition of possibility of the third (participation in governance) these two proposals are part of a single programme of social and political transformation which, *mutatis mutandis*, is recognizable in the actual transformations that have taken place since the nineteenth century – regional, national and continental variations notwithstanding.

Whatever Plato's[2] intentions in its initial presentation, various forms of one crucial aspect of his main argument in favour of these proposals have been central, either implicitly or explicitly, to both liberal and socialist feminism. Concomitantly, as feminists of a different theoretical and political persuasion have criticized aspects of these liberal and socialist variants, so too have they criticized the assumptions animating Plato's argument.

Before investigating this argument, and the fundamental presupposition, hitherto, of all the feminist responses, one might summarize their popular forms as follows. According to Socrates in Plato's *Republic*, the difference between the sexes (which is not, in itself, denied) is not such that men or women, *qua* men or *qua* women, are suited to any one kind of work or any distinct social or cultural existence. The difference between the sexes is reduced to the different roles of men and women in reproduction and is said to be *irrelevant* to their capacities for work. Plato's generalized sexism notwithstanding – his apparent belief that men are superior to women in all things – the argument seems to support the view that it is the different treatment and cultural expectations of boys and girls and men and women that produce many of the differences in capacity and character that people are wont to ascribe, erroneously, to the 'natural' differences between the sexes.

Those in agreement with a modern version of one crucial part of Plato's argument – that culture, not nature, is the relevant arena here – have nevertheless disagreed profoundly in their interpretations of Plato's position and its wider implications. For some, Plato anticipates the chief demands and assumptions of modern feminism; for others, the underpinnings and intention of his argument are either non- or anti-feminist. These interpretations fall into three main groups. The first, broadly liberal position, arguing for Plato's proto-feminist credentials, draws its strength from the favourable comparison of Plato's proposals with the actual legal and social position of women in classical Athens, and from the obvious parallels between Plato's emphasis on education and access to public and political life and the same emphasis in the history of feminism.[3] The second position is also broadly liberal but interprets Plato as a non- or anti-feminist, pointing to the lack of or hostility to other concepts central to the history of feminism (notably those of rights, equality and happiness), to the excessively utilitarian impetus of Plato's argument, and to the many passages elsewhere in the *Republic* and in other dialogues in which women are denigrated, pronounced inferior or held in contempt.[4] For the third position, associated with the so-called 'feminism of difference' largely inspired by Luce Iriga- ray, Plato merely demonstrates (according to some, even inaugu- rates) a disregard for sexual difference that is not only inimical to, but destroys the foundations of, feminism in the 'de-sexing' of women and an overemphasis on equality according to a masculine ideal.[5] Support for this interpretation can be drawn from Plato's denial of any specifically feminine excellence or capacity, from the masculine, military emphasis of the proposed education for women, and its relation to the profoundly horrible treatment of motherhood and nurture in the first proposal.

What is at stake in these different and often opposed interpreta- tions and arguments? There is no single thing at stake in them all; rather, it is because different things are at stake for different readers that there are different interpretations. They all, however, share a common assumption, which I shall contest in what follows: namely, the assumption of the role of a modern concept of 'sex'. I use the term 'modern' in a very broad sense here, in distinction from the 'ancient'. Looking again at the famous proposals in the *Republic* the main claim in this chapter is that this modern concept of 'sex', as the general term for the categories of male and female which ground the categories of men and women ontologically, plays no role in the relevant arguments concerning women in Plato's *Republic*. Reading the *Republic* from the standpoint of this claim the familiar passages in Book V take on a different hue and invite a new interpretation. At the same time the peculiarity of the function of this modern concept of sex is thrown into relief. In what follows, then, I shall first examine Plato's main argument for the second and third proposals from the standpoint of some of the most familiar English translations and feminist responses. I shall then attempt to justify the claim that the modern concept of sex pre- sumed in these translations and responses is, strictly speaking, absent from the *Republic*, re-examining the argument and some related passages from the *Laws* accordingly. Finally, I shall consider some of the broader implications of this claim.

The relevance of sex

The most contentious of Plato's proposals first surfaces explicitly in
Book IV. If, Socrates says, the Guardians have been properly raised
and educated, they will be easily able to see or discover for themselves the instructions given by the pretend founders of the city
(Socrates and company, 379a) – both those instructions which have
already been discussed and those which are 'now' (in Book IV)
passed over or omitted, 'such as the possession of women, mar-
riage, and the production of children, all of which ought so far as
possible to be dealt with on the proverbial basis of "all things in
common between friends" '.[6] When challenged to justify and explain
these arrangements Socrates is more than usually diffident, in an
unusually convincing way, although his reticence should not gull
us into thinking that this was the first time such arrangements had
been discussed or recommended by Athenian gentlemen. There
were historical precedents for such arrangements, if Herodotus is
to be believed.[7]

In broaching the justification and explanation for these arrangements, however, the second proposal – for the equal education of
men and women in the Guardian class – arises and takes prece-
dence for a while. The issue, according to Socrates, is that of the
possession (*ktēsis*) and use (*chreia*) of women and children by men
with the origin (*phusi*) and education (*paideutheisin*) (451c1–3)
described earlier in the dialogue. Most importantly, in this context,
this refers back to the principle that each person should do the one
job for which they are most naturally suited and to the division of
superior and inferior natures, according to the myth of metals, into
the three categories of gold, silver and brass. The men in question,
Socrates reminds us, were previously (375a) likened to watchdogs.
Without contradicting what has already been agreed in the dialogue, then, the birth (*genesin*) and upbringing or rearing (*trophēn*)
(451d1) of these same men (so the symmetry of the text implies)
must now be described.

If here the discussion seems to switch topic, moving on to the
question of the education of the women who will be held in common,
and away from the men who will so hold them, the discontinuity
is only apparent, for the question of the birth and upbringing of
these men is inseparable from the question of who bears them
and brings them up.[8] Socrates' argument begins with actual
watchdogs:

'Ought female watchdogs [*tas thēleias tōn phulakōn kunōn*] to perform
the same guard-duties as male [*hoi arrenes*], and watch and hunt and
so on with them? Or ought they to stay at home on the grounds that
the bearing and rearing [*tokon te kai trophēn*] of their puppies inca-
pacitates them from other duties, so that the whole burden of the
care of the flock falls on the males?' 'They should share all duties,
though we should treat the females as the weaker and the males as
the stronger [*hōs asthenesterais chrōmetha, tois de hōs ischuroterois*].'
'And can you use any animal for the same purpose as another', I
asked, 'unless you bring it up and train it in the same way?' 'No.' 'So
if we are going to use men and women for the same purposes, we
must teach them the same things?' 'Yes.' 'We educated the men both
physically and mentally.' 'Yes.' 'We shall have to train the women
also, then, in both kinds of skill, and train them for war as well, and
treat them in the same way as the men.' (451d–452a)

For Socrates, this argument establishes that men and women should
receive the same education *if* they are to be used for the same purposes, but it does not establish that they can and should be so used.
The first question, whether the proposal is possible (*dunata*) (452e),
is answered some pages later in terms of its being not contrary to
nature (*mē para phusin*) (456b7); indeed 'nature' (*phusis*), in a slightly
different sense, is the central concept in the argument. If the issue
is thus whether Socrates' proposals are or are not contrary to nature,
objections based on the idea that they are contrary to *convention* or
law can be ruled out of court; the first to go is the objection (conservative, not philosophical) that the proposal will, at first, seem
ridiculous 'by present standards' (*en tō parestōti*) (452b).

It is of course easy enough to show, as Socrates does in reply to
the anticipated ridicule, that whether or not people exercise naked
or clad in the gymnasium is a matter of convention. The point of
this example, however, is to establish that both the current arrangements for the possession and use of women and children and those
proposed by Socrates are, as arrangements, wholly matters of convention. Although this point is arguably more radical than the
proposal of any particular set of arrangements, it passes Socrates'
interlocutors by. Polemarchus and Adeimantus draw Socrates back
into a justification of his apparently off-hand remark about the
desirability of one particular set of arrangements – the holding of
women and children in common – but nobody notices, in the
prelude to this justification, the claim that this most important
of issues is about '*customs* which are fair and good and just [*kalōn
te kai agathōn kai dikaiōn nomimōn peri*]' (451a8–9).[9] If, as Socrates'

argument suggests, what is possible in social arrangements is coextensive with what is not contrary to nature (*mē para phusin*), no one set of possible arrangements could have an exclusive claim to be 'natural' (*kata phusin*, in accordance with nature), ruling out other possible sets of arrangements as unnatural, though anything that was impossible would be unnatural. This may seem to be a sophistical trick, based on the substitution in the argument of what is not contrary to nature for what is possible, but the connection in Greek between *phusis* and *dunamis* (power, giving us *dunatos*, possible, within one's power) implicitly carries the argument conceptually.[10] Accordingly, if Socrates can show that his proposed arrangements are possible, it cannot successfully be objected that they are contrary to nature – although this is precisely the form that the major objection to them will take.

Because of the limitations of the guard-dog analogy, Socrates is aware that most of the work in the argument is still to be done, a point that Aristotle's surprisingly literal objection ('it is absurd to argue, from the analogy of animals, that men and women should follow the same pursuits, for animals have not to manage a household'[11]) seemingly fails to acknowledge. According to Socrates:

> The first thing we have to agree on, then, is whether these proposals are feasible [*dunata*] or not. For, whether it's asked in joke or in earnest, we must allow people to ask the question, Is the female of the human species naturally capable of taking part in all the occupations of the male [*poteron dunatē phusis hē anthrōpinē hē thēleia tē tou arrenos genous koinōnēsai eis hapanta ta erga*], or in none, or in some only? And if in some, is military service one of them? (452e5–453a3)

The subject of the question is the grammatically feminine noun 'nature' (*phusis*) qualified with the appropriate forms of the adjectives *anthrōpinos*, 'human', and *thēlus*, 'female'; Shorey's 'female human nature' is thus the more literal translation.[12] This is an important point, and not simply linguistic pedantry, as Plato's phrase brings to the argument, as if it is a position already established, that there is a human nature with male and female variants, and not two quite distinct natures, male and female.[13] The 'occupations of the male' are, more specifically, the occupations of the male 'race' or 'kind' (*tou arrenous genous*). As the question is introduced with the interrogative particle *ara* a negative answer is expected. The implication, then, is that the capability of the female is 'in question', in the sense of 'in doubt'.[14] Accordingly, Socrates formulates a serious objection to his own proposals, on behalf of the doubters, by referring back to the previously agreed-upon principle that 'each man was naturally [*kata phusin*] fitted for a particular job of his own':

> 'Well', he [the doubter] will continue, 'isn't there a very great natural difference between men and women [*estin oun hopōs ou pampolu diapherei gunē andros tēn phusin*]?' And when we admit that too, he will ask us whether we ought not to give them different roles to match these natural differences [*oukoun allo kai ergon hekaterō prosēkei prostattein to kata tēn hautou phusin*]. When we say yes, he will ask, 'Then aren't you making a mistake and contradicting yourselves, when you go on to say that men and women should follow the same occupations, in spite of the great natural difference between them [*pleiston kechōrismenēn phusin echontas*]?' (453b7–c5)

More succinctly: 'We admit that different natures ought to have different kinds of occupation, and that men and women have different natures; and yet we go on to maintain that these admittedly different natures ought to follow the same occupations' (453e2–5).

Socrates' answer to this objection, which aims to clear away the appearance of internal inconsistency, constitutes the main argument for both the second and the third proposals. It is the objection, he says, that is faulty, in not being able to distinguish between merely verbal oppositions and more important 'distinctions in kind' (*mē dunasthai kat' eidē diairoumenoi*) (454a4–5), and in not considering 'what kind [*eidos*] of sameness or difference of nature we mean, and what our intention was when we laid down the principle that different natures should have different jobs, similar natures similar jobs' (454b6–9). If this is not considered, the same principle that 'different natures should have different jobs', coupled with the agreement that the bald and the long-haired have opposite natures, would lead to the conclusion that we should 'allow bald men to be cobblers and forbid long-haired men to be, or vice versa' (454c). This is a clever, and not a trivial, example. It works by suggesting both that the difference between bald and long-haired men is analogous to the difference between men and women, and that it is not. It suggests, first, that the difference between bald and long-haired men is inconsequential in relation to their professional capacities, and that the difference between men and women is a difference of the same calibre. Simultaneously, given its immediate context, it pre-empts the objection that the first suggestion is based on an illegitimate comparison between sorts of differences (the objection

that the difference between the bald and the long-haired is not the
same kind of difference as that between a man and a woman) as
the whole point of the example is allegedly to highlight the importance of drawing distinctions between kinds of differences, or differences in kind. (And as we shall see later, there might be even
more to it than this.)

The absurd conclusion that jobs might be allocated differentially
to bald and long-haired men can only arise, according to Socrates,
because it applies the principle that different natures should have
different jobs without understanding its nuances:

> 'we never meant [Socrates says] that natures are the same or different
> in an unqualified sense [*ou pantōs tēn autēn kai tēn heteran phusin eti-
> themetha*], but only with reference to the kind of sameness or differ-
> ence which is relevant to various employments. For instance, we
> should regard a man and a woman with medical ability as having
> the same nature [*hoion iatrikon men kai iatrikēn tēn psuchēn ontas tēn
> autēn phusin echein elegomen*]. Do you agree?' 'Yes.' 'But a doctor and
> a carpenter [*iatrikon de kai tektonikon*] we should reckon as having
> different natures.' 'Yes, entirely.' 'Then if men or women as a sex [*to
> tōn andrōn kai to tōn gunaikōn genos*] appear to be qualified for different
> skills or occupations', I said, 'we shall assign these to each accord-
> ingly; but if the only difference apparent between them is that the
> female [*to thēlu*] bears and the male [*to arren*] begets we shall not
> admit that this is a difference relevant for our purpose, but shall still
> maintain that our male and female Guardians [*tous te phulakas hēmin
> kai tas gunaikas*] ought to follow the same occupations.' (454c8–e4)

The argument of this passage is extremely condensed. If it is to
work without reneging on the agreement that men and women
have different natures, it must imply that the sense in which men
and women have different natures is yet to be determined. Granted
that there is, indeed, 'a very great natural difference between men
and women', in what, precisely, does that difference consist, and to
what and in what way is that difference relevant?

Socrates' first point is that 'a man and a woman with medical
ability have the same nature [*hoion iatrikon men kai iatrikēn tēn psuchēn
ontas tēn autēn phusin echein*]'. Here the use of the masculine and
feminine adjectival forms of 'medical' (*iatrikos, iatrikē*) emphasizes,
linguistically, the primary importance of the being-medical of the
soul, its masculine and feminine variants being, secondarily, merely
different instances of this kind. In contrast, in the second point –
that 'a doctor and a carpenter' [*iatrikon kai tektonikon*] have different

natures – the two masculine forms of 'doctor' and 'carpenter' emphasize the difference of the kinds of soul despite the identity of gender. Given the previous agreement on the 'very great' natural difference between men and women, the situation is now that the interlocutors are agreed both that men and women have different natures (as men and women), and that some men and women have the same nature (as doctors, for example). This is not a contradiction in Socrates' argument, but the exposition of an apparent contradiction in the beliefs of his interlocutors, due to the same mistake that Socrates identified earlier: failure to ask in what the difference between the natures of men and women consists and how that difference is relevant. The next step will be to determine just this:

> 'Then if men or women as a sex [*to tōn andrōn kai to tōn gunaikōn genos*] appear to be qualified for different skills or occupations', I said, 'we shall assign these to each accordingly; but if the only difference apparent between them is that the female bears [*to men thēlu tiktein*] and the male begets [*to de arren ocheuein*] we shall not admit that this is a difference relevant for our purpose, but shall maintain that our male and female Guardians [*tous te phulakas hēmin kai tas gunaikas*] ought to follow the same occupations.' (454d6–e5)

Having reached his conclusion in this passage – that the only difference in nature between the female and the male is that the one bears and the other begets – Socrates next asks, in relation to the principle that each nature is fitted for a particular job, whether there are any 'professions or occupations in the structure of society [to which] men and women are differently suited by nature' (455a1–3). That is, what occupation in the structure of society (Lee), or what pursuit concerned with the conduct of a state (Shorey) (*pros tína technēn ē tí epitēdeuma tōn peri poleōs kataskeuēn*), is there that is associated with women's nature, to the exclusion of men? Casting the issue in terms of the administration of the state is clever. It rules out the objection, from Socrates' traditionalist interlocutors, that the rearing of children is women's special task because, as far as they are concerned (one conjectures) this is not part of the administration of the state. From Socrates' point of view, on the other hand, it precisely *is* a part of the administration of the state, but not something for which women have a special natural capacity. Females bear (*tiktein*), Socrates says; he does not say that they rear.

Before the imaginary opponent can suggest for what profession or occupation in the structure of society women are suited by nature, Socrates says that he will show that there is none. If one with a natural capacity (*euphuē*) for something reveals this in learning how to do that thing quickly and in being well co-ordinated mentally and physically (implying, perhaps: if bodily strength is adequate to mental strength), then 'is there any human activity at which men [*to tōn andrōn genos*] aren't far better in all these respects than women?' (455c3–4). Gaining easy consent to this claim, Socrates leaps forward to his conclusion:

> There is therefore no administrative occupation which is peculiar to woman as woman or man as man; natural capacities are similarly distributed in each sex [*all' homoiōs diesparmenai hai phuseis en amphoin toin zōoin*], and it is natural for women to take part in all occupations as well as men, though in all women will be the weaker partners. (455d7–e1)

If all natural capacities are distributed between men and women, some men and women will have the same nature with respect to the qualities necessary for guardianship of the city, although women will be weaker than men here as elsewhere: 'We must therefore pick suitable women to share the life and duties of Guardian with men, since they are capable of it and the natures of men and women are akin [*epeiper eisin hikanai kai xuggeneis autois tēn phusin*]' (456b1–4).

There is obviously a lot wrong with this argument. The assumption of the general superiority of men is unsupported (except by the consent of the characters in the dialogue) and fatuous.[15] It is argumentatively weak (to say the least) since it could just as easily lead to the conclusion that there must be some things that women cannot do or things that are best left to men, and it in no way follows from it that there are no occupations peculiar to man as man – that would need a separate argument. The argument is philosophically and politically objectionable at almost every turn. Because of its weaknesses, its presuppositions and its distance from the kinds of considerations animating the history of feminism, Julia Annas' conclusion is hard to resist:

> Plato has established the undeniable point that while women are different from men in some ways and similar in others, discussion at that level is sterile; the interesting question is whether the undisputed differences matter when we decide whether women should be able to hold certain jobs. This is the crucial point not only for Plato but for any sensible discussion of the topic. But Plato's argument is seriously incomplete.[16]

Although this aspect of the overall discussion pinpoints the issue at the centre of feminist politics, on the basis of the argument itself, 'the proposals made in *Republic* V are irrelevant to the contemporary [feminist] debate'.[17]

Extrapolating from Annas' argument, the 'crucial point' in (liberal and socialist) feminism is that sex difference, which is certainly relevant in procreation, is only illegitimately used to justify women's exclusion from participation in education, administration of the state, governance, and so on. This much, according to Annas and many other feminist readers, Plato was able to see. For some, this insight extends to Plato's ability to see that what women currently are and do is not what women *could be* and *could do* under different, more favourable conditions (principally, with more favourable educational opportunities).[18] Translating Plato's arguments into a modern vocabulary, Janet Farrell Smith describes Plato's 'basic premise' as the claim 'that in the absence of scientific evidence, social and moral assumptions [not sex difference] account for political structuring of sex roles', a claim that 'can be extrapolated to contemporary democratic and egalitarian arguments'.[19]

Given the conservative or reactionary role that appeals to 'sex' tend to play in discussions of the capabilities, characteristics and proper pursuits of men and women, it is not surprising that feminists should emphasize the general irrelevance of the fact (if such it is) of sex difference to professional capability, and to argue that the fact of sex difference does not translate into necessarily determined intellectual or psychic differences.[20] To the extent that readers have found Book V of the *Republic* to contain arguments congenial to feminism it is therefore also not surprising that Plato's position is couched in these terms. Thus Elizabeth V. Spelman, although by no means wholly sympathetic to Plato, explains that Socrates' argument suggests 'that a difference in bodily features is not necessarily a sign of a difference in nature', and that 'people ought to engage in different pursuits only when their differences are relevant to the capacity to carry out the task . . . [H]e was trying to get his companions to see that it is irrational to differentiate between people on the basis of sex if sex is irrelevant to the point at hand.'[21] According to this interpretation, Socrates' argument is pitted against his interlocutors' assumption that sex difference – the fact that women bear and men beget – is the basis of their doubt that women are capable of sharing in men's work (most specifically in governance). As Vlastos says, 'The most radical innovation in Plato's vision of a new society . . . is the reasoned rejection of the age-old dogma,

never previously questioned in Greek prose or verse, that difference
of sex must determine difference of work allocation.'[22] The guard-
dog analogy is then meant to show that as this reproductive function in the female dog is not determining so it is not in the female
human being; the introduction of the difference between bald and
long-haired men functions to highlight the fact that any difference
(but specifically sex difference) will often be irrelevant.

These readings, despite their varying degrees of sympathy for
Plato, agree that the 'crucial point' concerns the irrelevance of sex
difference, the denial of the presumption that sex difference determines what men and women can or cannot and should or should
not do. They therefore share the assumption that a modern category
of 'sex' is somehow operative in, or can be read back into, the arguments in Book V of the *Republic*.

The relevance of *genos*

However, there is a conceptual problem here that most English
translations and interpretations – including the feminist interpretations already discussed – do not merely miss but conceal. This is
the case, moreover, in precisely that passage in which, according to
Annas and others, the crucial point is made, namely:

> 'Then if men or women as a sex [*to tōn andrōn kai to tōn gunaikōn genos*]
> appear to be qualified for different skills or occupations', [Socrates]
> said, 'we shall assign these to each accordingly; but if the only dif-
> ference apparent between them is that the female bears [*to men thēlu
> tiktein*] and the male begets [*to de arren ocheuein*] we shall not admit
> that this is a difference relevant for our purpose, but shall maintain
> that our male and female Guardians [*tous te phulakas hēmin kai tas
> gunaikas*] ought to follow the same occupations.' (454d6–e5)

What is perhaps most interesting about this – the crux of Socrates'
argument – is obscured by the translation of *genos* as 'sex', and by
the use of the English terms 'male' and 'female' in the final line.

In classical Greek there is no distinct word for 'sex'. The word
genos, which is sometimes translated as 'sex', means, primarily,
'race', 'stock', 'kin'; also 'offspring', 'tribe', 'generation', and 'kind'.
For example, in the first five books of the *Republic*, Plato uses the
word *genos* to speak at 368a5 of the 'race' of the sons of Ariston; at
429a1 and 460c7 of the 'class' of the guardians; at 459b5 of the

'breeds' of birds and dogs (*to te tōn ornithōn kai to tōn kunōn genos*); at 470c2 of the Hellenic 'race'; at 473d7–8 of 'the human race'; and at 477c1 of the 'class' of faculties or powers. In the *Sophist* Plato uses *genos* as the word for the five major 'kinds' of *being, rest, motion, same* and *other* in such a way that its meaning is virtually indistinguishable from that of '*eidos*', familiarly translated as 'form' or 'idea'.[23] In an essay concerned with the possibility of translating *genos* as 'race', Rachana Kamtekar notes the variety of kinds of *genē* across Plato's dialogues:

> Examples of *genē* include the elements or principles (*Timaeus*, 48e ff, *Philebus*, 23d ff), the branches of expertise (*Sophist*, 223c ff, *Statesman*, 263e), kinds of perception (*Theaetetus*, 156b) or capacities in general (*Republic*, 477c–d). . . . A *genos* may also be a species (*Protagoras*, 321c), for example, there is the *genos* of the cicada (*Phaedrus*, 259c) . . . or a still more inclusive class, such as the winged *genos* (*Sophist*, 220b) or the *genos* of tame and herd-living creatures (*Statesman*, 266a). Finally, there is the *genos* of gods and that of humans (*Hippias Major*, 289a–c; *Charmides*, 173c).[24]

This Borgesian catalogue includes, of course the *genē* of men and women and those of males and females, and every time Plato's use of *genos* is translated into English as 'sex', the more general 'race' or (better) 'kind' would make equally as much sense. To translate *genos* as 'sex' is therefore to *introduce into* Plato's dialogues a specification of the *kind* of kind that males and females or men and women are, when this specification is not linguistically marked in the texts themselves.[25] As this has significant consequences for the interpretation of *Republic* V it is worth explaining in some detail.

In modern English, 'sex' is an abstract noun of classification referring to 'the sum of the characteristics that distinguish organisms on the basis of their reproductive function', and also to 'either of the two categories, male or female, into which organisms are placed on this basis.'[26] 'Sex' as a conceptually distinct term is aligned with nature itself, in contrast with the conventional attributes of 'gender'. As such, 'sex' functions conceptually (and also allegedly empirically) as the basis for, though it is not identical with, the categories of 'man' and 'woman' (a species-specific version of the adult forms of male and female) and the characteristics of gender. If 'sex' is a general term referring to the two categories of male and female – the category according to which the 'nature' of men and women is ultimately determined – then there is, *strictly speaking*, no concept of sex in Plato's *Republic*. For each time *genos* is used in the *Republic* in relation to men or women or male or female it is attached *to one or the other* in order to specify men or women or male or female as a class in distinction from this or that man or woman or male or female animal. The word is never used – indeed it *cannot* be used – as a singular term to refer to a distinction in kind covering both men and women or male and female (or any other distinction in kind, for that matter). That is, it is *never* used as the general term 'sex' is used in English.[27] The very broad generality of the concept of a *genos*, which may refer indifferently to any content (the *genos* of this, that or the other – it does not matter), is most unlike the very narrow specificity of the concept of sex, which is identical with its limited content. Sex *as a general term* designates what kind of categories 'male' and 'female' are; there is nothing equivalent in classical Greek.[28]

To say that, strictly speaking, there is no concept of sex in the *Republic* is *not* to say that Plato and his contemporaries had no concept of what we now call 'sex' at all, in the sense that they did not distinguish between male and female or understand that both played a role – however misunderstood or mysterious – in the reproduction of the species. Of course they did. Consequently, although the fact that there is no distinct word for 'sex' in classical Greek is important for the claim that there is, strictly speaking, no concept of sex in Plato's *Republic*, the argument is not to be confused with the type of argument used by Bruno Snell in support of his claim that, for example, the early Greeks (and Homer in particular) 'did not, either in their language or in the visual arts, grasp the body as a unit', that their language and consequently their 'mentality' 'made no provision for the body as such'.[29] The presumption behind this, and Snell's similar claims for the early Greek lack of any knowledge of, or interest in, the intellect or the soul in the modern senses, is that 'if they had no word for it, it follows that as far as they were concerned it did not exist'.[30] According to Snell the 'objective truth' of the unity of the body 'does not exist for man until it is seen and known and designated by a word; until, thereby, it has become an object of thought. Of course the Homeric man had a body exactly like the later Greeks, but he did not know it *qua* body, but merely as the sum total of his limbs.'[31] The problem with this argument, as Bernard Williams pointed out, is that whilst it may be true that Homer had no word exactly equivalent to the English word 'decide', for example, this did not mean that he did not have the 'notion'. For, as Williams says, 'he has the idea of coming to a conclusion about what to do later, and doing that thing at that later time because of that conclusion'. Similarly, if Homer had no precise word to cover our concept of 'will' (in the sense of volition), what he did have was rich enough to cover what covers 'will' in English, and it cannot therefore be said that he did not have the 'conception'.[32]

My claim that there is, strictly speaking, no concept of sex in Plato's *Republic* is not the result of a Snellian nominalism, although it does, like Snell's claims, acknowledge that the differences between languages are intriguing and may sometimes be taken to suggest significant and interesting differences in their respective conceptual orderings of the world. (Williams' critique of Snell's nominalism is just, but he downplays the linguistic differences to the extent of depriving them of any interest at all.) To repeat, to say that there is, strictly speaking, no concept of sex in the *Republic* is not to say that the distinction between male and female is absent from it. It is also not a claim about Plato's biological knowledge or commitment to any particular biological theory or the representation of any bio-logical theoretical position in the *Republic*. It is the claim that there is an important conceptual difference between *genos* and sex that must be taken into account when these are the crucial terms in Socrates' argument and in modern interpretations of it. This claim is based on an analysis of and comparison between the two differ-ent concepts (*genos* and sex). The argument is made with reference to the context and function of the word *genos* in Plato's dialogue, in comparison with the function of the modern English 'sex'. Any objection to the claims must therefore be made at the same level. The fact that generations of highly respected classical scholars and philosophers have routinely employed the category of sex in com-mentary on and interpretation of Plato's text does not *demonstrate*, but merely *presumes*, that the same concept is operative there, and it is precisely this presumption that this chapter aims to question. This puts us in a position to say that knowledge of the distinction between male and female – which certainly is evident in the *Republic* and in classical Greek literature quite generally – is *not identical with the modern natural-biological concept of sex*, that the modern concept of sex *means* a lot more than the identification of different types with distinct roles in reproduction.[33]

What, then, are the consequences – philosophical and otherwise – of the translation of *genos* as 'sex'? The specificity of the concept of sex lies not just in its reference to a particular kind of difference in comparison with the generality of the concept of a *genos*. It lies

also in the ontological status afforded this kind of difference in relation to others. What does 'sex' *mean*? 'Sex' means, in the vast major-
ity of modern discourses, the immutable biological basis that
determines one's being as either a man or a woman. 'Sex' operates
as a distinct concept – distinct, for example, from 'gender' or 'sexuality' – with reference to this foundational status and ontological
function.[34] The presumption that constitutes the specificity of the
concept of sex is that sex difference is a foundational difference, that
amongst any given set of differences between a group including
men and women sex difference is, as it were, the *Ur* difference in
the categorization of men and women, a difference beyond or prior
to which one will not find any more significant. However, Plato's
use of *genos* in Book V of the *Republic* not only does *not* warrant this
same presumption in its interpretation, it explicitly argues against
it. The considerable grammatical and semantic differences between
the two terms '*genos*' and 'sex' mean, therefore, that the translation
of the former as the latter effects a conceptual transformation. The
ontologically indifferent relations between the kinds of kinds that
compose the catalogue of *genē* in the *Republic* is displaced by the
translation of *genos* as 'sex', establishing the ontological priority of
the distinction between two types of kinds – male and female –
where no such priority is suggested in the text.

This is most evident in Socrates' main argument concerning the
division of people into groups on the basis of their having different
natures. He shows that the different 'natures' of bald men and long-
haired men do not disqualify them from undertaking the same
occupation in order to underscore the importance of specifying
'what kind of sameness or difference of nature we mean' (454b6–7)
when we say that different natures ought to have different occupations; that is, what kind of sameness or difference 'is relevant to
various employments' (454d1–2). Accordingly,

> 'we should regard a man and a woman with medical ability as
> having the same nature [*hoion iatrikon men kai iatrikēn tēn psuchēn ontas
> tēn autēn phusin echein elegomen*]. Do you agree?' 'Yes.' 'But a doctor
> and a carpenter [*iatrikon de kai tektonikon*] we should reckon as having
> different natures.' 'Yes, entirely.' 'Then [*Oukoun*] if men or women
> as a sex [*to tōn andrōn kai to tōn gunaikōn genos*] appear to be qualified
> for different skills or occupations', I said, 'we shall assign these to
> each accordingly; but if the only difference apparent between them
> is that the female [*to thēlu*] bears and the male [*to arren*] begets we
> shall not admit that this is a difference relevant for our purpose, but
> shall still maintain that our male and female Guardians [*tous te phu-*

lakas hēmin kai tas gunaikas] ought to follow the same occupations.' (454d2–e5)

This is usually interpreted to mean that sex difference, reduced to function in reproduction, is irrelevant to employment, to the extent that it does not dictate that either men or women have any particular aptitudes for any particular kinds of work, and this surely is part of what Socrates means to say. But Socrates' argument also does more than this. In moving through the distinctions between i) bald men and long-haired men, ii) those with the nature of a doctor and those with the nature of a carpenter, and iii) men and women, only the last pair are *explicitly* said to be different *genē* (*to tōn andrōn kai to tōn gunaikōn genos*), but the other classes of people (bald men, long-haired men, doctors, carpenters, males, females) do also, of course, constitute specific *genē* too. This is why Socrates can move argumentatively *from* bald men and long-haired men, doctors and carpenters, *to* men and women, the seemingly inconsequential word '*oukoun*' ('so', 'therefore') making the link. The precise point of Socrates' argument is that, in this instance, the division into the *genē* of carpenters and doctors is more significant than the division into the *genē* of men and women. The implication is that all these *genē* exist on a plane of ontological equivalence, none standing out a priori as more important than any other, but various of them assuming an importance in different contexts. This makes sense in the context of the overarching point in the social-political discourse of the *Republic* which is, of course, that no distinction is more important in the organization of the polis than the division into the three *genē* of philosopher kings (Guardians proper), auxiliaries and the rest.[35] That is, the argument suggests that the divisions between the two *genē* of men and women and of males and females are ontologically equivalent in the discussion of human nature to the division between bald and long-haired men. But this argument is obscured by the translation of *genos* as 'sex' to the extent that the translation cannot but mark out the division into the two *genē* of men and women *as sexes* as a particular kind of *privileged* difference – sex difference – when the argument attempts to secure precisely the opposite conclusion.

It is open for an objector to argue, at this point, that the translation of '*genos*' as 'sex' is inconsequential here, because the dominant interpretations of Socrates' argument, interpretations based on this translation, concur with the downgrading of the importance of sex anyway. That is, even with 'sex' in the mix the ontologically indifferent relations between the *genē* are preserved in the interpretation that sex differences ought not to be privileged *in this instance*, in assigning occupations. But this presumes that Socrates' argument is pitted against a certain view of the determining role of sex in the being of men and women; that is, it presumes the general context of the ontological privilege of the modern concept of sex. Is this presumption warranted?

According to the presumption that a certain view of the role of sex in determining the being of men and women drives the position that Socrates opposes, what is contentious and radical in Socrates' argument is the claim that the fact that females bear and males beget is irrelevant to employment and governance. That is, it is assumed that all parties are agreed that the 'very great natural difference' between men and women – the first real stumbling block to Socrates' proposals – can be boiled down to the difference in their roles in reproduction, the fact that one begets and the other bears, and that Socrates' innovative suggestion is that sex is irrelevant to the matter at hand. But this reduction is precisely what Socrates *introduces into* the discussion, this is his contribution – the possibility that all of the differences between men and women can be reduced to this one difference: that females bear and males beget. The objection, expressing a general opinion, is not that the very great natural difference between men and women is identical with the difference in their reproductive functions – quite the contrary. Socrates' argument only really makes sense when viewed as a reply to a much more far-reaching objection that asserts a difference between men and women *in every aspect of their existences*, an assertion governed by the assumption of a set of 'natural' characteristics peculiar to women, including (as Socrates emphasizes) a generalized inferiority and weakness. It is this nature that Socrates' imagined opponents believe to be incompatible with membership of the *genos* 'ruler', not specifically their reproductive function as females.

Of course, the question of what Plato means by 'nature' (*phusis*), along with its cognate verbs and other parts, is extremely complex. In the ancient Greek context more generally the concept of nature is very pliable. Kenneth Dover points out, in relation to a wide range of sources, the tendency for ancient authors in diverse genres to use the concept opportunistically as their argument or political point demanded it.[36] *Phusis* could be used as an 'enforcement' word, claiming legitimacy for certain laws or customs, or it could be used to name what was recalcitrant to law and custom; it could be both a regulating principle and that which had to be regulated.[37] It could be used to refer to a nature shared by a whole group or to name 'one's own unnegotiable bent'.[38] One could heroically rise above one's nature, or pervert it into wickedness; it is sometimes admirable to conform to it, sometimes ignoble to submit to it. In the *Republic, phusis* plays a prominent role in referring to the nature of each individual man, woman, girl and boy. It is also used to speak of a human nature shared by all, as well as the nature of a Guardian shared by a few. Throughout Plato frequently assumes or states that one's nature is innate, but the emphasis on education is also justified with the idea that, as he says in Book IV, 'maintaining a sound system of education and upbringing you produce [*empoiei*] citizens of good character [*phuseis agathas*]' (424a5–7). The different possible translations of *phusis* as, variously, 'nature', 'constitution', 'character', 'temperament', 'bent', and so on, also demonstrate its semantic breadth.[39]

To the extent that the concept of nature can be pinned down in its philosophical function in the *Republic*, it seems that it determines the *genos* to which one belongs. This being so, what is the 'nature' of a woman? What determines membership of the *genos* 'woman'? Granted that women share a set of characteristics, what is the presumed basis of this set of characteristics peculiar to women? With the ready availability of the modern concept of sex the answer is easy: the basis of the characteristics peculiar to women is their sex, their being-female. Their nature as women is determined by their sex. But if the modern concept of sex is not presumed then it is possible that what women *are* as a *genos* is constituted by the *totality* of this set of characteristics itself. Without the presumption of the modern category of sex to carry the explanatory burden, it is possible that the 'nature' of women is not attributable, ultimately, to a singular sexual 'essence', in the modern sense, but is composed of a unified multiplicity of behavioural and other characteristics, the totality of which bears the ontological weight.

This is not just the claim (common to all of the feminist interpretations discussed above) that social and political conditions, rather than differences in capability emanating from the natural fact of sex, determine in any given culture what women can and cannot *do*. It is to suggest the possibility that the set of womanish characteristics and attributes are the ontological basis of what a woman *is*, that they – and not reference to a modern concept of sex – define what it is to *be* a woman in the strong sense.

As has often been pointed out, Plato's dialogues are littered with casual references to women determined by this set of (wholly negative) characteristics and are historically typical in that respect. To the extent that this is also presupposed as the background to the *Republic*, it is what Socrates tries to put into question. What Socrates (unlike modern feminists) must oppose in the *Republic* is thus not the presumption of the determining role of sex difference, but the presumption that women as a race (*genos*) are different – indeed opposite – to men *in every respect, in every aspect* of their 'nature'. Accordingly, Socrates' contentious move in the relevant passages in the *Republic* is *not* the claim that the different roles of the male and the female in reproduction are irrelevant to the matter at hand. It is the *reduction of* 'the very great natural difference between men and women' *to* the distinction between male and female, which reduces to the fact that one begets and the other bears. Philosophically, that is, Socrates' contentious move is the definition of the nature of men and women, for the purposes of the argument, in terms of being-female and being-male, the *substitution of* different roles in reproduction *for* the 'very great natural difference'.[40]

In making this reduction Socrates' argument exploits a consequence of the generality of the concept of *genos*, a possibility that is closed off when the concept of sex, and all that it entails, is introduced into the argument. That is, Socrates' argument exploits the possibility of distinguishing between the conceptual pairs of men and women and males and females as different *genē* amongst which there is no ontologically privileged pair. Having drawn the distinction between the conceptual pairs of men and women and males and females the question arises: what is the relation between these conceptual pairs? The modern concept of sex answers this question for us because of the ontological presumption that it carries within it: male and female are the determining ontological bases for the being of men and women. Sex makes a man a man and a woman a woman. But if, strictly speaking, there is no concept of sex in the *Republic*, the relation between male and female and man and woman should not be presumed to be the same, and there is reason to interpret the arguments in Book V without presuming that 'sex' underpins the presumptions there on the nature or being of men and women.

The presumption of the modern concept of sex is that sex is a baseline supporting and regulating the characteristics of men and women. Accordingly, when Socrates moves from 'the very great natural difference between men and women' to the reproductive categories of 'male' and 'female' it is a descent to the bottom line, a movement downwards on a vertical plane. On this presumption the move to male and female is the distillation of the essence of men and women. However, without the presumption of the modern category of sex, the move from 'man' and 'woman' to 'male' and 'female' can be seen as a shift on a horizontal plane, to a different pair of *genē*, not foundational descriptions – two more *genē* in a general economy of the ontological equivalence of *genē*. Without the presumption of the foundational category of sex, 'man' and 'woman' and 'male' and 'female' are different groups or kinds across which the distinction of conditioned/conditioning, dependent/foundational is not distributed. Socrates substitutes the *genē* of males and females for the *genē* of men and women, which is precisely what Aristotle objected to. Substituting function in reproduction for the social and political being of men and women, Socrates moves from a discussion of differences that would be seen as specifically human to a discussion of a difference that is common to all animals (his use of the verb *ocheuein* for the male role in reproduction emphasizes this). Aristotle objects to this reduction of men and women to their being-male and being-female precisely because these latter *cannot* be seen to determine one aspect of their social existences (broadly speaking, the division of labour) that for him is crucial to the definition of the existences of men and women.

In an essay on the relation between Aristotle's biological and political theory Chloë Taylor Merleau has argued something very similar to this. In the *Politics*, Taylor Merleau argues, Aristotle ascribes great importance to the differences between men and women in terms of social functions and characteristics, 'what are now referred to as "genders" '. In his scientific treatises, on the other hand, the distinctions between what we now call the sexes 'are very slight and often precarious'.[41] Not only, according to Taylor Merleau, is there no biological justification for gender in Aristotle, but gender, 'or a gendered division of labour, demands or is used to explain the existence of male and female bodies . . . In explaining sex difference, therefore, gender serves as necessitating cause and sex as effect.'[42] Drawing on Thomas Laqueur's argument for the operation of the 'one-sex' model in classical antiquity (and beyond), Taylor Merleau emphasizes the 'transitivity' of male and female sexual substances in Aristotle's biology, and his apparent belief that 'the sexes are merely two variations on a theme, or two stages of development upon a continuum towards human perfection'. For Aristotle, the semen and the menstrual blood of humans, 'along with breast milk and body hair (signs of sex difference to moderns), are merely blood concocted to different degrees and released in different forms. Hence if the female were a bit warmer, she would produce semen, whereas if the male ejaculates under-concocted semen, it will be bloody like catamenia.'[43] Convinced of the naturalness of the social and political difference in function between men and women – a division of labour necessary to the economic functioning of society in the service of the ends of the human being – Aristotle explains biological sexual difference as necessary for (but not the cause of) the social and political differ-ences.[44] Nothing in the biology accounts for the politics; the politics accounts for the biology.

Becoming women, becoming men

To recap, without the presumption of the modern concept of sex, Socrates' argument and more particularly the reconstruction of the position that it opposes, suggests the view that what it is to be a man or to be a woman – what constitutes a man as a man and a woman as a woman – is not primarily the identification of sex, but equally or even chiefly the socio-historical norms of what we now call 'gender', where this includes the attributes of masculinity and femininity and most importantly the normative social and political roles prescribed for each. Thus, we could say, to be part of the *genos* 'woman' or of the *genos* 'man' is to have the set of womanly or manly attributes and characteristics respectively, and the associated presumption of inferiority or superiority, and to occupy a certain social and political position. 'Women' and 'men' *are* groups or *genē* defined socio-politically, not biologically. This is of course not incompatible with an awareness of the anatomical differences between males and females. But it does imply that the recognition of what we call sex difference need not necessarily play the explana-tory role in the definition of the being of men and women that it tends to play today, that the *genē* of male and female, because of their insertion in a general economy of ontologically indifferent relations between *genē*, do not necessarily determine what it is to be a member of the *genos* of men or a member of the *genos* of women.

This sheds an interesting light on the social prohibition of 'wom-anish' behaviour for men in ancient Athens and illuminates the arguments in Plato's *Republic* and *Laws* against certain forms of poetry and against men taking women's parts in dramatic perfor-mance. These arguments are, in part, the extension of the familiar social prohibition taken to its limit. 'The gravest charge against poetry', in Book X of the *Republic*, concerns 'its terrible power to corrupt even the best characters, with very few exceptions' (605c7–9). Even the best of us, Socrates says, on hearing Homer represent the sufferings of a hero, will be carried away by our feelings and, moreover, praise the poet who can affect the listener most powerfully in this way (605c–d): 'Yet in our private griefs we pride ourselves on just the opposite, that is, on our ability to bear them in silence like men [*hōs touto men andros on*], and we regard the behaviour we admired on the stage as womanish [*gunaikos*]' (605d7–e2). Admiring this behaviour, feeling sympathy with this behaviour, entails a loosening of the control of the best part of the soul over the lowest and *leads to* this kind of behaviour itself (606a–d). It leads to *becoming* womanish.

The danger is arguably even greater in playing the part of the grieving hero or – worse – a grieving woman. In Book III, in the discussion of the education of the Guardians, it is said that they

> should neither do a mean action, nor be clever at acting a mean or otherwise disgraceful part on the stage for fear of catching the infection in real life [*hina mē ek tēs mimēseōs tou einai apolausōsin*]. For have you not noticed how dramatic and similar representations, if indulgence in them is prolonged into adult life, establish habits of physical poise, intonation and thought which become natural [*eis ethē te kai phusin kathistantai kai kata sōma kai phōnas kai kata tēn dianoian*]? (395c7–d4)[45]

As, at this point in the *Republic*, the Guardians should be *men* of worth (*andras agathous*), they will not, *being men* (*andras ontas*) be allowed to take the parts of or to imitate women (395d). For if the set of womanish characteristics (rather than anything like the modern concept of sex) defines what it is to be a woman, a man for whom these characteristics have become natural will, in some sense, *become* a woman. If it is not the case that men and women are defined solely according to their being-male or being-female, the set of behavioural characteristics and attributes that define what it is to *be* a woman are not mere predicates, they have existential status, a state of affairs which is no doubt encouraged, if not explained, by the lack of linguistic distinction in classical Greek between what we now call the existential and the predicative senses of the verb 'to be'. These womanly characteristics in a man are not therefore accidents attached to a manly substance; they entail an existential transformation.

This existential transformation is possible, moreover, despite the fact that males are always male. In the *Laws*, in the context of a discussion affirming that educational utility and 'correctness',[46] not simply pleasure, are the criteria of judgement for music (*mousikē*), the Athenian notes that judgement is often difficult because of the fallibility of mortal composers and their inferiority in relation to the Muses themselves (whose music, one may infer, would be easy to judge as it would always be 'correct'):

> The Muses would never make the ghastly mistake of composing the speech of men to a musical idiom suitable for women [*rhēmata andrōn poiēsasai to schēma gunaikōn kai melos apodounai*], or of fitting rhythms appropriate to the portrayal of slaves and slave-like people to the tune and bodily movements used to represent free men. (669c3–6)

Speaking later of the regulation (rather than judgement) of music, the Athenian says:

> we shall have to distinguish, in a rough and ready way, the songs suitable for men and those suitable for women [*eti de thēleiais te prepousas ōdas appresi*], and give each its proper mode and rhythm. It would be terrible if the words failed to fit the mode, or if their metre were at odds with the beat of the music . . . One possibility is simply to ensure that the songs men and women sing are accompanied by the rhythms and modes imposed by the words in either case; but our regulations about female performances must be more precise than this and be based on the natural difference between the sexes [*autō tō tēs phuseōs hekaterou diapheronti*]. So an elevated manner and courageous [*andrian*] instincts must be regarded [*phateon einai*] as characteristic of the male [*arrenōpon*], while a tendency to modesty and restraint must be presented [*paradoteon*] – in theory and law alike – as a peculiarly feminine [*thēlugenesteron*] trait. (802d9–e12)

This passage is controversial. Susan Moller Okin takes it to be an example of Plato's prescriptive, not descriptive, attitude towards what counts as male and female nature. It is, she says, 'a ruling about how the two sexes must come to think about themselves and about each other'.[47] Criticizing Okin, Natalie Harris Bluestone defends Glen Morrow's interpretation that the passage is about 'the specific differences between the psychical nature of women and that of men'.[48] According to Harris Bluestone, Okin has 'superimposed the modern ideas of self-image and sex-stereotyping instituted for a hidden purpose', whereas (she claims) the translation of *autō tō tēs phuseōs hekaterou diapheronti* as 'the actual natural distinction of sex' 'captures Plato's unequivocal meaning well'. She continues:

> we have every reason to believe that as Plato wrote these lines he was expressing his belief in a fixed female human nature. It is evidently difficult for Okin to think herself into the position of one who wants the political order to reflect, be based on, be in tune with a 'natural' ontological order which exists independently of what anyone legislates.[49]

However, one reason we do have to believe that Plato was *not* expressing the kind of belief that Bluestone here ascribes to him is the absence of her modern concept of 'sex' in the ancient text, a concept which the translation introduces (here *phuseōs* is certainly not, *unequivocally*, sex).[50]

It is perfectly possible, as Okin suggests (contra Bluestone), that *Laws* 802e does endorse a normative set of behaviours and characteristics that *constitute* – rather than stem from – the 'natural' differences between men and women. On this model, womanliness and manliness can commute across male and female, and the idea of the womanly male seems to crystallize in the category of the *kinaidos*. According to John J. Winkler, the *kinaidos* was conceived of as 'a man socially deviant in his entire being, principally observable in behaviour that flagrantly violated or contravened the dominant social definition of masculinity',[51] the latter often represented as fulfilled in the figure of the (ideal) hoplite. Although the word *kinaidos* is not used, the type is evoked at the end of the *Laws*. Plato's Athenian imagines the ideal punishment for a man who, in the face of his enemy, deliberately abandons his weapons 'preferring a coward's life of shame to the glorious and blessed death of a hero' (944c6–8). This is a man who lacks *andreia*, 'courage' or 'manliness',[52] the chief virtue of the hoplite. It is not, he says, within mortal power to change such a man into a woman (*eis gunaika ex andros metabalousa*) as a god once changed Kaineus the Thessalian into a man – that is, it is not within mortal power to effect a *physical* transformation. But the decreed punishment shall be the next best thing, 'the closest possible approximation to such a penalty: we can make him spend the rest of his life in utter safety' (944e3–4), never being appointed to any soldierly position, as he has, because of his own nature, given up on or been debarred from the risks that only men can run (*apheisthai tōn andreiōn kindunōn kata phusin*) (945a7–8). The man who lacks manliness shall be treated like the woman he really is by nature,[53] a nature that his male anatomy does not override. In this case, indeed, anatomy *contradicts* 'nature'. In his Funeral Speech Lysias says much the same thing of the mythical Amazons: 'They were looked upon as men, because of their valour, rather than as women, because of their [bodily] nature [*enomizonto de dia tēn eup-suchian mallon andres ē dia tēn phusin gunaikes*], for they were thought to transcend men in soul more than they fell short of them in appearance.'[54]

The ontological significance of the set of womanish characteristics and attributes is also often dramatized, exaggerated and satirized in Aristophanes' plays. The effect is, of course, comic, but the plays also stage (though not necessarily consciously) some of the anxieties and fantasies associated with women defined in this way. *Ecclesiazusae* – or *Assemblywomen* – provides perhaps the best example. In this play a group of women, fed up with the men of Athens' inability to govern the polis in a stable or fair way, decide to sneak into the Assembly disguised as men, swinging the vote in favour of a proposal for the women to take over the administration of the state. The play opens with the women, led by Praxagora, effecting their disguise. To this end the relevant differences between men and women boil down to the following: the women have oiled their bodies and stood in the sun to brown their skins like men. They have given up their usual depilations so that, as one says (gleefully), 'I've let my armpits get nice and bushy'; another 'I threw my razor out of the house so I'd get all hairy and not look female at all! [*hina dasuntheiēn holē kai mēden eiēn eti gunaiki prospherēs*]'.[55] (In classical Athens the razor – a symbol of modern masculinity – was, symbolically, more a woman's than a man's implement.) They put on men's cloaks and shoes, carry men's clubs, and try to remember to address each other with the appropriate masculine forms and to swear masculine oaths. The only marked masculine feature that the women cannot acquire through the transformation of their own bodies is the beard; false beards are thus required for all. However, even the status of this as an exclusively masculine natural attribute is put into question with a rude joke. Beware when clambering over the seats in the Assembly, Praxagora says, not to flash your 'Phormisios', Phormisios being a man noted for his hairiness. It may be presumed that the women's regrowth of hair extends to their previously trimmed and singed pubic hair. As Lauren Taaffe says, the implication of the joke is that women simply have their beards in a different place.[56]

The womanliness of these women, prior to their transformation, is thus defined through their clothes, their artificial hairlessness, their sun-starved skins, and their use of language, as well as their social and political status and roles. These are also the markers of womanliness assumed superficially by Euripides' disguised kinsman in Aristophanes' *Women at the Thesmophoria* but more significantly by the character of Agathon in the same play: 'My clothing always matches my thoughts. To be a poet a man must suit his fashions to the requirements of his plays. If, say, he's writing plays about women, his body must partake of women's ways.'[57]

All this, perhaps, might lead us to reconsider Socrates' example in the *Republic* of the difference between bald and long-haired men. As this brief discussion of a few details from a couple of Aristophanes' plays has shown, in their common context the distinction between hairiness and hairlessness is intimately bound up with the distinction between men and women, and Socrates' example is perhaps carefully chosen with this is mind. Further, according to Aristotle's biology, the transitivity of sexual substances implies that the difference between male and female itself is in many respects *like* the difference between those with and those without hair – a difference in degree (degrees of heat, degrees of perfection), not a difference in kind. In this context, then, Socrates' example may be much more deeply embedded, culturally and metaphysically, than the superficial interpretation of it as a mockery of absurd discrimination allows.

Para doxan

I have argued that, without the presumption of the modern concept of sex in the interpretation of Plato's *Republic*, it is possible that it is the set of womanish characteristics and attributes that define what it is to be a woman.[58] The possibility for womanishness, understood in this way, to commute across male and female is recognized in the *Republic* and the *Laws* in the prohibition of behaviours that would encourage it. This same commutability of womanishness and manliness is also the ultimate basis for the possibility of Socrates' proposals concerning women in the *Republic*. For Plato and his contemporaries the set of characteristics and attributes that define women as women includes lack of self-control, tendency to extremes of emotion, flightiness, untrustworthiness and secretiveness (the list could be much longer). As these are the precise opposites of the

characteristics of the Guardians, and as Socrates argues that some
women have the nature befitting a Guardian, his argument must
imply that some women do not have the characteristics and attributes that define women as women, but have rather the characteristics that define men as men – that is, some women (those with the
nature of a Guardian) are, in fact, men.

This, then, is the *implicit* conclusion: some women are, or could
be, men, although they remain, incontrovertibly, female.[59] This conclusion seems very odd and contradictory in relation to the modern
concept of sex, according to which being female would determine
that one was a woman, but not in the context of the ontological
significance of the set of womanish and manly characteristics and
attributes in the definition of what it is to be a woman or a man. To
the extent that this conclusion intensifies, rather than contradicts,
the assumptions of Socrates' interlocutors, it is 'paradoxical' (*para
doxan*, as Socrates frequently says), not in being contrary to logic or
possibility, but contrary to *convention* and to what is taken to be
desirable. In this context it is always possible that women might
become men or men become women, a possibility that is both
feared and socially prohibited. Socrates' innovation is to endorse
and promote the possibility that some women might become men,
eschewing the set of conventional characteristics and attributes of
women described elsewhere in Plato's dialogues.

The idea that some women might – indeed ought to – become
men has been the basis of one form of the feminist criticisms of
Plato, articulated most strongly, perhaps, by Arlene W. Saxonhouse,
who speaks of the 'de-sexed and unnatural females' of Socrates'
imagination, repeating the objection of Socrates' imaginary opponent in a modern form:

> As Socrates attempts to turn women into men by making them equal
> participants in the political community, he ignores the peculiar
> natures of each and thus undermines the perfection of the political
> society in the *Republic*. . . . If one's *phusis* is defined by that which one
> does better than anyone else, then Socrates has disregarded the *phusis*
> of the female.[60]

Saxonhouse makes this argument in the context of a defence of what
she sees as the 'natural role' of women, determined by their 'peculiar biological qualities'.[61] It is based on the unexamined modern,
natural-biological concept of 'sex' functioning as both the 'real
property' securing the arguments and the thing secured by them,

the thing mortgaged and the loan itself. Although Saxonhouse is by no means representative of the many feminist readings of Book V of the *Republic*, this modern concept of sex is the common assumption that cuts across them all. Without this assumption, I have argued, the context of the discussion of Socrates' proposals is realigned and the specificity of his argument – its simultaneous immersion in and divergence from the assumptions of his contemporaries – emerges more clearly.

This analysis also reveals the specific function of the modern, natural-biological concept of sex, a concept whose general, conservative ideological tendency, in its association with the idea of a fixed, immutable 'nature', is to mark a universal and unchallengeable difference, now located at the level of the biological, with reverberations throughout the social and political spheres. Without claiming that Plato was a proto-feminist, without claiming that the arguments in Book V of the *Republic* might provide resources for feminists looking for arguments in the twenty-first century, and without being forced into the choice of a feminist position for or against Plato, it might at least be suggested that our exposure to the possibility of an alternative ontology of 'men' and 'women' in Socrates' argument calls into question the otherwise overwhelming presumption of the givenness of the modern, natural-biological concept of sex.

It is telling, however, that in our modern societies, apparently so committed to this concept of sex, we are yet unable to *trust* sex to make our boys and girls into men and women, as the hyper-gendering of babies, children and young adults seems to reveal. Indeed, despite the function of the modern, natural-biological concept of sex, the contemporary anxiety that females might, to all intents and purposes, become men, is regularly revealed in the anti-feminist discourses that still warn of the 'de-sexing' of modern women and the feminist 'perversion' of their natural roles. In July 2004, in a statement of doctrine on gender issues, the then-Pope's chief theological spokesperson, cardinal Joseph Ratzinger, accused feminists of 'blurring the biological difference between man and woman' with dangerous claims about the constructed nature of gender roles which cause women to 'neglect their family duties'.[62] Having become Pope Benedict XVI, Ratzinger reiterated the danger in 2008, warning that 'gender theory blurred the distinction between male and female and thus could lead to the "self-destruction" of the human race'.[63] How could this happen if sex performed its allotted role, making men, men and women, women, according to the dictates of nature? If, on the other hand, what it is to be a woman or a man is determined by a set of womanish or manly character- istics that can commute across, and are not determined by, the distinction between male and female, the Pope's worry becomes intelligible. It seems that 'man' and 'woman' are, as in this chapter's interpretation of the *Republic*, social and political, not natural, cat- egories. 'Sex' is the modern talisman with which we pretend to ward this knowledge off, while all the time acknowledging it.

2

The Origin of Sex: Aristophanes, Freud and Lacan (Symposium)

I have suggested in Chapter 1 that the widespread and common-sense assumption that Socrates opposes in the *Republic* with his main argument for the admittance of women to the governing Guardian class may concern not the determining role of sex (in the modern sense, with all that that entails), but the assertion of a very great natural difference between men and women in every aspect of their existence. If, strictly speaking, the modern concept of sex is absent from Plato's *Republic*, it is possible that, for his interlocutors, it is the purported set of womanish characteristics and attributes (something more like the modern concept of gender) that constitutes, ontologically, what a woman *is*, that defines what it is to *be* a woman in the strong sense, and that Socrates' redefinition of the *genē* of men and women, reduced to their biological function, is his controversial innovation. This amounts to the claim that the *genē* of men and women are primarily socio-political, not biological, groups. If 'womanishness' and 'manliness' are understood in this way it is possible for them to commute across the distinction between female and male. This possibility is the ultimate basis both for Socrates' arguments in the *Republic* (the set of characteristics and attributes that constitutes manliness also determines the character of those females suitable for guardianship) and for the fear driving the prohibition of womanly behaviour in the *Republic* and the *Laws*. As well as reconfiguring the way in which the relevant passages in the *Republic* are interpreted, these claims also suggest the historical specificity of the modern concept of sex (with all that that concept implies), and that 'sex' should be treated as an object of philosophical investigation rather than an unquestionable natural given.

This chapter continues the investigation of 'sex', this time via a consideration of aspects of the theory of love attributed to Aristophanes[1] in Plato's *Symposium*. Amongst other things, Aristophanes' speech seems to offer an explanation for the origin of the two sexes. Moreover, unlike the 'official' myths of the origins of the first Athenian (Erichthonius) and the first woman (Pandora) – myths which were a central part of the ancient Athenian imaginary and the concomitant social and political structure of the polis – Aristophanes' myth seems to describe the simultaneous origin of male and female as we now know them from the same human source. In marked contrast to the official myths, in which the divine origin of the autochthon Erichthonius and the divine fashioning of Pandora sit uneasily with the question of the successive generation of their human ancestors, Aristophanes' myth also seems to provide an explanation for the origin of sexual reproduction. Although the overall narrative and the details are clearly fabulous it thus appears to work with something like the modern concept of sex, eschewing the creationist vision of the official myths.

Aristophanes' tale is thus usually seen as a mythic account of the non-mythic phenomena of sex, sexuality and love. But can 'sex' support a distinction into its mythic and non-mythic forms? This chapter investigates this question through an analysis of the status of the concepts of male (*arren*) and female (*thēlus*)[2] in Aristophanes' myth, and a discussion of the relevant aspects of the work of two modern thinkers who are explicitly indebted to it: Freud and Lacan.

Human nature, then and now

The characters in Plato's *Symposium*, no doubt ensconced in the *andrōn*, the male-only quarters of a private house, agree to amuse and edify themselves with competitive speeches, composing – apparently spontaneously – encomia to the god Eros, or Love. According to Aristophanes, in the fourth speech, there is a necessary anthropological propaedeutic to any discussion of the power of the god Eros. In Rowe's translation:

> First, you need to learn about the nature of human beings and what has happened to it [*ta pathēmata autēs*]; for our nature as it was, once upon a time, was not the same as it is now, but of a different kind.

In the first place, human beings were divided into three kinds [*prōton men gar tria ēn ta genē ta tōn anthrōpōn*], not two as they are now, male and female [*arren kai thēlu*] – in addition to these there was also a third in which both of these had a share [*kai triton prosēn koinon on amphoterōn toutōn*], one whose name now survives although the kind itself has vanished from sight; for at that time one of the kinds was androgynous [*androgunon*], in form as well as in name shared in by both the male and the female [*eidos kai onoma ex amphoterōn koinon tou te arrenos kai thēleos*], whereas now it does not exist except as a term of reproach. . . . The reason why they were divided into three kinds, and kinds like this [*ēn de dia tauta tria ta genē kai toiauta*], is that the male was in the beginning born from the sun, the female from the earth, and what shared in both male and female from the moon [*to de amphoterōn metechon tēs selēnēs*], because the moon too shares in both [*amphoterōn metechei*]. (189d4–190b3)[3]

Each of these original three kinds was, according to Aristophanes, round in shape, four-legged, four-armed, one-headed but two-faced, with each possessing two sets of genitals on the 'outside' (191b). Strong, powerful and ambitious, these beings 'made an attempt on the gods'. As punishment, weakening without annihilating human beings, Zeus set about cutting each human being in two 'like people who cut up sorb apples before they preserve them, or like people cutting eggs with hairs' (190e8–9). Healing Apollo drew the skin from all sides over the wound, like a drawstring pulling the edges of a purse, catching it in the middle to make what we now call the navel. All of these newly stitched half-humans longed to be whole again; they locked themselves together in an embrace and 'because of their desire to grow back together, they died from not eating or indeed doing anything else, because they refused to do anything apart from each other' (191a7–b2). Out of pity Zeus came up with another plan. Whereas previously, with their genitals on what was originally the outside, the humans 'did their begetting and child-bearing not in each other but in the ground, like cicadas', now Zeus moved their genitals round to the front 'and brought in reproduction through these in each other' at least for the halves of the original androgyne, and 'satisfaction in their intercourse' (191c) for the rest.

The elaboration of this tale into a universal theory of love is the imaginative extension of the condition of the halved creatures to ourselves: we are creatures of lack; in love we long to be complete, to be one with our 'other half'. Love is, as Aristophanes says, 'the desire and pursuit of the whole' (192e10–193a1). Furthermore, this seems to explain the range of sexual preference. Today's men who are cut from the original composite being are attracted to women; women cut from this kind are attracted to men. Men cut from the original male 'pursue male halves'; women cut from the original female are inclined towards women (191e).

To the extent that the myth appears to explain the origin of the two sexes, as we know them today, its relation to the 'official' myths of origin in ancient Athens is interesting. These latter myths (or their variants) could be said to be 'official' by virtue of their privileged place in the Athenian imaginary and their physical inscription in the temples of the Acropolis. The origin of the first Athenian is both divine and earthly. According to one version of the myth, Hephaestus pursued Athena in desire. The goddess escaped, but not before Hephaestus' semen splashed her thigh. She wiped the semen from her thigh with a scrap of wool that she then threw to the ground. Earth (Gē) was thus inseminated and from her the child Erichthonius was 'born', passing into the care of Athena, after whom he later named the city he founded. This myth, in which the birth of Erichthonius bears similarities with the myth of the birth of Athena and other divinities, provided the Athenians with a satisfyingly Olympian heritage and legitimized Athenian hegemony, imagining the Athenians as the sole original inhabitants of the Attic soil in contrast with barbarian immigrants.[4] The myth is also intimately connected to the masculine hegemony within Athens. To refer, on the basis of the myth, to the collective citizenry of Athens as autochthonous feeds the fantasy of a purely masculine origin, symbolically eliminating the female from reproduction. (This fantasy is, of course, articulately expressed in the *Symposium*.) The myth provides Athenian men with a symbolic masculine heritage that justifies or explains the absence of the female Athenian political subject.

The myth of Pandora, the first woman, created or fashioned by Zeus and Hephaestus, is notably more general in scope. Pandora is the first of the whole race (*genos*) of women. From Pandora, through the genesis of the race of women, the principle of sexual reproduction and – what may be the same thing in this mythic universe – the principle of human death and destruction is introduced.[5]

However, these myths fit only uneasily with both the subsequent legal definition of the Athenian citizen and the fact of sexual reproduction. First, according to the Periclean law of citizenship the Athenian citizen is the person born from *two* citizen parents. But in the absence of an account of the first female Athenian – indeed, in the absence, as Loraux suggests, of the category of the female Athenian itself[6] – Erichthonius is the first of a line of exclusively masculine Athenians and the requisite bilateral citizen parentage is impossible (unless, as Loraux says, the male Athenian's two citizen parents are his father and his mother's father[7]). Second, these two myths stage the origins of two distinct *genē* (kinds), male Athenians (from Erichthonius) and generic women (from Pandora).[8] Neither refers to the origins of human beings in general, and, indeed, to the extent that Pandora was created to punish the human race, she and her female ancestors are not imagined, strictly speaking, as part of it.[9] The problem, then, is twofold: How does the generic dissymmetry between the two *genē* of Athenian men and women in general reconcile itself into the sexual reproduction of the one *genos*, the human race? And what is there of a specifically *human* nature in either the first Athenian or the first woman, if neither is born of human parents? In what does their humanity consist?

To the extent that Aristophanes' myth appears, at first sight, to avoid these problems, and to offer a – fantasmatic – physical anthropogony, it is tempting to read it, in modern terms, as an account of the origin of the two sexes, its fictional status notwithstanding. Aristophanes' myth *is*, unlike the two 'official' myths, an account of the origins of human beings as a whole, restricted neither in relation to men or women nor in relation to non-Athenians. Further, human beings as they are 'now' (where 'now' may be taken to mean 'now we are divided into two kinds', encompassing both classical antiquity and modernity) are said to derive from a specifically human ancestor, their physical deviation from the form of this ancestor being a result of the nature of the derivation. The theme of autochthony is still present. According to Aristophanes, the original race of human beings 'did their begetting and child-bearing not in each other but in the ground [*eis gēn*], like cicadas' (191c1–2). While this is not true autochthonous birth, in which no human parent is involved, it recalls two details of the myth of Erichthonius – the idea that the earth is inseminated and that the child is 'born' from out of the earth. This form of autochthony was sufficiently acceptable in relation to the myth of Erichthonius for the Athenians to adopt the cicada as a symbol of their autochthonous origin. But while the official myth of Erichthonius has no explanation for the origin of the non-autochthonous from the autochthonous (the evolution of sexual reproduction from autochthonous production), Aristophanes' version does attempt this, describing both a physical transformation and the reason for this. This part of the myth is afforded a retrospective plausibility parasitic on the psychologically powerful description of passionate love. Aristophanes' speech was often dismissed in nineteenth- and early twentieth-century readings of Plato as a Rabelaisian burlesque obsessed with the 'lower bodily stratum', to use Bakhtin's phrase.[10] In fact, though, there is no obscenity in Aristophanes' speech and – a fact that has been read as an anticipation of the metaphysical doctrine of Socrates' report of Diotima's speech – its climax is in the paradoxically clear expression of the inexpressible yearning of desire, a desire which does not aim at, and is not satisfied by, sexual congress. Lovers who refuse to be separated from each other 'wouldn't even be able to say what they want for themselves from one another. For no one would suppose this to be sexual intercourse . . . it is something else that the soul of each manifestly wants, which it cannot express, but dimly grasps what it wants and talks of it as if in riddles' (192c8–d2).

Aristophanes' speech also contains a frank admission of diversity in sexual preference (and purportedly explains it), including women's sexual love for women, explicit mention of which is extremely rare in ancient literature.[11] In contrast with the other speeches, and with the official myths of origin, Aristophanes' tale, despite its incredible details, thus speaks more recognizably of actual human experience according to what seem like modern categories. The anthropological genealogy of the derivation of the two kinds – male and female – from a common human origin and the presentation of this sexual duality as the condition of human being in general, as it is now, seems then to be an account of the origin of sex difference, of human being as sexual duality, and of human sexual reproduction.

Aristophanes: One, two, three, four . . .

But things are a little more complicated than this. Examining Aristophanes' speech in detail, the question of the meaning of the Greek '*genos*' presents itself again. Human beings were once, Aristophanes says, divided into three *genē*, which Rowe translates each time as 'kinds' (the primary and most general meaning of the Greek word). In Dover's famous commentary, a note on Aristophanes' first use of *genē* offers the explanatory translation 'sexes', the correctness of which, Dover says, 'is clear from what follows'.[12] In fact, it is not clear at all. As two of the original three 'kinds' of human being are immediately identified with the two 'kinds' 'as they are now' and specified as male and female (*arren kai thēlu*), the interpretation of the 'three kinds' as three sexes is hardly unmotivated, but it is strictly unjustified, since anything that could distinguish them as sexes is absent. 'Sex', in the sense of sex difference, is what distinguishes organisms within the same species on the basis of their function in reproduction, or is used to refer to each of the two categories, male and female, into which organisms are divided on this basis. Accordingly, Aristophanes' three kinds are *not* sexes. As they do not reproduce sexually, none are distinguished by their role in reproduction. None are distinguished by any relation between sex and sexual desire, since they have no sexual desire. None are distinguished on the basis of what we could recognize as genital morphology, since in this respect they are all rather unusual, having two sets of genitals (*aidoia*) the exact form of which, adapted to 'begetting and child bearing (*egennōn kai etikton*) . . . in the ground', is mysterious. There is, then, nothing of that alleged 'nature' and, especially, none of that duality which grounds the presumption that would let us distinguish them *as* sexes, and as the precise sexes that they are, rather than simply as different kinds.[13] Similarly, to the extent that 'male' and 'female' are zoological categories, distinguished for the ancient Greek as much for us by their roles in reproduction (as Plato says in the *Republic*, the one begets, the other bears), nor is it, strictly speaking, legitimate for Aristophanes to call two of these original three kinds male and female, unless, as another interpretation suggests, 'male' and 'female' mean something else. If two of the original three kinds were 'male' and 'female', 'male' and 'female' do not mean here what we usually take them to mean, since they are clearly not identical to the 'male' and 'female' that is the result of the subsequent division into three kinds.

The definition of these terms is even more difficult when we try to untangle what Aristophanes says about 'form' (*eidos*) in relation to the original three kinds:

> In the first place human beings were divided into three kinds, not two as they are now, male and female, for in addition to these there was also a third in which both of these had a share (*alla kai triton prosēn koinon on amphoterōn toutōn*) . . . for at that time one of the kinds was androgynous, in form as well as in name shared in by both the male and the female (*androgunon gar hen tote men en kai eidos kai onoma ex amphoterōn koinon tou te arrenos kai thēleos'*). (189d7–e4)

Other translations of this passage reverse the relation of sharing and shared. Hamilton (translating *alla kai triton prosēn koinon on amphoterōn toutōn*) has 'the third partook of the nature of both the others'; Lamb: 'there was a third kind as well, which had equal shares of the others two'; Gill: 'a third one, a combination of these two'. Dover's gloss explains that the androgyne was 'made up' from both male and female.[14] These different translations boil down to two different types of interpretation, both of which can be supported by the grammatically ambiguous text. First, as Rowe's translation suggests, the androgyne is originary; second, as the other translations make explicit, the androgyne is a secondary construction from the more original male and female.

Rather than trying to decide between these two interpretations, it makes sense to read this detail in Aristophanes' myth as the expression of an originary ambiguity common to all references to the idea of androgyny – broadly understood – in Plato's ancient Greek predecessors. The idea of what, in modern terminology, Luc Brisson calls 'dual-sexed' beings (referring to beings designated *androgynos*, *Hermaphroditus*, *arrenothēlus*) is prominent in ancient Greek and other cosmogony, theogony and mythlogy. Brisson defines 'dual sexuality' as 'the simultaneous or successive possession of both sexes by a single individual'.[15] The primordial beings in Orphism, Hermeticism and Gnosticism – beings who were at the same time personified principles or archetypes – were dual-sexed, expressing, as Brisson says, 'the total coincidence of opposites that characterizes the origin of all things'.[16] In these myths the unity of male-female is prior to the separation between male and female. To the extent that Aristophanes' myth is about original beings, the subsequent division of original beings and the nostalgia for original unity it is likely that there is in it an implicit reference to these earlier accounts (and specifically to variants of Orphism, famous for its dual-sexed Eros).[17] If this is the case, it also seems likely that it is meant to evoke the idea of the originary androgyne, the primordial male-female from which the secondary division between male and female is derived.

But in Aristophanes' myth the move from unity to division is of course complicated by the fact that the original human beings are already divided into three kinds. Furthermore, whereas the division in the earlier myths is a halving that produces double the original amount of units (one kind – male-female – is divided into two, male and female), Aristophanes' division results either in a reduction of the kinds of units (three kinds – male-male, female-female, male-female – are divided into two, male and female) or their proliferation (three kinds are divided into four: women who like men, women who like women, men who like men and men who like women). However, what is common to both mythic structures in their result – the division into male and female – is also their common presupposition. If the earlier myths try to mask or deny this in their manifest content, Aristophanes' myth makes it explicit. The division of the three original kinds into male and female is their *resolution* into their constituent parts. This is no less true of the earlier myths, despite their ostensible claim to describe an originary *unity* before any kind of division. In both cases, the distinction between male and female is presupposed, even if they are said to be originarily united. This is the originary constitutive ambiguity of the idea of the androgyne or of what Brisson calls 'dual-sexed' beings.

If, then, 'sex' figures in Aristophanes' myth it is located not in the distinction between the three original kinds (as Dover supposes) but in the components which make up each of the three kinds, components into which the split beings are resolved or fragmented. If 'sex' figures in Aristophanes' myth it is in the presupposition of the categories of male and female that structure the idea of the original three kinds, but not in the division of the three kinds themselves. However, in that case, what precisely is the nature of the presupposition of 'male' and 'female', or to what, precisely do these terms refer?

That the categories of male and female are not derived but presupposed is clear in Aristophanes' explanation of the origin of the three kinds:

> The reason why they were divided into three kinds, and kinds like this [*ēn de dia tauta tria ta genē kai toiauta*], is that the male was in the beginning born from the sun, the female from the earth, and what shared in both male and female from the moon [*to de amphoterōn metechon tēs selēnēs*], because the moon too shares in both [*amphoterōn metechei*]. (190b1–3)

Here 'male' and 'female', as originarily – and hence fundamentally – attributes of the sun and the earth, are not the two categories of sex distinguished on the basis of an organism's role in reproduction but are structuring cosmic principles. In the structure of Aristophanes' myth male and female as a distinction between kinds of humans is *derived from*, and is *not the basis of*, this cosmic principle of the division of all things into male and female, a cosmic principle which is not narratalogically justified but rather foundational – a first principle. Reading strictly according to the structure of Aristophanes' myth, the distinction between male and female in human beings is thus a projection of the cosmic principle into the human realm, meaning that the distinction between kinds of humans on this basis is, precisely, *mythic*.

Freud: two to infinity

Most modern interpretations of Aristophanes' myth understand its various elements in terms of the non-mythic ideas or structures that they are taken to express. Accordingly, the myth of the origin of the two kinds that we are now and the mythic cosmic principle of the division of male and female that precedes this structurally in Aristophanes' tale *express* or otherwise refer us to the non-mythic modern categories of sex, even if those categories are not explicit in it. The confident assumption in this interpretation of Aristophanes' myth, using the modern category of sex, is that the *non-mythic* status of the latter is not in doubt. In that case, the story would have no interesting or productive philosophical consequences for it would not lend itself to any kind of philosophical interpretation. Indeed 'sex' itself, it is presumed here, is not a proper object for philosophical interrogation.[18]

However, when the story reappears in the context of a theoretical discipline for which sex or sexual difference[19] *is* a central and contested category – psychoanalytical theory, specifically the psychoanalytical theories of Sigmund Freud and Jacques Lacan – the outcome is somewhat different. Freud, of course, put ancient Greek myth centre stage in his psychoanalytical theory with the naming of the Oedipus complex, but the influence of classical literature – and of Plato in particular – on Freud is more far-reaching than this.[20] Although his explicit references to Plato are few, what Freud identifies as the agreements between aspects of Plato's philosophy and psychoanalytical theory are profound. Most important of these, for Freud, was the virtual identity, as he saw it, of the extension of the psychoanalytical concept of sexuality or libido and 'the Eros of the divine Plato' or the 'Eros of Plato's *Symposium*'.[21] Freud's brief references to Plato on this point serve both an explanatory and a justificatory function, but they are not the occasion for theoretical speculation. It is as if, once discovered, Freud took the agreement for granted, supposing each – Plato's concept of Eros and the psychoanalytical concept of sexuality – to be mutually reinforcing. The few references to Aristophanes' myth (explicit and implicit), on the other hand, indicate that it was rather more provoking, and precisely on the question of the origin of sex.

Freud's most concerted attempt to grapple with the psycho-biological problem of sex difference, and his most intriguing references to Aristophanes' speech, appear in his 1920 essay 'Beyond the Pleasure Principle'. Here Freud defines the 'drives' (*die Triebe*) as 'the representatives of all the forces originating in the interior of the body and transmitted to the mental apparatus'.[22] Here, as elsewhere, he also affirms that although the drives are the most important element in psychological research, they remain the most obscure. Struggling to understand the compulsion to repeat, especially when that compulsion seems to override the pleasure principle, Freud is led to propose, as 'a universal attribute of drives and perhaps of organic life in general', that '*a drive is an urge inherent in organic life to restore an earlier state of things*', an expression of the 'inertia inherent in organic life' or of 'the *conservative* nature of living substance'.[23] This claim seems strange, Freud says, because we are accustomed to think of the drives as dynamic forces of change and development in the organism. He proposes, instead, 'that the phenomena of organic development must be attributed to external disturbing and diverting influences'. Change is forced upon the organism which, if left to its own devices, would 'have no wish to change'.[24] But the organism is never left to its own devices, simply because it exists in an environment which impinges on it. In striving to counteract the influence of the environment and to restore itself to its earlier state, the work of the drives appears to tend towards change and progress, but this is change in the name of (progress towards) the restoration of the earlier state.

If animate organisms developed from the inanimate, it follows that the drive towards the restoration of an earlier state is the drive towards the inanimate state, a state which, from the point of view of the animate organism, is death. Thus, Freud is compelled to conclude, '*the aim of all life is death*'.[25] Even the so-called self-preservative drives, which ward off death from external sources, have as their ultimate aim the restoration of the earlier state, attempting to assure only that the organism shall die in its own way, according to a process immanent to the organism itself.

However, Freud points out, the function of the sexual drive seems to contradict these general claims. In so far as the sexual drives tend towards the reproduction of the organism, 'winning for it what we can only regard as potential immortality',[26] they work against the restoration of an earlier state of things; that is, they work against death. This contradiction suggests the drawing of a sharp distinction between the 'ego-drives' (tending towards death) and the sexual drives (tending towards the reproduction of life). But Freud soon finds this distinction inadequate, not least because of the libidinal aspects of the ego-drives (sexual instincts operate in the ego, hence narcissism) and of the obvious destructive elements of the sexual drives (for example in sadism). This distinction is thus replaced with that between life drives and death drives, what Freud will later call Eros and Thanatos. Both sexual instincts and ego-drives can work in the service of both life and death.

Although the argument is not explicit, this shift enables Freud to relocate at least one aspect of the sexual drives within the earlier, general description of the drives as the urge inherent in organic life to restore an earlier state of things. Freud reminds us that he was led to this general claim, and thence to the hypothesis of the death drive, by trying to understand the function of the compulsion to repeat. Here again, though, the sexual drive poses a problem: 'what is the important event in the development of living substance which is being repeated in sexual reproduction?' Further, how can sexual reproduction – 'the coalescence of two germ cells' working 'against the death of living substance'[27] – be understood in terms of the death drive?

Freud is very clear that the hypotheses presented in 'Beyond the Pleasure Principle' are speculative and far from certain. Although other aspects of psychoanalytical theory – the phenomenon of repression, for example – are, for Freud, amply attested to in analytic experience, the claims in 'Beyond the Pleasure Principle' cannot be confirmed in this way. Freud's method here, then, is to 'borrow' from the science of biology, to look for answers in the findings of biology and construct speculative psychological theories on that basis. The question of the relation between the sexual drive and the compulsion to repeat – the question of which event is being repeated in sexual reproduction – marks the limit, in this essay, of the usefulness of biology. To answer these questions, Freud says, we would need more information on the origin of sexual reproduction and of the sexual drives in general,[28] but science has so little to say here that the problem may be likened to 'a darkness into which not so much of a ray of hypothesis has penetrated'. Or, rather, the only hypothesis in this darkness comes not from science but from myth, a myth of so fantastic a kind, Freud says, 'that I would not venture to produce it here were it not that it fulfils precisely the one condition whose fulfilment we desire. For it traces the origin of a drive to *a need to restore an earlier state of things.'*[29]

This myth is Aristophanes'. Borrowing from the myth, in a reversal of his method previously, Freud constructs a speculative biological theory on the basis of an analogy with his psychological insight:

> Shall we follow the hint given us by the poet philosopher, and venture upon the hypothesis that living substance at the time of its coming to life was torn apart into small particles, which has ever since endeavoured to re-unite through the sexual drives? That these drives, in which the chemical affinity of inanimate matter persisted, gradually succeeded, as they developed through the kingdom of the protista, in overcoming the difficulties put in the way of that endeavour by an environment charged with dangerous stimuli – stimuli which compelled them to form a protective cortical layer? That these splintered fragments of living substance in this way attained a multicellular condition and finally transferred the instinct for reuniting, in the most highly concentrated form, to the germ-cells?[30]

Freud mentions earlier that although sexuality and the distinction between the sexes did not exist when life began, 'the possibility remains that the drives which were later to be described as sexual may have been in operation from the very first'.[31] Thus the instincts of the protista, endeavouring to reunite the small particles of its living substance, would develop into what we now call the *sexual* drives when the distinction between the sexes also developed. Harmonizing this with Freud's general theory of the drives in 'Beyond the Pleasure Principle', the distinction between the sexes would arise as a convoluted means towards its own abolition. The distinction between the sexes would arise with sexual reproduction as a strategy in the overall aim of the abolition of all distinctions in the organism. That is, the origin of the distinction between the sexes would be in the attempt of a non-sexed organism to restore itself to a previous wholeness. The development from the non-sexed organism to the sexually distinguished organism would not be a process of development immanent to the organism itself, nor would it be 'progress'. It would be a change forced upon the organism 'by an environment charged with dangerous stimuli' and a change that the organism would seek to undo by restoring an earlier state of things. But in this case the organism is doomed to failure. Sexual reproduction only reproduces the sexual division, a trauma[32] that the human organism is compelled, endlessly, to repeat. The

parallels here with Aristophanes' myth are so obvious that one need
not spell them out.

In Freud's account the postulation of the origin of the distinction
between the sexes is derived from the prior hypothesis that 'living
substance at the time of its coming to life was torn apart into small
particles'. Freud thus implies that sexual division is the result – at
the level of both the germ cell (gamete) and the phenotype (the
individual organism) – of a rending of an initially unified substance.
Freud was clear about the speculative and uncertain nature of these
hypotheses. He did not know himself, he wrote, how far he believed
in them, though 'they seemed to me to deserve consideration'. He
claims, furthermore, that the basis of these speculations in biology
makes them more, not less, uncertain, as developments in this
science might very well 'blow away the whole of our artificial structure of hypotheses',[33] thus acknowledging that the biological theory
itself was unstable.

As an elaboration of an ancient myth, built on an admittedly
insecure biological basis, Freud's account of the origin of sex is
obviously shaky as a scientific theory, though none the less interesting for that. Indeed, Freud's speculations here seem to have more
in common with the mytho-poetic philosophies of the pre-Socratics
than with the scientific discourses of his contemporaries. To this
extent Freud seems to borrow not just the content but also the form
or genre of Aristophanes' tale, and both are easily interpreted as
purveyors of a mythic account of a non-mythic fact: sex difference.
But in Freud's theory, the 'fact' of sex difference itself is a complicated matter.

Given the content of Freud's hypotheses on the origin of sex,
their relation to Aristophanes' myth, and Freud's remarks about
biology, it is perhaps surprising that Freud does not refer – as
he does on numerous occasions elsewhere – to one of his most
staunchly held and enduring theoretical commitments: his endorsement of Fleiss' theory of bisexuality. This is, explicitly, a theory of
anatomical (organic, constitutional), not psychological or psycho-
pathological, bisexuality (though the former may, according to
Fleiss, Freud and others, explain much about the latter and about
homosexuality in particular). In the section headed 'Bisexuality' in
the first of Freud's 'Three Essays on the Theory of Sexuality' he
writes:

> It is popularly believed that a human being is either a man or a
> woman. Science, however, knows of cases in which the sexual char-

acters are obscured, and in which it is consequently difficult to determine the sex. This arises in the first instance in the field of anatomy.
The genitals of the individuals concerned combine male and female
characteristics. (This condition is known as hermaphroditism.) . . . The
importance of these abnormalities lies in the unexpected fact that
they facilitate our understanding of normal development. For it
appears that a certain degree of anatomical hermaphroditism occurs
normally. In every normal male or female individual, traces are
found of the apparatus of the opposite sex. These either persist
without function as rudimentary organs or become modified and
take on other functions.

   These long-familiar facts of anatomy lead us to suppose that an
originally bisexual physical disposition has, in the course of evolution, become modified into a unisexual one, leaving behind only a
few traces of the sex that has become atrophied.[34]

Freud goes on to discuss 'inversion', but makes it clear that 'bisexuality' is to be understood 'in the sense of *duality of sex*'.[35] A bisexual
disposition 'is somehow concerned in inversion, though we do not
know in what that disposition consists, beyond anatomical
structure'.[36]

   In lecture XXXIII, 'Femininity', of the *New Introductory Lectures*
Freud draws his audience's attention to the scientific fact that

   portions of the male sexual apparatus also appear in women's bodies,
   though in an atrophied state, and vice-versa in the alternative case.
   It [science] regards their occurrence as indications of *bisexuality*, as
   though an individual is not a man or a woman but always both –
   merely a certain amount more the one than the other.[37]

This notion of anatomical or constitutional bisexuality may be and
is 'transferred . . . to mental life', or to the psychological notion of
bisexuality, the 'bisexuality' that twenty-first-century readers are
most likely to understand in terms of sexual preference or orientation. For Freud, anatomical bisexuality was an established fact, and
one much easier to understand than psychological or behavioural
bisexual dispositions. Furthermore, the presumption of anatomical
bisexuality was, for Freud, one of the most basic in psychoanalysis.
Since becoming acquainted, via Fleiss, with the notion of bisexuality, Freud says, 'I have regarded it as the decisive factor, and without
taking bisexuality into account I think it would scarcely be possible
to arrive at an understanding of the sexual manifestations that are
actually to be observed in men and women.'[38]

The problem of the origin of sex difference, the nature of the sexual drives and the theory of bisexuality are brought together explicitly in Freud's 'Civilization and its Discontents' (1929). Writing of the, often intolerable, impediments to the satisfaction of the sexual drives in civilized society, Freud raises the possibility that the sexual drives are, in themselves, unsatisfiable: 'sometimes one seems to perceive that it is not only the pressure of civilization but something in the nature of the function itself which denies us full satisfaction and urges us along other paths. This may be wrong; it is hard to decide.'[39] Freud adds, in a footnote:

> The view expressed above is supported by the following considerations. Man is an animal organism with (like others) an unmistakably bisexual disposition. The individual corresponds to a fusion of two symmetrical halves, of which, according to some investigators, one is purely male [*männlich*] and the other female [*weiblich*]. It is equally possible that each half was originally hermaphrodite.[40]

Out of context, this claim sounds fantastic, but the idea has a rational basis in anatomy and more specifically in embryology, as the explanation of bisexuality from the 'Three Essays on the Theory of Sexuality' showed. The external genitalia and sexual reproductive organs of both male and female human beings develop from the same originally sexually indifferent structures, some of which continue to develop and some of which atrophy (but, as Freud pointed out, only imperfectly and sometimes not at all). This is the claimed scientific basis for Fleiss' theory of bisexuality, and Freud was most likely aware of it as early as 1874, when he studied with zoologist Carl Krauss who specialized in anatomical bisexuality (successive and simultaneous hermaphroditism) in existing species.[41]

Although Freud's reference to 'a fusion of two symmetrical halves' and the idea of an original hermaphroditism evokes Aristophanes' myth – contributing to the fantastical air surrounding his claim – it is, at the level of its manifest content, incompatible with it. Aristophanes' hermaphrodite describes only one of three kinds of original human beings, and his individuals (men and women as they are now) are precisely *not* a fusion of two halves, though this is what they seek in love. Moreover, Aristophanes' myth was invoked in 'Beyond the Pleasure Principle' with reference to the idea of a splitting into two from an original, non-sexed, unity, whereas the theory of bisexuality in 'Civilization and its Discontents', which does not speculate on the origin of the human organism from a non-human ancestor, refers only to the already sexed nature of the human organism, a duality of two kinds of organisms (male and female), *and* an internal duality in each kind of organism itself. There is no original non-sexed unity in this account, though there is in the hypotheses concerning the origins of sex in 'Beyond the Pleasure Principle'. Nevertheless, the theory of bisexuality in 'Civilization and its Discontents' shares with Aristophanes' myth a structural presupposition about the 'male' and the 'female' that problematizes them for Freud. Freud's remarks on bisexuality and Aristophanes' myth share an unresolved – indeed unresolveable – ambiguity in the idea of originary hermaphroditism. The division into male and female that follows on from the original hermaphroditic state is always already presupposed within it. The conceptual distinction that is the result of division in fact already structures what allegedly precedes it.

In Aristophanes' myth the distinction between 'male' and 'female' in human beings is, strictly speaking, the projection of the cosmic principle of the division of all things – including the sun and the earth, 'parents' of two of the three original kinds of human beings – into male and female. The distinction between male and female human beings is derived from, and is not the basis of, the mythic cosmic structuring principle. Although Freud's considerations on bisexuality and the original, multiply hermaphroditic ancestor seem, on the contrary, to be based firmly on a non-mythic, scientific concept of sex (the distinction between male and female on the basis of their roles in reproduction), the status of this basis is questionable, to say the least. The theory of bisexuality displaces the location of the division of sex from the level of kinds of organism, or kinds of germ cells possessed by kinds of organism, to an intra-organismic duality. Sex duality – the distinction between 'male' and 'female' – exists within each organism regardless of which kind ('male' and 'female' in a different sense, presumably) it is. Freud's footnote, however, goes even further than this, displacing the division of sex from the intra-organismic duality of each individual to a yet more basic distinction within each of the halves which together make up the whole organism. The individual is composed of two halves which were themselves, Freud speculates, originally hermaphroditic, that is, themselves composed of two halves, 'male' and 'female'. But if at each stage 'male' and 'female' are revealed to be hermaphroditic unities composed, again, of 'male' and 'female', an infinite regression can be only arbitrarily halted. Although Freud apparently wished to distance himself from Otto Weininger's elaboration of the theory of bisexuality, in which bisexuality is attributed to or located in the vital activities of every organ and every cell,[42] the implications of the potential regress of 'male' and 'female' in the footnote from 'Civilization and its Discontents' is difficult to distinguish from it. By this stage it is very difficult to imagine in what 'maleness' and 'femaleness' could consist. Ostensibly derived from hermaphroditism, they in fact operate as a priori principles of division very much like Aristophanes' mythic cosmic principle of division but projected on a micro scale. What, then, is 'sex' if 'male' and 'female' are intra-organismic, or even intra-cellular, characteristics at every level of division?

It is interesting that the same kind of problem arises in the ancient Hippocratic Treatises that deal with sexual reproduction, treatises that perhaps form part of the background to the speech Plato gives to Aristophanes. Accordingly to Lesley Dean-Jones, the ancient Greeks did not dissect bodies in their physiological researches. The biological distinctions between male and female were therefore based on the observation of exterior sexual characteristics, but 'the archetype of the male or female body could not be substantiated by referring simply to the actual bodies that men and women possessed'. Claims about the archetypes had to be supported 'by demonstrating that typical male or female observable characteristics . . . were evidence of a more perfectly male or female invisible nature (*physis*)'.[43] But according to the theory of sexual reproduction expounded in the Hippocratic treatise 'The Seed', 'maleness' and 'femaleness' were not to be found exclusively in male and female bodies respectively. This treatise teaches that both male and female produce 'sperm'. Moreover, both male and female produce both male and female sperm, the male sperm being the stronger. If both male and female produce the stronger (that is, male) sperm, a male child is the result. If both produce the weaker (that is, female) sperm, then a female is the result. If one produces the stronger and one produces the weaker type of sperm 'then the resultant sex is determined by whichever sperm prevails in quantity'.[44] According to some commentators, this means that there are six possible ways in which the sex of a child can be determined, including where the female parent's male seed is determining in producing a male and the male parent's female seed is determining in producing a female.[45] The picture is further complicated by the fact that, according to the treatise, the sperm 'is a product which comes from the whole body of each parent, weak sperm coming from the weak parts, and strong sperm coming from the strong parts',[46] which implies, as Dean-

Jones points out, that both male and female must have both male and female parts of the body.[47] Once again, what are 'male' and 'female' here, and how does, for example, the male seed coming from a possibly male part of the female body relate to the perfectly male or female nature (*physis*) that allegedly determines the outwardly, but imperfectly, male or female body of the individual?

Freud, who thought about these things more than most, was clear that the a priori assumption of the categories of 'male' and 'female' was far from being unproblematic:

> Psychoanalysis has a common basis with biology, in that it presupposes an original bisexuality in human beings (as in animals). But psychoanalysis cannot elucidate the intrinsic nature of what in conventional or in biological phraseology is termed 'masculine' and 'feminine': it simply takes over the two concepts and makes them the foundation of its work. When we attempt to reduce them further, we find masculinity vanishing into activity and femininity into passivity, and that does not tell us enough.[48]

For Freud, then, Aristophanes' tale does not express in mythic, symbolic form the straightforward and non-mythic fact of sex. Rather, it reveals the complexity masked by the straightforward assumption of the 'non-mythic' fact of sex. Of course Freud's biological speculations yield a concept of sex that is, in its own way, every bit as mythical as Aristophanes' cosmic principle of the division of all things into male and female. But the question is, can *any* concept of sex claim to divorce itself entirely from myth?

Lacan: m/f

'Sex', we might say, is a problematic presupposition functioning as the modern site of the existential problem with which Aristophanes' myth grapples: what is the origin and nature of human being? The crossing of the existential problem and the principle of the division of male and female in Aristophanes' myth is illuminated even more sharply in certain of Jacques Lacan's allusions to Plato's text, especially in his *The Four Fundamental Concepts of Psychoanalysis*. Indeed, to the extent that Aristophanes' tale explains the phenomenon of human love through an account of 'the nature of human beings and what has happened to it' (189d4), where 'what has happened to it' [*ta pathēmata autēs*] is also what the nature of human beings has

undergone or *suffered*, the myth is emblematic of the Lacanian psychoanalytical attempt to account for the human subject. What has
the human being suffered or undergone in order to be the human
subject that it is? How has this 'suffering' marked the subject, or
how is this 'suffering' marked in the constitution of the subject?
These questions – referring to the genesis of the human subject as
such, rather than the psycho-pathological history of any human
individual – are inseperably bound up in Lacanian psychoanalysis
with the question of 'sexual difference', where 'sexual difference' is
a specifically psychoanalytical category that it is important to distinguish from the non-psychoanalytical category of 'sex' or 'sex
difference'. 'Sex' or 'sex difference' distinguishes organisms as
either male or female solely in relation to their function in reproduction; 'sexual difference' refers to the distribution of subject positions
within the realm of signification, a distribution that, for Lacan,
hinges on the subject's relation to the phallus, the allegedly empty
signifier of difference, distinguished from the penis as an anatomical organ. Sexual difference is thus a psychic structure that is an
effect of signification, inscribed in the subjectivity of the subject, not
anything like a natural fact.

The Lacanian psychoanalytical account of sexual difference and
sexuation is intended to displace the biological and zoological category of sex as an explanans in psychoanalytical anthropology. If
sex nevertheless continues to appear in psychoanalytical theory we
thus need to clarify its role and the relation between sex and sexual
difference. In this regard, it is not good enough to say that the word
'sex' is often used where the psychoanalytical category of sexual
difference is intended, as any confusion or failure to make the distinction has serious theoretical consequences. So what is the relation
between 'sex' and 'sexual difference' in psychoanalytical theory?
This question is of singular importance in understanding the originality and influence of the theoretical foundations of Lacanian psychoanalysis in particular. For if psychoanalysis could not distinguish
between sex as biological sex difference and the psychic structure
of sexual difference there would be no specificity to the psychoanalytical discourse of sexuation and Lacan's account of sexed subjectivation would amount to no more than a traditional psychology of
gender identification propped up by a dubious and untheorized
relation to a biological presumption.

In addressing these questions I will henceforth employ a strict
terminological distinction between 'sex' or 'sex difference' (the presumed biological difference between male and female) and 'sexual

difference' (the specifically psychoanalytical term for the distribution of subject positions within the realm of signification). Neither Freud nor Lacan mark the term 'sexual difference' as a conceptual innovation (Freud did not make any terminological distinction, speaking freely of 'the distinction between the sexes'; Lacan tended to speak of 'sexual positions'). However, the phrase 'sexual difference' became common in psychoanalytical feminism in the 1980s and 1990s precisely as a way of marking the specificity of the psychoanalytical account in distinction from any biological conception of sex difference. For the purposes of this discussion, the differences in the details of various contemporary psychoanalytical accounts of sexual difference – or in various different explanations of the meaning of 'sexual difference' in psychoanalytical discourses – are less important than the basic shared presumption that 'sexual difference' is something other than a biological fact.

Lacan does not address the question of the relation between sex and sexual difference explicitly – indeed, that is the problem. Although there is a conceptual distinction between sexual difference ('sexual positions') and sex difference, Lacan himself makes no terminological distinction between the categories of sex (male/female), gender (masculine/feminine) and sexual difference (man/woman). (Occasionally words from all three categories appear in one sentence: 'That is what the other sex [*l'autre sexe*], the masculine sex [*le sexe masculin*], is for women [*les femmes*].'[49]) Nevertheless (and despite sentences like this: 'There is thus the male [*mâle*] way of revolving around [the fact that there is no such thing as a sexual relationship] and then the other one . . . the female [*femelle*] way'[50]) the specificity of sex difference is generally marked as 'biological', rather than psychic. It would thus not be true to say that, for Lacan, what has traditionally been understood as sex difference is reinterpreted as sexual difference, even if the explanatory force of biology in the definition of what it is to be a man or a woman gives way to a psychoanalytical account. But if sex difference is not sexual difference, there is nevertheless a relation between them that needs to be clarified. What is this relation? It is in Lacan's – admittedly oblique – references to Aristophanes' speech in the *Symposium* that the question permits itself to be seen, and in which (so I will argue) an answer presents itself.

The formulas of sexuation in Lacan's Seminar XX (*Encore*, 1972–3) distinguish between the two 'poles' of 'so-called man or woman' (where 'man and 'woman' are, he says earlier, abbreviations for the articulation of these formulas).[51] According to Lacan, every speaking being must situate itself at one pole or the other. On the side of man, the formula expresses the claim that the whole of man, or all men, are determined in relation to the phallic function, or, perhaps, that man is wholly determined, *qua* man, in relation to the phallic function; at the same time – and the contradiction is deliberate – there is at least one not submitted to the phallic function ('that is what is known as the father function').[52] On the other side, the formula expresses the claim that not all here are submitted to the phallic function (that woman *qua* woman is not wholly determined in relation to the phallic function; what is not thus determined is called feminine *jouissance*). At the same time, there is not one for whom the phallic function does not operate. These positions are, explicitly, not identified with male and female, that is, they are explicitly not identified with the categories of sex. They are determined by the subject's relation to the phallus, a relation 'that forms without regard to the anatomical distinction between the sexes'.[53] Thus, '[a]ny speaking being whatsoever, as is expressly formulated in Freudian theory, whether provided with the attributes of masculinity – attributes that remain to be determined – or not, is allowed to inscribe itself in [the woman portion]';[54] '[o]ne ultimately situates oneself there [the pole where man is situated] by choice – women are free to situate themselves there if it gives them pleasure to do so'.[55] Although Lacan says that women can situate themselves on the side of men, the claim that the formulas of sexuation 'are the only possible definition of the so-called man or woman portion for that which finds itself in the position of inhabiting language'[56] means that it is, strictly speaking, more correct to say that female speaking beings can be men; male speaking beings can be women. This is why '[t]here are men who are just as good as women'[57] – they *are* women.

But this still leaves the question of the relation between sex and sexual difference unanswered. What is at stake in this question can be seen most clearly when it is posed in response to Lacan's earlier discussions of the role of the Oedipus complex and the phallic function in the subject's 'assumption' of or 'identification' with their 'sex'. When Lacan says, for example, that 'one can indicate the structures that govern the relations between the sexes by referring simply to the phallus's function',[58] in what sense are these 'sexes' to be understood? Are humans divided biologically into two sexes – represented by the little boy and the little girl – each of which will subsequently 'assume' their sex in the process of sexuation, taking up a sexual position structured with reference to the phallus? Or are these 'sexes' only specifiable *as sexes* from the perspective of a structure of sexual difference?

The latter *must* be the case. Biological sex difference could not somehow be 'discovered' as a sexual difference in the loose sense of the phrase independently of the logic of sexuation. The 'discovery' of sex difference could not, if the psychoanalytic account is to retain its specificity, be independent of sexuation – it is *part of it*.[59] The distinction of sex difference (like all distinction, *tout court*) does not subsist outside of the symbolic order or the order of significa-tion. So, how could it be separated off – as an allegedly natural division – from sexuation and sexual difference? The 'discovery' of sex difference can only be understood, in Lacan's terms, as a psychi-cally mediated interpretation of otherwise meaningless aspects of anatomical diversity, according to what he sees as the necessity to take up one of two sexual positions; that is, according to the relent-less duality of the logic of sexuation.[60] If it is nevertheless the case that references to biological sex difference continue to appear in Lacan's work, what part do they play? What is the status of 'sex difference' in Lacan's account of sexuation?

At first sight Lacan's scant references to biology and to sex dif-ference in Seminar XX seem designed not to illuminate, but rather to intensify the mystery of this question. This is especially the case where Lacan – like Freud – considers the fact of human sexual reproduction. In Seminar XI, *The Four Fundamental Concepts of Psy-choanalysis*, Lacan reintroduces the myth of the lamella, the impos-sible 'organ' that is the libido '*qua* pure life instinct, that is to say, immortal life or irrepressible life', representing what is subtracted from or lost to 'the living being by virtue of the fact that it is subject to the cycle of sexed reproduction . . . that part of himself that the individual loses at birth'.[61] Lacan later distinguishes 'two lacks', by way of which 'sexuality' (by which he seems to mean both sexed subjectivity and sexual being) is established. The first, he says, 'emerges from the central defect around which the dialectic of the advent of the subject to his own being in the relation to the Other turns – by the fact that the subject depends on the signifier and that the signifier is first of all in the field of the Other'.[62] This lack-in-being, which is the very condition of the subject's insertion into language 'takes up', Lacan says,

> the other lack, which is the real, earlier lack, to be situated at the advent of the living being, that is to say, at sexed reproduction. The real lack is what the living being loses, that part of itself *qua* living

being, in reproducing itself through the way of sex. This lack is real because it relates to something real, namely, that the living being, by being subject to sex, has fallen under the blow of individual death.[63]

Lacan refers here to an idea familiar from Freud: sexual reproduction and the death (the mortality) of the organism are two sides of the same coin. Like Freud in 'Beyond the Pleasure Principle', Lacan then refers us to Aristophanes' myth of the origin of sexuality in Plato's *Symposium*:

> Aristophanes' myth pictures the pursuit of the complement for us in a moving, and misleading, way, by articulating that it is the other, one's sexual other half, that the living being seeks in love. [For] this mythical representation of the mystery of love, analytic experience substitutes the search by the subject, not [for] the sexual complement, but [for] the part of himself, lost forever, that is constituted by the fact that he is only a sexed living being, and that he is no longer immortal.[64]

Lacan does not reject Aristophanes' myth, but reinscribes its account of lack within a psychoanalytical register. Aristophanes' claim that there is a division and that the result of this is sexual (as opposed to autochthonous) reproduction is interpreted as a mythical representation of the lack within the subject itself, a lack traced back to the division of sex difference and the relation between death and sexual reproduction. Thus sex difference and sexual reproduction ostensibly account for the constitutive lack in the subject, for the division between 'the living subject and that which it loses by having to pass, for its reproduction, through the sexual cycle'.[65]

How should we interpret this? Does Lacan suggest that for the Aristophanesian myth we are to substitute the non-psychoanalytical finding that the subject's lack has a biological foundation? That the lack in the subject can be explained with reference to the biological 'fact' of human reproduction, without the need to understand the subject's constitutive relation to signification? Unless Lacan lapsed, on this point, into a biologism quite inexplicable in relation to the foundations of his theoretical project, the reference to biological lack must be explained in relation to what is surely the *more fundamental psychoanalytical* claim: 'the subject as such is uncertain because he is divided by the effects of language. Through the effects of speech, the subject always realizes himself more in the Other, even if it is no more than half of himself that he searches for there.'[66]

The biological lack is not elaborated in terms of its most obvious existential significance – the constitutive finitude of the subject, its being-towards-death – but at the cellular level, ultimately in the process of meiosis that precedes conception.[67] How could division at this level constitute the subjectivity of the subject? How could the fact of cell division be understood as in any way related to the constitution of subjectivity *except as* a *representation* of it in or from another discourse, a story told (*muthōs*), a tale, a legend: a mythic representation or symbolization of the condition of the subject of language? Lacan, we may recall, substituted the Aristophanesian myth with the myth of the lamella, the mythic immortality of pure libido before sex distinction, 'the myth intended to embody the missing part'.[68] The reference to the biological 'lack' is part and parcel of this myth. The biological lack is the mythic representation of the psychic lack (what Lacan earlier called the 'lack in being' or 'lack of being', *manque à être*) that constitutes the subject in its inscription in the order of signification.

To the extent that subjectivation *is* sexuation in Lacanian psycho-analytical theory, the biological concept of sex difference functions as the 'mythic' representation of sexual difference, a symbolization or a 'biological metaphor'[69] for 'that division of what is improperly called humanity insofar as humanity is divided up into sexual iden-tifications'[70] – the necessity for speaking beings to situate them-selves at one of the two poles of sexual difference. We can now see how, for Lacan, Aristophanes' myth can be interpreted as teaching much the same thing. The human condition, constituted through/ as lack, is symbolized mythically as the cut of sex, the division into two. The myth of origin does not symbolize the non-mythic fact of the division into male and female; the division into male and female functions mythically to symbolise the subject constituted through lack. Of course, not all commentators see it this way. Paul Verhae-ghe, for example, reads Lacan's account of the 'original lack' quite literally:

> The Real of the organism functions as a cause, in the sense that it contains a primordial loss which precedes the loss involved in the chain of signifiers. What kind of a loss is this? It is the loss of eternal life, which paradoxically enough is lost at the moment of birth as sexed being. Non-sexual reproduction implies in principle the pos-sibility of eternal life (single-celled organisms and clones), whereas sexual reproduction implies in principle the death of the individual. Each organism wants to undo this loss and tries to return to the previous state of non-sexual being . . . the primordial loss on the

level of the organism is re-interpreted as a phallic lack in the relation between subject and Other . . . The loss at the level of the Real is the cause by means of which life is turned into one elongated, elaborate attempt to return to eternal life . . . the original lack gets re-interpreted in phallic terms.

This reinterpretation, according to Verhaeghe, gives rise to a 'gender identity' that is 'a result of the loss of chromosomal gender'.[71] But how, even at the level of the unconscious or of an unconscious ontology of the human being, could this be a real cause that did not need to be understood, interpreted, symbolized – in some way *psychically mediated* – by the subject?

In commenting on the same passage from *The Four Fundamental Concepts of Psychoanalysis* Žižek glosses it thus: 'The myth of the lamella presents the phantasmatic entity that gives body to what a living being loses when it enters the (symbolically regulated) regime of sexual difference.'[72] Žižek seems, then, to agree that this is not to be read literally as a reference to the ultimate biological basis for the explanation of psychic phenomena. But in glossing the passage in this way he avoids the question of the relation of the biological concept of sex and 'the (symbolically regulated) regime of sexual difference'.

Refusing to avoid this question, we should have to say that, within psychoanalytical theory, the biological concept of sex difference can have no other legitimate function than the mythic representation of sexual difference, and it can certainly have no explanatory power in relation to the alleged necessity of the sexual positions. Indeed, it is the ubiquitous *illusion* of its explanatory power in everyday life that demands a psychoanalytical explanation: why is the speaking subject seemingly compelled to misrecognize the logical exigency of sexual positioning (as Lacan has it) as a biological fact? Why is the speaking subject seemingly compelled to misrecognize the inherently unstable assumption of their sex ('which, you know, always retains a certain ambiguity in analysis'[73]) in terms of a supposedly unambiguous and essentially immutable sex difference? This is the paralogism of sex: why does the speaking subject mistake a logical necessity for a substantial reality?[74]

Lacan's account of sexuation ostensibly affords an explanatory priority to the terms 'man' and 'woman' in relation to 'male' and 'female', with the latter understood as a way of representing the necessity of the former (*qua* sexual positions) to ourselves. The correlation male-man/female-woman is therefore, in one sense, conventional. But if we nevertheless find, throughout Lacan's work, a presumption that the former determines one's sexual position (for example: 'man – I mean he who happens to be male without knowing what to do with it'[75]), it is not because Lacan mimics the paralogism that psychoanalysis should explain – it is because his own account of sexuation is paralogistic. The separation of sex and sexual difference is most radical in Seminar XX: 'The sexed being of . . . not-whole women does not involve the body but what results from the logical exigency of speech.' Further, '[t]here isn't the slightest prediscursive reality, for the very fine reason that what constitutes a collectivity – what I call men, women and children – means nothing qua prediscursive reality. Men, women and children are but signifiers.'[76] But if the logical conclusion of this account of sexual positions is, as I have said, that female speaking beings can be men and male speaking beings can be women this is, nevertheless, not a conclusion that Lacan ever seriously entertains. At every turn it is in fact presumed that females will be women and males will be men. The 'mythic' function of the concept of sex difference is still at work in the discourse that reveals it, propping up the account of sexual difference to the extent that the latter claims to uncover an inflexible necessity. For what grounds this necessity in Lacan's theory is of course sex difference itself.[77] Lacan does not just describe or explain a normative function ('the Oedipus complex has a normative function, not just in the moral structure of the subject, nor only in its relations to reality, but as regards the assumption of his sex')[78] – Lacan's psychoanalytical theory *is* normative on this point. This normativity – which becomes an undisguised moralism in much contemporary Lacanian theory – is perhaps most evident in the pathologization of homosexuality, which rests on the presumption that the instance of the feminine male is the result of a failure, a short circuit, in the assumption *'de son propre sexe'*.[79] If the only justification for the alleged necessity of the two sexual positions and their formulas is that 'analysis teaches us' that it is so, it needs to be explained how the analyst can so easily distinguish between history and necessity, especially when the relation between pathology and the vicissitudes of 'civilization' is basic to Freudian theory.

For Joan Copjec the foregoing argument would no doubt fall under the heading of what she calls, in her essay 'Sex and the Euthanasia of Reason', the 'deconstructionist' approach to the theoretical analysis of sex exemplified in Judith Butler's *Gender Trouble*.

In this essay, Copjec argues that Butler's powerful critique of the substantial concept of sex (of the idea that sex is the determining essence of human existence) cannot be extended to encompass 'the rejection of the notion that there is anything constant or invariable about sexual difference'.[80] Whilst it may be true, according to Copjec, that the meaning of the term 'woman' has shifted histori- cally, this cannot be the basis of an argument for the fundamental instability of sexual difference. That meanings shift because signi- fication is always 'in process' is not an argument against the stabil- ity of sex as Lacan conceives it, because sex, Copjec argues, is not a signifier whose meaning forever remains complete, it is, itself, the 'impossibility of completing meaning . . . sex is the structural incompleteness of language'.[81] In fact Butler's argument is not, as Copjec claims, based on the fact that the meaning of the term woman has changed historically, and Butler's position has never been to 'deny' sexual difference, as Copjec suggests.[82] But Copjec is right that Butler's argument is directed against the claims for the 'com- pulsory' inevitability of the structure of sexual difference described by Lacan.

Copjec claims that sexual difference (which she does not distin- guish terminologically from sex), because it is produced by the failure of signification – indeed, it is this failure – is not inscribed in the symbolic. As such it is a difference unlike all other differ- ences: it 'is a real and not a symbolic difference'.[83] As she puts it elsewhere, the structures described by Lacan, including that of sexual difference, are 'not to be located among the relations that constitute our everyday reality; they belong, instead, to the order of the real'.[84] According to Copjec, Butler locates sexual difference in the realm of culture, and hence assumes that it is deconstructible. There is, Copjec writes, a psychoanalytical objection to this:

> Freud argues . . . that sex is to be grasped not on the terrain of culture but on the terrain of the drives, which – despite the fact that they have no existence outside culture – are not cultural. They are, instead, the other of culture and, as such, are not susceptible to its manipulations.
>
> Sex is defined by a law (of the drives) with which . . . 'one does not bargain', which one does not 'trick'. . . . [F]rom the standpoint of culture, *sex does not budge*. This is to say, among other things, that sex, sexual difference, cannot be deconstructed, since deconstruction is an operation that can be applied only to culture, to the signifier, and has no purchase on this other realm.[85]

This argument is straightforwardly fallacious, since it slips from the sexual drive to sexual difference as if the two terms were synonymous (a slippage facilitated in the English by the ambiguous word 'sex'). This is especially egregious, given that Freud goes to some pains to insist on the independence of the analysis of the sexual drive from sex.[86] Even apart from this, the claim that sexual difference is a dimension of the real (where this is understood in Lacan's sense) is very hard to understand, given the conventional acceptance that 'the real' is, for Lacan, undifferentiated and unsymbolized (indeed, unsymbolizable).[87] These arguments are, however, beside the point, when what Copjec needs to make her case is an argument for the alleged invariable constancy of the structure of sexual difference, an account of the necessity of its 'compulsion' *in this form*, rather than a mere presumption of it.

In the absence of any such argument Copjec's 'real' sex is a mythic structure, a paralogistic inference drawn from a transcendental ground (the formal conditions of subjectivation).[88] Without an argument for, rather than a normative social injunction in favour of, the necessity of the sexual positions in Lacan's account of sexuation, 'sexual difference' in Lacanian psychoanalysis cannot answer for itself without secret recourse to the mythic function of a biological concept of sex difference, borrowing its sheen of necessity.

X, Y, Z, etc.

To all this it may be objected that although the account of the principle of the division of all things into male and female in Aristophanes' tale, the projection of male and female into ever smaller intra-cellular parts in Freud's speculations, the role assigned to biological sex difference in Lacanian psychoanalytical theory, and the paralogism of the substantiality of sex in Copjec's misguided anti-Butlerianism are all mythic, in the broadest sense of the word, nevertheless there is a non-mythic natural-biological concept of sex which is not vulnerable to this kind of analysis, whose status is not questionable and the meaning of the terms of which are clear. What we mean when we say this is that there simply are male and female human beings and biology can explain to us how this comes about, in the sense that it can explain what makes an embryo develop into one or the other. This, we learn in school, is determined by chromosomes: genotype XY for males, XX for females. As the X chromosome is found in the typical genotype of both males and females but the Y only in the typical genotype of males the Y is sometimes seen as the sex-determining chromosome. But, emphatically, the X chromosome is not 'female' and the Y chromosome is not 'male'. What we do not usually learn about in school are the significant number of males and females who do not possess either of these genotypes, or possess the 'opposite' genotype for their sex: XXY or XXXY or XXXXY (or 46XY/47XXY) males (Klinefelter Syndrome, affecting between 1 in 500 and 1 in 1000 males), XY females, XO females (Turner Syndrome), and XX males (no doubt there are other chromosomal variations found in human beings too).[89]

What does 'male' mean when we can speak of XX males? What does 'female' mean when we can speak of XY females? These are not questions about these sexual 'anomalies', but questions about the norms from which they apparently diverge. Can we be sure, when the diversity of our bodies and genotypes is so great, that 'sex' does not impinge on us primarily and most profoundly as a structuring presupposition or an organizing metaphysical principle? That our modern, natural-biological concept of sex does not function much like Aristophanes' mythic principle of the division of all things into male and female?

3

'Erōs' *and* 'Sexuality', *Plato and* Freud (Symposium)

The role of Aristophanes' account of the origin of male and female in the *Symposium* in Freud's avowedly *speculative* meditations on the origins of sex difference was, it seems, primarily inspirational. The speculation of 'Beyond the Pleasure Principle' is, Freud wrote, 'an attempt to follow out an idea consistently, out of curiosity to see where it will lead',[1] with Aristophanes providing a hint, a provocation or spur, for the intellectual journey. Freud's references to Plato's concept of eros seem, on the other hand, designed to ground (as if on undisputed authority) a basic concept in his psychoanalytical theory, that of sexuality (*Sexualität*). Those who look down with contempt on psychoanalysis should, he says in the Preface to the fourth edition of 'Three Essays on the Theory of Sexuality' (1920), 'remember how closely the enlarged concept of sexuality of psychoanalysis coincides with the Eros of the divine Plato',[2] as if no one would look down with contempt upon that, or him. Speaking of the 'outbursts of indignation, derision and scorn' from the opponents of psychoanalysis, especially in relation to the apparent outrage of its concept of sexuality, Freud reminds his readers elsewhere that it is not so much desire for sex union that the concept implies; rather it has 'far more resemblance to the all-inclusive and all-preserving Eros of Plato's *Symposium*', as if that could not possibly cause any offence.[3] (Freud seems to forget, in appealing to his respectable predecessor, the moral outrage and disgust with which many modern commentators had viewed the *Symposium*, with its easy acceptance of the unnatural 'vice' or 'perversion' of what came to be called 'homosexuality'.) In 1921, in 'Group Psychology and the

Analysis of the Ego', Freud even goes so far as to claim that the apparently original concept of sexuality in psychoanalysis 'coincides exactly' with 'the "Eros" of the philosopher Plato'.[4]

As the fact of *some* conceptual relation – even if not, as Freud claims, an identity – between Plato's ancient concept of eros and Freud's modern concept of sexuality seems indisputable, the question of the influence of the one on the other certainly arises. But this chapter is concerned, instead, with a relation in the other direction, as it were – with the extent to which presumptions about one (sexuality) have influenced the way the other (eros) now figures in contemporary thought. It is concerned, specifically, with the way in which the failure to realize, theoretically, the specificity of Freud's concept of sexuality – a failure that Freud himself did not avoid – has influenced one particular debate in the literature on the *Symposium* concerning the meaning and interpretation of the concept of eros.

The nature of the interpretative problem is revealed already in the problem of the translation of the classical Greek *erōs*. For although the noun *erōs* is readily (if superficially) intelligible and easily transliterated, the meanings of the words we might use to translate it and its cognates into English – specifically, 'love' and 'eros' or 'the erotic' – overlap but do not coincide, to the extent that popular opinion presumes a non-erotic love to be no contradiction in terms. To distinguish between these different kinds of love in English we may introduce the qualifier 'sexual': *erōs* is sexual love, or has to do with sexual desire (*ta Aphrodisia* – sexual pleasures or those things pertaining to sexual pleasure), and this is indeed how the concept of *erōs* is frequently distinguished for us from the concept of *philia* (affectionate or friendly love). But this restriction (presuming for now that we understand the English 'sexual' in the generally accepted restricted sense) flies in the face of the expansion of the field of *erōs* in the *Symposium*, where ultimately *erōs* is considerably distanced – if not completely dissociated – from *ta Aphrodisia*.

This translational problem is at the heart of one of the central interpretative debates about the account of eros in Socrates' speech in the *Symposium*: does Socrates speak throughout of the nature and function of a specifically sexual passion, or is eros a metaphor for some more general kind of desire or existential force?[5] In what sense is the concept of eros originally sexual, and does it remain sexual in its transformation into the passionate contemplation of truth? In the twenty-first century, these questions inevitably invoke the theoretical context of Freudian psychoanalysis. For regardless of one's position in relation to Freud (for or against, or indifferent) the Western cultural-intellectual landscape has been so indelibly marked by Freudian theory that it is difficult to ignore in relation to a whole host of questions and impossible to ignore when the question is that of eros.

Freud's innovative concept of sexuality is different from the pre-vailing 'popular' conception of sexuality, which is understood as a phenomenon of physiological maturity, emerging at puberty and fully realized in adulthood, provoked by an 'object' of the opposite sex and fulfilled (or desired to be fulfilled) in genital stimulation (its ultimate aim and satisfaction: penetrative heterosexual inter-course). Freud's expanded conception of sexuality widens the field of the operation, objects, aims and possible routes of satisfaction of or for sexuality considerably (some might even say infinitely) and has of course not been uncontroversial. One aspect of Freud's theory of sexuality – the sublimation of the sexual drive – has been a major theme in the twentieth-century interpretation of Plato's concept (or, for some, theory) of eros. Nevertheless, making a formal parallel with the argument of Chapter 1, in particular, this chapter argues that interpretation of Plato's concept of eros has unwittingly been prejudiced by the assumption by commentators of versions of the popular modern conception of sexuality, effectively imposing the concept on to interpretations of Plato and thereby closing off an appreciation of the specificity of Plato's concept to the extent that the modern concept is essentially at odds with that of Plato.

What is *erōs*?

The account of *erōs* in Socrates' speech is not an attempt to arrive at a definition of the word, but an analysis of its nature and func-tion.[6] As such, we are obliged to follow through the argument ourselves if we are to understand the concept. The speech begins with ironic flattery and a devastating elenchus. Agathon (the previ-ous speaker) was right, Socrates says, to begin with an attempted definition of Eros, displaying 'the sort of character Eros himself has [*hopoios tís estin ho Erōs*], and then go[ing] on to what he does [*ta erga autou*]' (199c6–7).[7] But Agathon was, of course, wrong in rela-tion to his postulated characterization of Eros as the most beautiful and the best of the gods. Socrates first gets Agathon to agree that Love must be Love *of* something: given the choice between the claims that love is love of nothing or that love is love of something Agathon obviously plumps for the latter. In making the argument that leads to this conclusion Socrates uses the noun form *erōs*, and makes an analogy with such relative nouns as 'mother', father' and 'brother' (as a father is a father *of* someone, so love is love *of* something), though it is not at all clear that *erōs*, as an abstract noun, should be understood in this way. In fact, Socrates' argument works better in relation to the *act* of loving, which may well be intentional, in the phenomenological sense. Indeed, the introduction of three verbs (*eraō*, to love, *epithumeō*, to desire; *boulomai*, to wish) in the next few lines reveal that this switch from the abstract noun to the verbal form is indeed the hidden assumption in Socrates' argument:

> 'Now tell me this – does Love desire the thing he is love of, or not [*poteron ho Erōs ekeinou hou estin erōs, epithumei autou ē ou*]?' 'Absolutely', said Agathon. 'Does he desire and love [*epithumei te kai era*] the very thing he desires and loves as a consequence of having it or not having it?' 'Of not having it, probably', said Agathon. 'Then see', said Socrates, 'whether instead of your "probably" it isn't necessarily like this: that what desires desires what it lacks [*to epithumoun epithumein hou endees estin*], or, if it doesn't lack it, it doesn't desire it? To me this looks amazingly necessary, Agathon; how about you?' 'It looks so to me too', he said. 'Well said. So will anyone wish [*bouloit'*] to be tall if he is tall . . . ?' 'From what we've agreed it'll be impossible.' (200a3–b6)

Socrates' conclusion in this section of the dialogue, based on the added premise that love is love of beautiful and not ugly things, is therefore that 'Love is lacking in, and does not possess, beauty' (201b3), contrary to Agathon's eulogy to the beauty of Eros. At this point Agathon drops out of the discussion and Socrates continues his speech by reporting to the symposiasts the account of Eros that he claims to have heard from Diotima of Mantinea, 'the very person who taught me [Socrates] about erotics [*ta erōtika*]' (201d5). Now Socrates casts himself in the role previously occupied by Agathon and Diotima's contribution constitutes, in part, a refutation or denial of various assumptions in Agathon's speech, as well as aspects of the other speeches too.

The beginning of this section of the dialogue echoes that of the previous section, reiterating that it is right to begin by 'describing who Eros himself is and what sort of character he has, and then going on to what he does' (201d10–e1). Socrates (like Agathon pre-

viously) presumes that Eros is beautiful and good; Diotima corrects
him. Eros is neither beautiful nor ugly, neither good nor bad, but
something in between. Carrying forward from the previous section
– as if it had been part of the discussion between Diotima and
Socrates – the conclusion that 'a lack of good and beautiful things
is what makes [Eros] desire the very things he lacks' (202d1–2), it
is agreed that Eros cannot be a god as the gods possess beauty and
goodness (in the sense that they *are* beautiful and good). Eros,
Diotima says, is something in between god and mortal, 'a great
spirit [*daimōn*]' (202d14), whose 'function' (or 'power', *dunamin*) is
to act as intermediary between gods and mortals. In claiming that
it is 'through this that the whole expertise of the seer [*hē mantikē*]
works its effects' (202e7), Diotima, herself a 'seer',[8] implicitly suggests the daimonic origin of her erotic knowledge and its ultimately
divine provenance.

The peculiar intermediate nature of Eros is explained by his parentage. At the gods' feast held to celebrate the birth of Aphrodite,
Resource (Poros) got drunk on nectar. Poverty (Penia) 'lay down
beside him and became pregnant with Eros' (203c1–2). Reflecting
the joint inheritance of the characteristics of both of his parents Eros
is poor, barefoot, homeless and lacking; but also a clever schemer.
Neither mortal nor immortal, 'on the same day he flourishes and
lives, when he finds resources, and now he dies, but then comes
back to life again'. Neither wise nor ignorant he is yet 'passionate
for wisdom and resourceful in looking for it, philosophizing through
all his life'. Indeed, Eros is 'necessarily a philosopher, and as a philosopher necessarily between wisdom and ignorance' (203d6–
204b5). In fact it is the need to arrive at this conclusion that drives
all of Diotima's previous characterization of Eros, including the
story of his birth. This enables her to reach, explicitly, the position
that was implicit in Socrates' questioning of Agathon:

> you thought Love to be what is loved, not what does the loving
> [*ōēthēs de . . . to erōmenon Erōta einai, ou to erōn*]; that, I imagine, is why
> Love seemed to you to be supremely beautiful. What is loveable [*to
> eraston*] is in fact what is really beautiful, graceful, perfect, and to be
> counted as blessed; whereas what does the loving [*to erōn*] is of quite
> a different character, of the sort I described. (204c1–6)

Having thus described 'who Eros himself is and what sort of character he has', Diotima must, as promised earlier, go on to describe
'what he does' [*ta erga*, his 'work'] (201–e1). But this point marks an

important shift in Socrates' speech. From this point the speech is no longer structured as an interrogation of the previous speech or previous assumptions and gradually builds up to its quasi-mystical climax. At the same time the discussion moves decisively from what is loved to 'what does the loving' or (more simply) the act of loving, as the subject of the speech shifts (silently) from Eros to eros. Thus both the questions of what Eros is and does (or, as Socrates puts it, what 'use' he is to human beings [204c8]) become questions about the lover (*ho erōn*) who loves beautiful things or about loving itself: '*era ho erōn tōn kalōn; tí era*'? (204d5). The one who loves, loves beautiful things; but why does he love them? Or, the one who loves, loves beautiful things, but what is it that he desires in loving them, what is his aim?[9] Shifting the discussion in this way Socrates has in fact introduced a new object, and the definition of love, despite appearances, is still to be achieved.

The next steps in the argument (204 d6–205) introduce several claims, as if they were self-evident, in order to arrive at a new definition of eros as power or passion (rather than, as previously, Eros the god). If we love beautiful things because we desire to possess them, or to make them our own, what do we gain by possessing them? If this question is difficult to answer, Diotima says, substitute 'the good' for 'the beautiful' (for in fact, it is claimed, 'there is nothing else that people are in love with except the good' [205e6–206a1]) and we see that we desire to possess good things because such possession makes us happy, and we do not need to go on to ask why we desire to be happy. This wish, this love (*tēn boulēsin kai ton erōta*) for good things, is common to all human beings, who wish (*boulesthai*) to possess them forever (205a5–7). In that case, Diotima concludes, 'we can sum up by saying that love is of permanent possession of what is good [*ho erōs tou to agathon hautō einai aei*]' (206a11–12).[10]

Before reaching this conclusion explicitly, Diotima established another, very important point:

> Why is it . . . that we don't say that everyone is in love [*pantas eran*], if in fact everyone loves [*erōsi*] the same things, and always loves them, but rather say that some people are in love [*eran*], others not? . . . The fact is, as we can now see, that we separate off one kind of love [*tou erōtos ti eidos*] and apply to it the name which belongs to the whole – 'love' [*erōta*] – and for the other kinds we use other names. (205a9–b6)[11]

The situation is similar, according to Diotima, to the restricted use of the word *poiēsis*. Although, strictly speaking, this latter includes all productive activity (all 'making'), it is often reserved for that kind of *poiēsis* concerned with music and verse. As is even more obvious in English translation, only this is called 'poetry' and only practitioners of this activity are called 'poets', when in fact the names should extend to 'what causes anything whatever to pass from not being into being' (205b9) and those who bring this about. Similarly, only those associated with one kind of love are said to be 'in love' (*eran*) or to be 'lovers' (*erastai*) (205d5–6). The breadth of the ordinary use of the English 'love' (according to which we say, for example, that we love tennis or peaches) means that the translation here makes the argument for Diotima. It should not blind us to the fact that the point about *erōs* is controversial.[12]

This extension of *erōs* is not included explicitly in Diotima's new definition ('love [*ho erōs*] is of permanent possession of what is good' [206a11]), but it is presumed. Now, it seems, Diotima is ready to go on to the second part of her account. If this is what love *is*, she says, what really is it that love *does* (*tí touto tugchanei on to ergon*) (206b3)? What is the function of love? The answer comes surprisingly briskly: 'It's giving birth in the beautiful [*tokos en kalō*], in relation both to body and to soul' (206b7–8).

Understanding how Diotima gets here is complicated. First, in an alleged clarification of the matter, Diotima tells Socrates the following: All human beings are pregnant in soul and body and, at the appointed age, desire (*epithumei*) to give birth. This 'giving birth' is something divine to the extent that it is the immortal aspect of the otherwise mortal human being. This divine giving-birth can only be brought about 'in the beautiful': beauty 'assists' at birth like the goddesses of childbirth.[13]

> For these reasons, if ever what is pregnant approaches something beautiful, it becomes gracious, melts with joy, and gives birth and procreates; but when it approaches what is ugly, it contracts, frowning with pain, turns away, curls up, and fails to procreate, retaining what it has conceived, and suffering because of it. This is why what is pregnant and already full to bursting feels the great excitement it does in proximity to the beautiful, because of the fact that the beautiful person frees it from great pain. (206d6–e1)

The extension of the meaning of conception, pregnancy and birth in this passage is not explained, but the previous discussion of the meaning of 'eros' suggests that the same justification could be offered here. (The 'intercourse of man and woman' is said to be 'a kind of giving birth' (206c5–6); a 'kind of giving birth' to which, we may extrapolate, the name of the whole – giving birth – has been restrictively applied.)[14] But what does it all mean, and how is this a clarification of the function of eros?

Given the mystical-declarative method of Diotima's teaching, it is not surprising that what follows is difficult to reconstruct as a series of logical steps. Eros is now said to be love of procreation and giving birth in the beautiful (206e5). Why? Because procreation is (as previously claimed) the mortal's claim to immortality, and if love is love of permanent possession of the good it follows (according to Diotima) that love must be love of immortality as well (206e7–207a1). Reporting what Diotima told him on another occasion, Socrates accounts for the relationship between love and immortality in a slightly different form. The desire for immortality is not part of love, but its *cause*, where love (for both animals and human beings) encompasses the desire for intercourse and the subsequent selfless nurture of offspring (207a5–d2). This is then extended even further: love of honour (*philotimian*) is explained by the desire to leave 'an immortal memory' of our courage, a 'glorious reputation' that outlives the mortal life (208c1–e2). Those who are pregnant in body attempt to achieve immortality through having children; those pregnant in soul through 'things that it is fitting for the soul to conceive and to bring to birth': wisdom and virtue as manifest, for example, in poetry, and in 'the setting in order of the affairs of cities and households' (208e6–209a7). A man pregnant in soul, eager to give birth, will warm to the beautiful body and soul of his beloved, and, educating the latter, associating with his beauty, 'brings to birth and procreates the things with which he was for so long pregnant . . . nurturing what has been born' – offspring of the soul of 'a more beautiful and immortal kind' than human children (209b1–d1).

We may summarize thus: eros is love of and desire for the perpetual possession of the good, hence love of and desire for immortality. The function of eros is to secure this immortality for the human; the way of eros is procreation in the beautiful. If this is what eros is and how it works, 'the final revelation' (210a1) – for which Diotima doubts even Socrates' readiness – is yet to come. Preparation for the final revelation is described as a journey to the correct approach to eros: the ascending progress of the initiate through the stages of love to the final vision and the true meaning of immortality for the human being.

First, the neophyte, if he is being 'led' correctly by an experienced lover, must 'fall in love [*eran*] with a single [beautiful] body and there procreate beautiful words' (210a6–7). Realizing that the beauty in any one body is closely related to that in any other, and that, in the pursuit of the outward form of beauty, the beauty in all bodies is therefore the same thing, 'he must [then] become a lover (*erastēn*) of all beautiful bodies' (210b4), outgrowing his previous passion for one body only. Next, 'he must consider beauty in soul more valuable than beauty in the body' (210b6–7), loving and caring for the beautiful soul, and giving birth to and seeking out the sort of words 'that will make young men into better men' (210c3). Having done this the lover 'may be compelled to turn to contemplate beauty as it exists in kinds of activity [*en tois epitēdeumasi*] and in laws, and to observe that all of this is mutually related' (210c4–7), leading in turn to 'the beauty that belongs to different kinds of knowledge' (210c8–d1). Each step in this ascent involves the realization that the previous form of beauty is worthless or petty in relation to the next. In this realization the lover frees himself from his 'slavish' attachment to any one kind of thing – but in particular from his slavish attachment to one person. Now he may gaze towards a beauty that is vast and may himself cease to be worthless and petty (as his previous attachment made him). Instead:

> turned towards the great sea of beauty and contemplating that, [he] may bring to birth many beautiful, even magnificent, words and thoughts in a love of wisdom [*philosophia*] that grudges nothing, until there, with his strength and stature increased, he may catch sight of a certain single kind of knowledge, which has for its object a beauty of a sort I shall describe to you. (210d3–7)

Moving correctly through the contemplation of beauty in its various forms the lover 'will come now towards the final goal of the matters of love [*tōn erōtikōn*]' (210e3), catching sight of an eternal beauty, absolute beauty, not located in any earthly thing: that beauty for the sake of which the work of love was done. The final step, then: ascent to the science (*to mathēma*) of beauty itself, 'in order that one may finally know what beauty is, itself' (211d1). Only then will the lover 'succeed in bringing to birth, not phantoms of virtue, because he is not grasping a phantom, but true virtue, because he is grasping the truth; and when he has given birth to and nurtured true virtue, it belongs to him to be loved by the gods, and to him, if to any human being, to be immortal' (212a4–7). The function of eros is thus to lead the lover towards philosophy and the contemplation of the form of beauty, of the contemplation of truth – to partake in immortality through 'catching sight' of the eternal and procreating the good.

Although this account of eros in Socrates' speech in the *Symposium* is presented as an attempt to answer the questions of what eros is and what eros does, the meaning of what we may summarize as its conclusion (eros is procreation of the good in beauty; erotics is the education of eros towards the true achievement of this aim) is still unclear. Indeed, for centuries, despite the summary conclusion, one stream of commentary on the dialogue has seemed to circle around the same question: yes, but really, what *is* eros in this account of eros? What is the meaning of this conclusion? In what sense, precisely, is the contemplation of truth *erotic*? Is eros a specifically sexual passion or some more general kind of existential drive or force? Is the terminology relating to a specifically sexual passion used metaphorically in relation to the contemplation of truth, or is this activity erotic in a more literal sense? If the latter, how is the erotics of philosophy related to the erotics of the sexual encounter? Does Plato mean to offer an account of the human experience of sexual passion, or is the human experience of sexual passion presupposed and deployed for other ends? (A defence of Socrates? A justification of philosophy? An apology for Plato's metaphysics?) All of these questions are further complicated by the narrative form of the dialogue, and specifically by the vexed issue of the status of the account attributed to Diotima, whose character may or may not be a distancing device (distancing the account not only from Plato the author but also from Socrates the character). How, then, can we begin to make our way through these questions?

What is the sexual drive?

To a very great extent, the contemporary understanding of the trajectory of the account of eros in Socrates' speech (from the physical expression of sexual passion to the intellectual achievement of philosophy) passes through the long shadow of Freud. This is more complicated than the ease of a Freudian interpretation suggests, for, as we have seen, in one very important respect Freud identifies one aspect of his own theoretical apparatus with Plato's concept of eros, appropriating it for his own purposes and borrowing Plato's intellectual authority and respectability for the defence of what were, initially, some of his most unpalatable and shocking claims.

At first sight, Freud's identification with Plato seems to centre on Socrates' expansion of the concept of eros, as if this provides a model for Freud's own expansion of the concept of sexuality, which he sometimes (at his most defensive), also called 'love' ('*Liebe*').[15] In his *Introductory Lectures on Psychoanalysis* (Lecture 20: 'The Sexual Life of Human Beings'), Freud points out that, although we tend to presume the opposite, 'it is not easy to decide what is covered by the concept "sexual" '.[16] Nevertheless, as he says in the 'Three Essays on the Theory of Sexuality': 'popular opinion has quite definite ideas about the nature and characteristics of [the] sexual drive', which popular orthodoxy it will then be Freud's goal to overturn in quasi-Socratic manner. (The terms 'sexual drive', 'sexuality', 'the sexual' and 'libido' are used interchangeably in many of Freud's essays.) Freud's description of the popular conception of the sexual drive dates from 1905, but is not so far removed from today's popular view:

> It [the sexual drive] is generally understood to be absent in childhood, to set in at the time of puberty in connection with the process of coming to maturity and to be revealed in the manifestations of an irresistible attraction exerted by one sex upon the other; while its aim is presumed to be sexual union, or at all events actions leading in that direction.[17]

In extending the concept of 'what is sexual' or 'sexuality', such that the kind of adult sexual practice which forms the basis of the popular conception becomes merely one expression of sexuality, Freud has, he says, 'given it [the concept of sexuality] back its true compass. What is called sexuality outside psychoanalysis relates only to a restricted sexual life, which serves the purposes of reproduction and is described as normal.'[18]

Freud's point – that the sexual drive is not restricted to the adult desire for heterosexual reproductive intercourse and manifests itself in surprising and unexpected forms – is justified, in part, as we have said, with reference to Plato. In the 1921 essay 'Group Psychology and the Analysis of the Ego', Freud defines 'libido' as 'the energy, regarded as a quantitative magnitude . . . of those drives which have to do with all that may be comprised under the word "love" '. This (for Freud) somewhat unusual use of the word 'love' (*Liebe*) and the description of its 'compass' is driven by the coming reference to Plato:

The nucleus of what we mean by love naturally consists (and this is what is commonly called love, and what the poets sing of) in sexual love with sexual union as its aim. But we do not separate from this – what in any case has a share in the name 'love' – on the one hand, self-love, and on the other, love for parents and children, friendship and love for humanity in general, and also devotion to concrete objects and abstract ideas. Our justification lies in the fact that psychoanalytic research has taught us that all these tendencies are an expression of the same instinctual impulses.[19]

This extension of the concept of love has

let loose a storm of indignation, as though it had been guilty of making an outrageous innovation. Yet it has done nothing original in taking love in this 'wider' sense. In its origin, function, and relation to sexual love, the 'Eros' of the philosopher Plato coincides exactly with this love-force, the libido of psychoanalysis.[20]

In fact, Freud dissimulates somewhat, as he effectively acknowledges on the next page. For what he calls 'the majority of educated people' object not to the extension of the use of the word 'love', but to the idea that phenomena that they are quite happy to call 'love' – in particular, the child's attachment to the parent, the parent's attachment to the child – are manifestations of the *sexual* drive. This is revealed in the conclusion of the discussion: 'Psychoanalysis, then, gives these love drives the name of sexual drives . . . and by reason of their origin.' (Those who cannot bear to use this terminology are, Freud, says, 'at liberty to make use of the more genteel expressions "Eros" and "erotic" '.[21]) It is thus more precisely the concept of the sexual drives or of sexuality that is identified with Plato's concept of eros, the extension of this latter being analogous to the extension of the concept of sexuality. This is explicit in the reference to Plato in the Preface to the fourth edition of the 'Three Essays on the Theory of Sexuality':

And as for the 'stretching' of the concept of sexuality which has been necessitated by the analysis of children and what are called perverts, anyone who looks down with contempt upon psychoanalysis from a superior vantage-point should remember how closely the enlarged sexuality of psychoanalysis coincides with the Eros of the divine Plato.[22]

What is the 'sexual drive'? Although it is hidden in most English translations, including Strachey's in the *Standard Edition*, Freud distinguishes terminologically (but with no explicit theoretical account) between the instinct (*Instinkt*) and the drive (*Trieb*).[23] In the absence of any definition from Freud himself, instincts, we may say, are for Freud 'animal' behaviours predetermined by heredity, their forms shared by all individuals of a given species. Freud's definition of the drive, on the other hand, is given in some detail in the 1915 essay 'Instincts [*Triebe*] and Their Vicissitudes'. Drives are specifically human dynamic forces: stimuli operating 'on the mind' from within the organism itself, inducing widely varying forms of behaviour in relation to a wide variety of objects and aims. Unlike the punctual external stimulus, from which the organism may, for example, flee or may dispose of 'by a single expedient action', the internal stimulus of the drive is a 'constant pressure', the demands of which can only be 'satisfied' 'by an appropriate ("adequate") alteration of the internal source of stimulation'.[24] If, as Freud believed, the function of the nervous system is to reduce or otherwise master stimuli, its task in relation to the drives is accomplished with much more complex manoeuvres than are provoked by external stimuli. Stimuli from the drives (*Triebreize*) make far higher demands on the nervous system 'and cause it to undertake involved and interconnected activities by which the external world is . . . changed'.[25] For Freud the 'drive' is thus a concept 'on the frontier between the mental and the somatic, as the psychical representative of the stimuli originating from within the organism and reaching the mind, as a measure of the demand made upon the mind for work in consequence of its connection with the body'.[26]

The discussion of the concept of the drive requires us to distinguish, Freud says, between the pressure (*Drang*), aim (*Ziel*), object (*Objekt*) and source (*Quelle*) of the drive. Its pressure is quantitative: 'the measure of the demand for work which it represents'. In each instance the aim is satisfaction, though there may be different paths to this ultimate aim and hence several intermediate aims; partial satisfaction may be obtained even when the ultimate aim is inhibited. Here 'satisfaction' seems to mean the quelling of excitation, the reduction of internal stimuli. However, the aim is also said to be 'the attainment of "organ-pleasure" ',[27] as if excitation were itself the aim.[28] The object of the drive is 'the thing in regard to which or through which the drive is able to achieve its aim. It is what is most variable about a drive and is not originally connected with it . . . It may be changed any number of times in the course of the vicissitudes which the drive undergoes during its existence [*im Laufe der Lebensschicksale des Triebes*].' Finally, the source is the somatic process, the internal stimulus which is psychically represented by the drive. Of these four only the study of the sources of the drives lies outside of psychology.[29]

There are, according to Freud in this essay, two groups of 'primal drives': the ego or self-preservative drives and the sexual drives. However, psychoanalysis is only able to say anything very much about the sexual drives, because only these can be observed 'in isolation, as it were, in the psychoneuroses'.[30] In fact, Freud's earlier study of the vicissitudes of the sexual drives – published in 'Three Essays on the Theory of Sexuality' (1905) – were the beginning of the theory of the drives in general and throughout Freud's work the sexual drives are the drives *par excellence*. Indeed, in the absence of any substantial discussion of the ego drives, and the very close relation of the thin outline of the latter to the self-preservative instincts, Jean Laplanche's claim that 'sexuality . . . represents the model of every drive and probably constitutes the only drive in the strict sense of the term'[31] is persuasive.

Freud's general characterization of the sexual drives in 'Instincts [*Triebe*] and Their Vicissitudes' is tightly packed:

> They are numerous, emanate from a great variety of organic sources, act in the first instance independently of one another and only achieve a more or less complete synthesis at a late stage. The aim which each of them strives for is the attainment of 'organ-pleasure'; only when synthesis is achieved do they enter the service of the reproductive function and thereupon become generally recognizable as sexual drives. At their first appearance they are attached to the self-preservative drives, from which they only gradually become separated; in their choice of object, too, they follow the paths that are indicated to them by the ego drives . . . They are distinguished by possessing the capacity to act vicariously for one another to a wide extent and by being able to change their objects readily. In consequence of the latter properties they are capable of functions which are far removed from their original purposive actions – capable, that is, of 'sublimation'.[32]

Two interconnected points here need to be emphasized. First, as explained at greater length in the 'Three Essays on the Theory of Sexuality', the sexual drive is originally attached to the functions of self-preservation, specifically suckling but also defecation, for example. These activities give rise to an excess of pleasure, over and above the satisfaction of hunger or relief of intestinal discomfort, pleasure obtained from the stimulation of the mouth, lips and anus. The sexual drive emerges in its independence as the desire to repeat this pleasure, for its own sake, irrespective of the needs of self-preservation.[33] Why call these pleasures sexual? Because, according to Freud, after passing through indisputably sexual material in the course of analysis we arrive back at these pleasures – hence on the basis of the inductive inference that a sexual symptom most likely arises from a sexual source.[34] If, however, the doubt about the sexual nature of these infantile pleasures arises because they do not look like adult genital (hetero)sexuality, Freud's whole point in the extension of the concept of sexuality – what can count as sexual – is missed. It is not that the popular definition of the sexual is retained and applied to more and varied phenomena, as is presumed when the Oedipus complex, for example, is crudely misunderstood as the claim that the child wants to 'have sex' with its parent. Rather, the sexual, which is not to be confused with the popular conception of sexuality, is reconceptualized *as* this independent seeking after pleasure/satisfaction. This is not an ad hoc and arbitrary redefinition of a common word, but a relocation of the specificity of the sexual. The justification for this relocation is the gain in explanatory power consequent upon it and the subsequent therapeutic advantages.

Second, the sexual drive is extremely labile and flexible in relation to its objects. For Freud this characteristic is explained by the origin of the sexual drive – its emergence as an independent drive in its peeling away from the instinctual satisfaction of needs. Although this origin 'indicates' certain objects for the sexual drive, it will go anywhere and to any object in the pursuit of its ultimate aim of satisfaction. The catalogue of the 'perversions' of the drive in Freud's 'Three Essays on the Theory of Sexuality', limited though it is, bears witness to its extraordinary opportunistic adaptability. The conclusion drawn from this section of the 'Three Essays' is precisely that the bond between drive and object in the popular conception of sexuality must be 'loosened', Freud says – although we may go further and say that that bond, in so far as it was presumed to be innate, has rather been severed: 'It seems probable that the sexual drive is in the first instance independent of its object; nor is its origin likely to be due to its object's attractions.'[35]

According to Freud, this apparent theoretical innovation in fact constitutes a return to the ancient Greek view. In a footnote to the claim about the coincidence of his concept of sexuality with Plato's concept of eros he writes that the difference between 'the erotic life of antiquity and our own no doubt lies in the fact that the ancients laid the stress upon the drive itself, whereas we [i.e. in the popular conception of sexuality] emphasize its object'.[36] This claim is complicated, for us, by the seeming conflation of the ancients' common view of eros with the specific concept of eros in Socrates' speech. But Freud's point does hold good in relation to the latter. Separating the 'popular' view of the relation between eros and its object from that of Socrates' speech is made difficult by the narrative context of the dialogue. However, in relation to the 'popular view' of the other speeches (particularly Agathon's) one of the conclusions in Socrates' speech is that 'love is not, as you think, of the beautiful' but 'of procreation and giving birth in the beautiful' (206e3–5). Beauty in the 'object' of desire traditionally conceived – the beautiful boy – merely facilitates eros' ultimate aim. Furthermore, the course of love is described as a process of substitution in relation to the various kinds of object such that the object as traditionally conceived (in a wider context) is itself superseded. Eros is conceived in such a way that this movement in relation to the object is not only possible, it is necessary to the satisfaction of the ultimate aim. Indeed, the field of eros is not determined by the specificity of its objects but by its aim (according to Socrates, immortality by way of procreation in the beautiful).

Freud claims that his theory of sexuality reinstates this ancient emphasis on the 'drive' and the aim. His stress on the indiscriminacy and indeterminacy of the sexual drive in relation to the object is more than a paean to its flexibility – it is a necessary propaedeutic to the claim that 'what is essential and constant in the sexual drive is something else',[37] something other than the object. This claim is crucial to Freud's reconceptualization of sexuality, for having shifted the analytical focus away from the object, most objections to the extension of the field of the sexual, an extension that is consequent upon its reconceptualization, are undermined. It can no longer be objected, for example, that the child's relation with the parent is not sexual because of any specificity of the parent *qua* object, for it is not in relation to the object (any object) that the determination of the sexual is decided.

However, Freud's claim about the aim(s) of the sexual drives bear little relation to the 'aim' of eros in Socrates' speech. In making the distinction between the object and the aim of the sexual drive Freud says that the latter is, in all cases, simply 'satisfaction' (whether through excitation or the cessation of excitation is a moot point). At the same time, the general characterization of the sexual drives and the conclusion of Freud's investigations into the 'perversions' and neuroses in the 'Three Essays' is that there must be a number of independent 'component drives', each distinguished from the others by their relation to their specific somatic sources and aims. Sexual excitation arising from specific somatic sources defines those somatic zones as 'erotogenic'. In keeping with the claim about the origin of the sexual drive in the self-preservative drive,[38] the mucous membranes of the mouth and the anus are obvious erotogenic zones, but *any* part of the body can be erotogenic.[39] Thus although, generally speaking, all drives aim at 'satisfaction', the component drives aim at satisfaction in their own particular ways. (At its simplest, this means that the aim of the sexual drive arising from the mucous membrane of the lips, for example, is satisfaction through sucking.) The identification of the component aims of these drives accounts for the infamous 'polymorphously perverse disposition' of the infant and the claim that 'this same disposition to perversion of every kind is a general and fundamental human characteristic'.[40]

Even so, the component drives usually undergo a process of organization or synthesis. The predominant socially sanctioned form of this synthesis is adult genital heterosexual sexuality ('sexual union, or at all events actions leading in that direction'[41]), a 'new aim' that Freud tends to identify with the aim of reproduction or the 'reproductive function'. In the popular conception of sexuality this organized aim is presumed to be innate, to the extent that sexuality is confused with reproduction, an error that, according to Freud, blocks the path to a true understanding of sexuality. For Freud, the organized aim is, rather, the perpetually unstable outcome of a more or less coercive subordination of the aims of the component instincts, a 'well-organized tyranny'.[42]

In contrast, the account of eros in Socrates' speech does, explicitly, have a definite and original aim to be satisfied. It is claimed that the cause of love is the desire for immortality, achieved through procreation in the beautiful (207b8–208b6). This glosses the earlier claim that all human beings are pregnant in soul and body and that they naturally desire to give birth (206c1–4). The semantic extension of 'pregnancy' and 'birth' and the privileging of the spiritual relegate physical reproduction to the status of just one expression of eros, and not a particularly noble one at that. But that is not the main point (not least because Socrates, unlike Freud, does not have to contend with a popular conception that mistakenly identifies eros with reproduction). What is eros? Eros is that power that drives human beings to the beautiful objects through which immortality may be achieved ('through the correct kind of boy-loving' [211b6]). To the extent that the aim of immortality is only truly achieved in the final stage of erotic education, it also identifies what is, ultimately, the proper 'object' of eros – the idea or form of beauty itself. Thus the account of eros in Socrates' speech is ultimately metaphysical, whereas there is no explicit metaphysics of the sexual drive.

The (non)-sexual: sublimation

In the face of this apparent gulf between the nature of the two men's theories, Freud's identification of his concept of sexuality with Plato's concept of eros looks to be based on a vulgar and ill-informed idea of the latter. The absence of any explanatory detail or justification for the identification seems to confirm this. But this is to suppose that Freud was not capable of an interpretation of the *Symposium* according to which the aim of immortality and the idealized object of beauty in itself are either the result of a process of sublimation or its narration. According to Freud, the capacity for sublimation is a consequence of the properties of the sexual drives, which 'are capable of functions . . . far removed from their original purposive actions'.[43] Here 'original purposive actions' (*ursprünglichen Zielhandlungen*) seems to mean those actions by means of which the original aims of the component drives were satisfied. To say that these aims are capable of 'sublimation' is to say that they are capable of being exchanged for other *non-sexual* aims, psychically related to the former.[44] These non-sexual aims are often said to be 'valued more highly' socially or ethically.[45] The account of eros in Socrates' speech could thus very easily be read, *mutatis mutandis*, as, if not itself a theory of sublimation, then an exceptionally good example of the process. (This would also mitigate the charge against Freud of an apparently vulgar identification of the account of eros in Socrates' speech – Diotima's account – with Plato's own position. An interpretation based on the concept of sublimation presupposes a distance between Plato the author and Socrates' narration of Diotima's account, or even more subtly between Socrates' narration and Diotima's account.) In either case the supposedly original aim of eros (immortality) would have the same status, of an unstable synthesis, as the organized aim of reproductive heterosexual intercourse presupposed in the popular conception of sexuality, even today.

The debate on the *Symposium* concerning the status of eros in its 'educated' forms, can be (and sometimes explicitly is) presented precisely in relation to Freud's concept of sublimation. Is it that a specifically sexual concept of eros is postulated as the driving force behind the higher, sublimated aims of the philosopher – that eros as sexual passion is responsible for all desire, including the desire to philosophize, and that philosophy is thus a sexual-erotic discipline? Or is it rather that a specifically sexual concept of eros is merely a metaphorical model – that a specifically sexual eros is just one kind of desire, figuring rhetorically in Socrates' speech as if all desire shared its structure and characteristics, such that philosophy *is not* sublimated eros? The first position is tenable on stylistic, rather than argumentative terms, and is persuasive to the extent that the speech clearly retains an erotic or sexual element, not just in its metaphors of excitation and ejaculation, but also in its general tenor (this is even more obviously true of the second speech in the *Phaedrus*).

The second position tends to base itself more securely on argument and analysis. Gerasimos Santas provides a good example, as he writes in the context of a general comparison of Plato and Freud. In 1909, R. G. Bury identified a distinction between generic and specific eros in Socrates' speech, its generic notion being 'the [universal] desire for the abiding possession of the good' and the specific notion the 'desire for procreation in the beautiful',[46] the latter – 'sex-love' – being one means by which immortality may be achieved. The justification for this lies, amongst other points, in the extension of the compass of eros on the model of poiesis – there must be a generic meaning if reservation of the word 'eros' for the specific meaning is an illegitimate limitation. Developing this distinction Santas denies that the erotic ascent in Socrates' speech can be accurately characterized in terms of the concept of sublimation because there is no reason to believe – and no textual evidence to support the idea that Plato believed – that the universal desire for the perpetual possession of the good, which entails the 'drive for immortality', is originally a sexual drive. For Plato, according to Santas, 'a desire is sexual only if it has a sexual object and/or sexual aim. The aims [for the good and for immortality] are not sexual, and at the highest step the Form Beauty is as non-sexual an object as one could possibly construct.' Whereas sublimation entails a transformation in the aims of a drive, Santas argues that Plato's lover's aim remains constant throughout: immortality. Far from explaining this generic aim, specifically sexual eros is explained by it. In making 'eros proper' a species of generic eros Plato was 'trying to desexualize even sexual love'.[47]

It seems to me that, with his *presumption* that the Form of beauty is a non-sexual object, Santas begs the question he claims to answer. (Indeed, in a footnote added to the 'Three Essays on the Theory of Sexuality' in 1915, Freud in effect claims precisely the opposite: 'There is to my mind no doubt that the concept of "beautiful" has its roots in sexual excitation and that its original meaning was "sexually stimulating".'[48]) But any decision about this and related interpretations, both those with and against Santas, needs to be clear about what Freud's concept of sublimation – identified as one of the two major vicissitudes of the sexual drive[49] – entails. However, 'sublimation' is a famously problematic concept in Freud's theoretical apparatus and an examination of its basic features will lead us to the heart of the conceptual complexity of 'sexuality'.

The second major vicissitude of the sexual drive is, according to Freud, repression. Although the neurotic symptom – the result of the repression of the sexual drive – does not look sexual, Freud is clear that it is. (The identification of the sexual nature of the apparently non-sexual neurotic symptom is, in a sense, the inauguration of psychoanalysis.) These symptoms, Freud says, '*constitute* the sexual activity of the patient'.[50] With sublimation, however, the situation is much less clear. In ' "Civilized" Sexual Morality and Modern Nervous Illness' Freud says that the process of the sublimation of the sexual drives 'places extraordinarily large amounts of force at the disposal of civilized activity'.[51] We know that this involves the substitution of the sexual aims with non-sexual aims, but what of the sexual nature of the drive or the force itself? Is the sublimated 'force' still, nevertheless, a sexual 'force'?[52] Can the sexual drive have non-sexual aims and still be a *sexual* drive? Do the activities enabled by sublimation constitute the sexual activity of, for example, the philosopher? Or has the rare individual (such as Socrates) who has succeeded in mastering the sexual drive by sublimation[53] substituted philosophy for sexual activity, in every sense of the word 'sexual'? As these questions show, even if we do choose to interpret the process of the education of eros in Socrates' speech in terms of sublimation, the question of the sexual-erotic nature of, for example, philosophical activity is by no means thereby answered unambiguously.

The basic tendency of Freud's theory of sexuality suggests that the sublimated sexual drives *do* remain sexual and that the satisfactions of the sublimated aims are substitute sexual satisfactions. The reconceptualization of sexuality certainly allows for this, and the same argument that was used to account for the sexual aetiology of the neuroses would hold good here in reverse form: that which is sexual in origin is most likely to be sexual as a 'symptom'. In the Preface to the fourth edition (1920) of the 'Three Essays' Freud seems to confirm this view when he writes of the book's 'insistence on the importance of sexuality in all human achievements and the attempts that it makes at enlarging the concept of sexuality'.[54] We should then have to say that Freud's description of the process of sublimation in terms of the exchange of sexual for non-sexual aims falls back upon the popular, restricted conception of 'sexuality' that it is otherwise the intention of the theory to overcome – and this is by no means the only example of such a regression in Freud's writings on sexuality.

It falls, as ever, to Lacan to point out in the starkest terms the consequences of this view. Freud's distinction between sublimation and repression insists that the former still constitutes the satisfaction of the sexual drive: 'In other words – for the moment, I am not fucking, I am talking to you. Well! I can have exactly the same satisfaction as if I were fucking. That's what it means. Indeed, it raises the question of whether in fact I am not fucking at this moment.'[55] For Laplanche, the 'extraordinary broadening of the notion of sexuality occasioned by psychoanalysis, a broadening as much in the extension of the concept as in its comprehension' compels us to the same conclusion. The broadening in extension means that 'sexuality' includes 'all of human activity, as the introduction of the concept of sublimation, for example, demonstrates'.[56] Any other conclusion would be a denial of the theoretical primacy of sexuality in psychoanalysis and the originality of Freud's work: 'With Freud, one should insist to the present day on the fact that people refuse to acknowledge what is sexual in their behaviour.'[57]

At the same time, Freud insists that the energy of the sexual drives are to be distinguished from psychical energy in general; thus that there *is* still a distinction between the sexual and the non-sexual to be made. In the 'Three Essays' Freud writes:

> We have defined the concept of 'libido' as a quantitatively variable force which could serve as a measure of processes and transformations occurring in the field of sexual excitation. We distinguish this libido in respect of its special origin from the energy which must be

supposed to underlie mental processes in general, and we also thus
attribute a qualitative character to it.[58]

In the later encyclopaedia article on 'The Libido Theory' (1923)
Freud is at pains to emphasize this again. Jung's proposal of

> a single primal libido which could be either sexualized or desexual-
> ized and which therefore coincided in its essence with mental energy
> in general . . . reduced the term 'libido' to the level of a superfluous
> synonym and was still in practice confronted with the necessity for
> distinguishing between sexual and asexual libido.[59]

This problem also haunts Freud: 'you must not forget that at
the moment we are not in possession of any generally recognized
criterion of the sexual nature of a process'.[60] Far from resolving
this problem, Freud's reconceptualization of the concept of sexuality compounds it. As the discussion of sublimation shows, it complicates any attempt to distinguish (as Freud insists we must)
between the sexual and the non-sexual. In numerous instances
Freud's attempts to draw such a distinction fall quickly back on
the popular conception of sexuality. Freud's reconceptualization
of sexuality entails a shift in the terrain of enquiry in relation to
the phenomena under discussion, from the empirical problem
of knowing whether this or that phenomenon may or may not
be classed as sexual to the prior, philosophical question of the ontology of the sexual itself. The specification of the concept of the
drive is part of Freud's attempt to wrest 'sexuality' away from its
popular interpretation, but the vocabulary of 'the sexual' – which
cannot be defined without reference to its correlate, the non-sexual
– continually frustrates him, always suggesting the popular conception even as Freud tries to twist away from it. Furthermore, the
concept of the drive brings with it its own contradictions. The aim
of the drive is 'simply satisfaction', the cessation of excitation. In
'Beyond the Pleasure Principle' this means the tendency to restore
an earlier state of things: homeostasis, complete discharge. At the
same time, in the 'Three Essays on the Theory of Sexuality', the
sexual drive (conceptualized as desire) *seeks* excitation, even to
the point of exhaustion.[61] The drive is the concept of something that
is inherently, ontologically ambiguous, bordering the psychic and
the somatic. The *sexual* drive is the concept of something that
doubles this ambiguity.

The ambiguity of *erōs*

It is tempting to speculate that it is this that Freud would signal in postulating the coincidence of his concept of 'sexuality' with Plato's concept of eros, which latter is itself constitutively ambiguous. This is most clearly marked in the story of the birth of Eros, always in the middle or in between – not occupying an empty space there but partaking of both sides, an intermediate being, including both/and, excluding neither/nor. The story of the birth of love allows for the shift in Socrates' speech from Eros as beautiful object of love (what is loved) to eros as love of the beautiful object (what does or is the loving itself). The philosopher, neither wise nor ignorant but desiring wisdom, retains at least one aspect of the ambiguity of Eros explicitly (203e6–8) and must continue to do so even in the contemplation of beauty in itself. But to the extent that the speech continues to speak of eros as force for good *in human life*, a 'co-worker with human nature' (212b3–4), it is constituted through its ambiguous relation to each of the pairs of distinctions that structure the account. Eros, in *all* its manifestations, is neither simply somatic nor psychical, but both. Even in the most physical urge to copulate Socrates' speech identifies a metaphysical desire for immortality shared by all animals, including the human. Correspondingly, intellectual procreation in the more abstract forms of beauty is described in the speech in ecstatic terms with reference to the physical acts of birth and orgasm (206c–e). And although the lover who achieves the contemplation of beauty in itself will understand the difference between the youths whose beauty once drove him out of his mind (211d5–6) and the nature of the beautiful in itself there is nothing in the speech to suggest that his passionate attachment will not remain; Socrates will still have his Isocrates.

It is strange then, that when, in his late work, Freud introduced a new concept of Eros, distinct from the concept of sexuality, little trace of this constitutive ambiguity remains, and it bears none of the distinctive features of the reconceived concept of sexuality. As briefly discussed in Chapter 2, in 'Beyond the Pleasure Principle', forced to rethink his previous distinction between the self-preservative or ego drives and the sexual drives, Freud proposed a more fundamental distinction between the 'life drives' (comprised only of the sexual drives) and the 'death drives' (incorporating what were previously called the self-preservative drives). On the basis of the biological fact of the separation of the 'germ cells' from the organism as a whole, and their combination with the germ cells of another organism (sexual reproduction), Freud now identifies the life drives or sexual drives with the ancient mytho-poetic view of Eros as the personified cosmic force of combination or reunification, the preserver of life. Thus if the concept of the sexual drives in the 'Three Essays on the Theory of Sexuality' and 'Instincts [*Triebe*] and their Vicissitudes' was meant to replace the popular biologistic concept of sexuality,[62] the late notion of Eros propels us straight back to it, restating as its characteristics precisely those supposed features (its instinctual nature, synthetic aim, innate attraction to a heterosexual object) that Freud destroyed point by point in the earlier essays.[63] The model for this concept of Eros is indeed to be found in Plato, but in the myth of the original 'whole' condition of human beings in Aristophanes' speech, and in Aristophanes' claim that eros is the pursuit of the whole, a model that, in the 'Three Essays', exemplified the popular conception of sexuality.[64] Freud's 'Eros' corresponds to the account of eros in Socrates' speech only to the extent that it embraces the general speculative mytho-metaphysical trajectory and synthesized aim of the latter, as Eros 'succeeds in winning for [the organism] what we can only regard as potential immortality'.[65]

Concomitantly, it is striking that most commentators on Socrates' speech in the *Symposium* presume some version of the popular conception of sexuality in its interpretation. This presumption underlies, for example, G. R. F. Ferrari's defence of the translation of *erōs* as 'love', when he argues that an insistence on its reference to the sexual would be too restrictive.[66] Irving Singer only 'finds great confusion in Plato' concerning the relation between sex and love precisely because, to a great extent, he presumes a popular conception of sexuality to be distinguished from love.[67] The popular conception of sexuality is presumed in Stanley Rosen's distinction between 'sexual' and 'psychic' eros, the former associated with the physiological, especially sexual reproduction, and in Allan Bloom's distinctions between sex and eros and between eros of the soul and eros of the body.[68] A. W. Price is certainly aware of Freud's attempt to offer an alternative to the popular conception of sexuality, but in presuming a straightforward distinction between the sexual and the non-sexual in his discussion of the relation between the erotic ascent in the *Symposium* and Freud's concept of sublimation he too falls back on the popular conception in his argument.[69] Rowe's rejection of the idea that Diotima's ladder of love could be anything like a theory of sublimation is based on a distinction between the specific and generic sense of eros where the former ('the ordinary sense of sexual desire or passion') presumes the popular concept of sexuality.[70] Even Santas' position, which is stated after a long chapter on the difference between Freud's new theory of sexuality and the popular view, is confidently reliant on our ability to distinguish between clearly sexual and clearly non-sexual objects and aims.

However, it is David M. Halperin who offers us the most sophisticated example of the operation of this presumption. Halperin begins his well-known essay 'Platonic *Erōs* and What Men Call Love' with an emphatic affirmation of the sexual nature of the concept of eros, against the idea that Plato is attempting to offer an adequate account of the romantic and affectionate phenomenon of love. For Halperin, then, the topic of the *Symposium* is, specifically, sexual desire, but sexual desire in so far as it is a species of desire more generally: for Plato 'the emphasis falls not on *sexual* desire but sexual *desire*'.[71] Although sexual appetite 'would be the blind urge to copulate, an instinctual drive to obtain the sexual pleasure afforded by genital stimulation', erotic sexual desire concerns a sexual object 'desired for the valued qualities it manifests to the lover, not merely for its usefulness as an instrument of sexual pleasure'.[72] Sexual desire is generic erotic desire that 'has become sexually thematized' because it is a response to beauty corporeally manifested. If beauty were not so manifested, no response to beauty could be called sexual; and if sexual response was not response to 'transcendent beauty', it could not properly be called erotic desire (but rather sexual appetite):

> Sexual desire is a response to the stimulus of physically instantiated beauty, as we have seen: it is sexual insofar as the particular instance of beauty which arouses it is carnally embodied, but it is erotic insofar as it is aroused by the presence of beauty, expresses itself as an endless desire to procreate excellence therein, and ultimately aims at the lover's perpetual possession of the good.[73]

Sexual desire so understood is 'continuous with the philosopher's desire for transcendental Beauty', for it too intends an object of metaphysical knowledge.[74] This means, according to Halperin, that we can understand 'Platonic *erōs*' without having to choose between an interpretation which sees the sexual as a 'racy metaphor, model, or analogy for the erotics of philosophical enquiry' and philosophical eros as reducible to a 'sublimated form of sexual energy' – without, that is, 'collapsing either its sexual or its meta-physical dimension to the other'.[75]

But although Halperin's argument moves beyond a simple sexual/non-sexual distinction in interpreting what the account of eros in Socrates' speech is basically *about*, he reinstates it at a more fundamental level in distinguishing between sexual appetite and sexual desire, where the former bears the characteristics of the popular conception of sexuality and the latter *is* effectively aligned with the non-sexual. Sexual desire, according to Halperin, is not a proper object of study for an 'erotic philosopher' in so far as it can be described as something 'specifically *sexual* – that is, as a biophysi-cal process',[76] but only in so far as it is an expression of generic, *metaphysical* erotic desire: '[s]o long as a sexual desire is erotic and not merely appetitive, in other words, there is nothing essentially or irreducibly *sexual* about it'.[77] Halperin, in fact, reduces sexuality to an instinct and expels it from the compass of philosophical investigation.

So long as the popular, modern conception of sexuality reigns in the interpretation of the account of eros in Socrates' speech in the *Symposium* we will continue to ask more or less the same question of it: is it, or is it not, a primarily sexual or a primarily non-sexual phenomenon? And as even Halperin's complex and nuanced argu-ment reveals, the popular, modern conception of sexuality, in which the sexual is quickly separated off from the non-sexual, on a variety of bases, carries with it an implicit set of related distinctions that structure the possible answers to this question: physical-corporeal/intellectual-incorporeal, body/soul, sex/love, genital/cerebral, base/elevated, female/male. Of course these distinctions are, implicitly and/or explicitly, deployed in the account of eros in Socrates' speech, along with others that map on to them (for example, mortal/immortal, particular/universal, illusion/truth). Further, the journey from the love of a single beautiful body to the contemplation of the Form of beauty seems to suggest a progressive movement from the first term of each pair to the second – it seems to suggest, that is, an *overcoming* of the first term in the achievement of the second which, in the context of the presumption of the popular conception of sexuality, means the overcoming of the sexual in favour of non-sexual forms.

However, what the presumption of the popular, modern concept of sexuality in the interpretation of the account of eros in Socrates' speech covers over is precisely the constitutive ambiguity of eros itself. The concept of eros is constituted through an ambiguity that the popular, modern conception of sexuality has, precisely, to disavow. Is eros a specifically sexual passion or is eros a metaphor for a more general non-sexual kind of desire or existential force? The answer is, of course, both, simultaneously. The specificity of the concept of eros lies precisely in the fact that the popular, modern distinction between the sexual and the non-sexual does not apply.

4

'I, a Man, am Pregnant and Give Birth' (Symposium)

'All human beings [*pantes anthrōpoi*], Socrates, are pregnant [*kuousin*] both in body and in soul, and when we come to be of the right age, we naturally desire to give birth [*tiktein*].' (*Symposium*, 206c1–2)

'Once, in the early hours of the morning, moreover, while he was in a state between sleeping and waking, the idea occurred to him "that after all it really must be very nice to be a woman submitting to the act of copulation".' (Freud, 'Psychoanalytic Notes on an Autobiographical Account of a Case of Paranoia (Dementia Paranoides)' [Schreber].)

The narration of the *Symposium* and the unfolding of the dramatic events – the lapses, the revelations, the enigmas and, most obviously perhaps, the predominantly erotic content (manifest and latent) of the dialogue – lend the proceedings the air of a dream. The dialogue begins by staging the narration as the not-altogether-reliable recollection, at second hand, of events 'a long time ago' (173a). The narrator, Apollodorus, addresses an unnamed friend or friends in such a way as to address the reader too. He is, he says, 'not unrehearsed' (172a1, 173c1) and not uninterested ('I've been spending time with Socrates, and have made it my business each day to know everything he is saying and doing' [172c5–7]). This leads us to expect the contribution of his own secondary revision. Apollodorus gets 'an amazing amount of pleasure' from talking about philosophy (173c). He has previously (outside the dialogue) described the symposium to Glaucon who, he says, once asked him if he could confirm what someone else had been told, by Phoenix, about the speeches on love. Glaucon has been misinformed and believes that Apollodorus was present at the symposium. Apollodorus puts him right (it happened when he and Glaucon were children) and he attributes his account to Aristodemus, who had been at the symposium, and was the same man who told Phoenix, who told someone else who told Glaucon (172a1–173b8). The rest of the dialogue then consists of Apollodorus reporting to his audience/us the speech of Aristodemus reporting the speeches at the symposium. Events, he says, happened 'something like this' (173e6). The narration is indirect ('Aristodemus said that Socrates said . . .') and although Socrates, apparently, confirmed to Apollodorus some of the things that Aristodemus told him, Aristodemus, according to Apollodorus, 'didn't remember everything each person said, nor in my turn do I remember everything he told me; but what he remembered best, and the people who seemed to me to say something worth remembering – I'll tell you the speech each of these gave' (178a1–3). The explicit attempts to authenticate the ensuing discussion only point, of course, to its fictional status.

But despite these very deliberate warnings, the speeches themselves are successful in drawing the reader into the atmosphere of the dialogue in long passages of reported speech. The irruption of Alcibiades and his drunken crew after the six speeches (those of Phaedrus, Pausanias, Eryximachus, Aristophanes, Agathon and Socrates) is a breach (not to say violation) of etiquette and a rupture in the narrative which is then resumed (peace is restored) until the dialogue ends in confusion ('everything was in uproar, and with things no longer in any sort of order' [223b5–6]) and finally tails off. Some leave, others drop off to sleep, and Aristodemus, himself 'nodding off', reports a fragment of an overheard speech from Socrates that finally puts his few remaining interlocutors to sleep. The day breaks; Socrates and Aristodemus leave. The dream is over.

If the attribution of the narrative at the beginning of the *Symposium* is unusually complicated, even by Plato's standards, it is rendered even more so by the introduction of the character of Diotima, whose speech is reported at fourth hand. There may or may not have been an actual Diotima. But even if Diotima was as real as Socrates, the fact of the introduction of this female character into the company of men, staging an historical-cultural impossibility, is a signal for our attention: something – we do not yet know quite what – is going on here. Furthermore, what Diotima says is extraordinary, notable especially for the centrality of the extended metaphors of pregnancy and birth in her account of the nature of eros.

An overlapping set of metaphors of sexual excitation, erection, frustration and ejaculation (also prominent in Socrates' second speech in the *Phaedrus*) complicates matters even further.

Metaphors of pregnancy and birth are not uncommon in philosophy, or elsewhere. But the prominence of the metaphors in the *Symposium* and their attribution to the female character of Diotima has meant that traditions of commentary which were not otherwise inclined to discuss issues of sex and gender have been forced to confront them, in however small a way. From the 1980s Diotima and her metaphors also became the focus of some feminist work on Plato, producing some widely divergent interpretations. A survey of this literature shows that one of the first questions to be answered, or one of the first issues upon which commentators must take a stance, concerns not so much the sex of Diotima, but the sex of the images of pregnancy and birth and the meaning of the choice of such metaphors. (Although, as we shall see, Diotima's sex is also an issue.) After setting out the detail of Plato's metaphors and their interpretation in the mainstream and feminist literature, this chapter identifies a common interpretative strategy of these different and even contradictory interpretations, tied to the question of the sex of the images of pregnancy and birth. This strategy, I will argue, does not do full justice to the literary specificity of the images which suggest, instead, another interpretation, in which Diotima and her images are less individual figures of fantasy or metaphorical or symbolic representation than the figuration of a specific *structure* of fantasy common to us all. (In the course of this chapter it will become clear why I do not distinguish between Diotima and Socrates in the exposition of the account of eros in Socrates' speech in the *Symposium*.)

The royal road

Although the metaphors of pregnancy and birth in the *Symposium* are confined to Socrates' speech, they are part of his critical, transformative development of aspects of some of the preceding speeches. In particular, Socrates' contribution to the discussion at the symposium replaces the question of parentage – common in the genre of speech practised here by Phaedrus, Pausanias and Agathon especially – with the characterization of eros as a giving birth. Echoing, citing and taking issue with their literary-cosmogonical heritage, Phaedrus declares that Love, one of the oldest of the gods, has no parents (178a8–9); Pausanias compares the dual parentage of Common Aphrodite, born of both male and female, with the motherless, male-born Heavenly Aphrodite (181c2–6); while Agathon, passing over Love's parental genealogy, takes a position on the birth order of the gods, insisting that Love is the youngest (195b1). In his preliminary interrogation of Agathon, in a notoriously puzzling passage, Socrates brings up the question of mothers and fathers, but only to redirect the discussion into new territory:

> [I]s Love of the sort to make him love of something, or of nothing? My question is not whether he is of some mother or father [*ei mētros tivos ē patros estin*] (for it would be ridiculous to ask whether Love is love of mother or father) [*ei Erōs estin erōs mētros ē patros*]; it's rather as if I were asking the same thing about a father – is a father a father of someone, or isn't he? (199d2–6)

Although the main point is to establish that Love always has an object, the genitive phrase on which the argument turns is ambiguous – that is, it is not clear in what sense Socrates is talking about Love being 'of' a mother and father. It can be understood as objective, referring to love *for* a mother or father, a reading which for some commentators has the virtue of confirming that what would be ridiculous is the suggestion that one feels eros for one's mother and father.[1] (Though *why* that would be thought ridiculous is not clear.) But it makes more sense, in the first phrase referring to parents, that it be read as a genitive of origin, as in Gill's translation: "I'm not asking whether Love is the child *of* a particular mother or father; it would be absurd of me to ask whether Love is Love *of* a mother or father in this sense."[2] Thus, Socrates seems to say, the issue is not whether Eros has parents, or who they are, but what kind of thing eros is.

This is the mature Socrates, expert in erotics. But when Socrates goes on to describe the encounter between his young self and Diotima, in which 'I myself was saying to her other things of pretty much the very sort that Agathon was saying to me just now' (210e4–5), his form of questioning regresses. Diotima gets Socrates to agree that there exists 'something between' (*ti metaxu* [202b4–5]) wisdom and ignorance, beauty and ugliness, good and bad, the mortal and the immortal, and that Eros is one of the spirits who inhabits this in-between realm. No doubt Diotima's mysticism may be enigmatic, but a sigh of weariness is almost audible after Socrates' next, misguided question: 'And who are his father and mother?' (203a8).

The ensuing story of the birth of Eros may very well be a tale told to an idiot, reiterating in just-so form the important point about the in-between, the middle or the neither-nor. The progress of the dialogue then retraces the moves in Socrates' earlier questioning of Agathon, moving on to the real issue of what love is and what it does, before arriving at the claim that love is love of permanent possession of the good (206a11) and the final question about its operation. What is it to love? What is love's work? (206b1–3) 'I'll tell you. It's giving birth in the beautiful, in relation both to body and to soul' (*tokos en kalō kai kata to sōma kai kata tēn psuchēn* [206b7– 8]). Diotima explains this as follows:

'All human beings [*pantes anthrōpoi*], Socrates, are pregnant [*kuousin*] both in body and in soul, and when we come to be of the right age, we naturally desire to give birth [*tiktein*]. We cannot do it in what is ugly but we can in what is beautiful. The intercourse of man and woman is a kind of giving birth [*andros kai gunaikos sunousia tokos estin*]. This matter of giving birth is something divine: living creatures, despite their mortality, contain this immortal aspect of pregnancy and procreation [*hē kuēsis kai hē genēsis*]. It is impossible for this to be completed [*genesthai*] in what is unfitting; and what is unfitting for everything divine is what is ugly, while the beautiful is fitting. Thus beauty is both Fate and Eileithyia for coming-into-being [*tē genesei*]. For these reasons, if ever what is pregnant [*to kuoun*] approaches something beautiful, it becomes gracious, melts with joy, and gives birth and procreates [*tiktei te kai genna*]; but when it approaches what is ugly, it contracts, frowning with pain, turns away, curls up, and fails to procreate [*ou genna*], retaining what it has conceived [*to kuēma*], and suffering because of it. This is why what is pregnant [*tō kuounti*] and already full to bursting [*spargōnti*] feels the great excitement it does in proximity to the beautiful, because of the fact that the beautiful person frees it from great pain [*ōdinos*]. For Socrates', she said, 'love is not, as you think, of the beautiful.'
    'Well, then, what is it of?'
    'Of procreation and giving birth [*tēs gennēseōs kai tou tokou*] in the beautiful.'
    'All right', I replied.
    'I can assure you it is', she said, 'Why, then, is it of procreation [*tēs gennēseōs*]?
    Because procreation [*hē genēsis*] is something everlasting and immortal, as far as anything can be for what is mortal; and it is immortality, together with the good, that must necessarily be desired, according to what has been agreed before – if indeed love is of permanent possession of the good. Well, from this argument it necessarily follows that love is of immortality as well.' (206c1–207a4)

Desire for immortality is at the bottom of love: 'mortal nature seeks so far as it can [kata to dunaton] to exist for ever and to be immortal. And it can achieve it [dunatai] only in this way, through the process of coming-into-being [tē genesei]'³ (207d1–3). Through reproduction, mortal nature – both animal and human – leaves behind something new in the place of the old, a process which Diotima identifies at work in the constant physical renewal of bodies and also, perhaps surprisingly, in the renewal of the soul: 'its traits, habits, opinions, desires, pleasures, fears – none of these things is ever the same in any individual, but some are coming into existence, others passing away' (207e4–6). So too with knowledge, which 'goes out of us' (we forget) and is replaced by 'going over something', creating a new memory which 'preserves our knowledge in such a way as to make it seem the same' (208a3–7). This is thus not the transformation of the mortal into the immortal, but the perpetual becoming-immortal of the mortal, which is to be distinguished from the being-immortal of the immortal.

'In this way everything mortal is preserved, not by always being absolutely the same, as the divine is, but by virtue of the fact that what is departing and decaying with age leaves behind in us something else new, of the same sort that it was. It is by this means, Socrates', she said, 'that the mortal partakes of immortality [thnēton athanasias metechei], both body and everything else; and what is immortal partakes of it in a different way [athanaton de allē].' (208a7–b4)⁴

This stretches the metaphor of 'procreation' [tē genesei] a long way, although this is the micro-detail of Diotima's explanation for animals' fervent desire to procreate and to nurture their offspring. The love and pursuit of immortality is the rational explanation for what would otherwise appear to be irrational behaviour, in both animals and humans. For the love of immortality, the weakest animals 'are prepared to join battle with the strongest on their offspring's behalf and even die for them, torturing themselves with hunger so as to rear them' (207b4–6). Similarly, the seemingly irrational desire for honour, for the sake of which human beings are 'ready to run all risks, even more than they are for their children' (208c6–d1), is the rational attempt to acquire a name for oneself, ' "laying up immortal glory for all time to come" ' (208 c5–6).

This moves the discussion on to an explanation of what Diotima means when she says that all people are pregnant in both body and soul. Those men

'who are pregnant [*hoi enkumones*] in their bodies turn their attention
more towards women, and their love is directed in this way, securing
immortality, a memory of themselves, and happiness, as they think,
for themselves for all time to come through having children [*paido-
gonias*]; whereas those who are pregnant in their souls – for in fact',
she said, 'there are those who are pregnant in their souls still more
than in their bodies, with things that it is fitting for the soul to conceive [*kuēsai*] and to bring to birth [*tekein*]. What then are these things
that are fitting? Wisdom and the rest of virtue; of which all the poets
are, of course, procreators [*gennētores*], along with all those craftsmen
who are said to be inventive. But by far the greatest and most beautiful kind of wisdom is the setting in order of the affairs of cities and
households, which is called "moderation" and "justice". When
someone is pregnant with these things in his soul, from youth on, by
divine gift, and with the coming of the right age, desires to give birth
and procreate, then I imagine he too goes round looking for the
beautiful object in which he might procreate . . . For I imagine it's by
contact with what is beautiful, and associating with it, that he brings
to birth and procreates the things with which he was for so long
pregnant [*ekuei tiktei kai genna*]'. (208e1–209c3)

These spiritual offspring are 'of a more beautiful and immortal
kind', which everyone would prefer, according to Diotima, to
human children (209c6–d2). They are the sort of children procreated
by Homer and Hesiod, and by the lawgivers Lycurgus in Sparta
and Solon in Athens (209d2, d6–7). The passion of the poets for
poetry and of the lawgivers for the law is erotics, that is, the procreation and giving birth in the beautiful for the sake of immortality. They are immortalized through these offspring in a way that no
one is through their human children (209e3–4). However, love's
work ascends beyond even this. In relation to a hierarchy of beautiful things, the spiritually pregnant give birth through, and to, philosophy. The love for a single beautiful body enables the procreation
of beautiful words (*logous kalous*). Love of beautiful bodies in general
and then beauty of souls enables the birthing of 'the sorts of
words . . . that will make young men into better men' (210c2–3).
Love of 'beauty as it exists in kinds of activity and in laws', then
'the beauty that belongs to kinds of knowledge' and 'the great sea
of beauty' thus disclosed, enables the lover to 'bring to birth many
beautiful, even magnificent, words and thoughts in a love of wisdom
[*philosophia*]' (210c4–d6). Finally, with the love of beauty in itself,
'pure, clean, unmixed, and not contaminated with things like human
flesh, and colour, and much other mortal nonsense' (211e1–4), the

lover succeeds 'in bringing to birth, not phantoms of virtue, because he is not grasping a phantom, but true virtue, because he is grasping the truth; and . . . when he has given birth to and nurtured true virtue, it belongs to him to be loved by the gods, and to him, if to any human being, to be immortal' (212a3–7).

The odd image

In the mid to late twentieth-century Anglophone literature on the *Symposium* the meaning and function of the metaphors of pregnancy and birth became a discrete topic. Two main issues are of most concern in this literature: the basic structure of the metaphors of pregnancy and birth and the distribution of roles, literal and metaphorical, between male and female, on the one hand; and the contribution of these metaphors to the metaphysical argument of Diotima's speech on the other. Attempts to sort out the basic structure of the metaphors and explain how they work are often motivated by a perceived need to account for the oddity of the idea of male pregnancy, an oddity both for Plato's contemporaries and his modern readers. M. F. Burnyeat's claim that there is a 'compelling naturalness' to the metaphor of the intellectual conception of ideas and their 'birth'[5] is perhaps supported by fact that the notion of the 'conception' of ideas is now hardly metaphorical in the languages that use versions of this Latinate word, but the idea of male pregnancy is still at risk of appearing comic, even Aristophanesian.

And it is specifically pregnancy, and not conception or birth, which is at issue here, for linguistic reasons. The verb translated, mostly, as 'to give birth' is *tiktein*, which also means 'to beget'. In Liddell and Scott the first definition is '*bring into the world, engender*; of the father, *beget*, of the mother, *bring forth*'. Thus in the first introduction of the theme in the *Symposium* – the definition of love as 'giving birth [*tokos*] in the beautiful, in relation both to body and to soul' (206b7–8) – it is not clear that there *is* any metaphor of birth, since there is not necessarily any transfer of vocabulary to do with the female to the male (it could equally be translated as begetting or procreating in the beautiful).[6] In the next lines, however, the elaboration of this gnomic pronouncement claims that 'All human beings [*pantes anthrōpoi*] . . . are pregnant [*kuousin*] both in body and in soul, and when we come to be of the right age, we naturally desire to give birth [*tiktein*]' (206 c1–2). The verb *kuein*, '*bear in the womb, be pregnant with*', is a verb usually only used of the female,[7] and hence seems to be used metaphorically here. In its proximity to *kuein*, a metaphorical use of *tiktein* is also suggested, prompting – although not necessitating – its translation as 'giving birth'.

In itself, a metaphor of male pregnancy, *qua* metaphor, need not necessarily be odd. However, in the *Symposium* the repeated use of the verb *kuein* with *tiktein*, the increasingly explicit shift from 'all human beings' to 'men' and the insistence on the extension of the metaphor, carrying it through to its end, produce an alienating effect, where one might have expected, instead, the attempt to produce a certain comfort with it. Indeed, its dogged pursuit throughout Diotima's speech has a strangely literalizing effect, to the extent that it becomes less and less discreet. Its repetition, the casual use of the verb in various ways, its insertion into the discourse as if it were something unremarkable means that stylistically it is used as if it were meant literally. The manner of its use is the manner of the literal use of a word. So how are we to understand the idea of male pregnancy? And what are we to make of the extended metaphor of birth?

In 1964 J. S. Morrison offered an explanation for Plato's use of *kuein* in relation to the male: 'his rather peculiar notion of what happens in human generation'.[8] In the *Timaeus* Plato seems to suggest that the generative 'seed' that originates in the brain or 'marrow' of the male produces a 'desire for emission . . . and so produce[s] the love of procreation' (91b4–5). This desire for emission, felt at the 'place of venting', has its counterpart in the female, in the womb's desire to bear children (*paidopoiias*). When they are brought together,

> like plucking the fruit from a tree, they sow the seed into the ploughed field of her womb, living things too small to be visible and still without form. And when they have again given them distinct form, they nourish these living things so that they can mature inside the womb. Afterward, they bring them to birth, introducing them into the light of day. (91c9–d5)

Morrison interprets this to mean that the male and female sexual organs 'have a similar function as receptacle and in due course outlet for this seed', such that it makes sense to describe ejaculation, as well as actual parturition, as 'birth'. Indeed, both 'are births, and both are accompanied (though in varying degree) by pangs: *kuein* in male and female is strictly parallel, it is the condition of readiness to bear a child; *kuēsai* is the act of producing whether in male or female.'[9]

This leaves us, Morrison admits, with a problem of translation. Although it is 'strictly correct' to translate *kuein* as 'to be pregnant' this is bound to seem ridiculous and confusing, he says, unless we bear the proposed biological rationale in mind.[10] Dover reaches the same conclusion, suggesting 'fertile' as a 'less paradoxical translation', so 'all human beings are fertile both in body and soul'.[11] For Morrison and Dover, then, *there is no metaphor* of pregnancy in the *Symposium*, in the sense that a word referring to the female is applied to the male, only a metaphorical extension of a physical process in the male to a spiritual process, also in the male, based on a highly unusual – indeed unique – use of the verb *kuein*. On these interpretations the references to specifically female functions are only apparent; they are explained away, relieving a certain anxiety, perhaps, about the (only apparently) female images. This is most explicit in A. W. Price, who notes – disconcertedly – that the clear distinction in fact between the female role of bearing and the male role of begetting and impregnating is blurred in the images in Socrates' speech, 'effectively subsuming begetting under bearing, as if sperm were a kind of foetus, and orgasm a release from birth-pangs'. For Price this intrusion of the female image seems to threaten to overwhelm the male vocabulary of begetting, but the ambiguity is resolved (the male imagery triumphs) 'in the case that most interests him [Plato], that of sowing seed through personal contact in another's mind'.[12]

In another, more complicated, interpretation E. E. Pender broadly agrees with Morrison's biological explanation for what she calls the 'male type' spiritual pregnancy, but she argues that spiritual birth also requires a 'female type' spiritual pregnancy for the male. Morrison, Stokes and Dover fail to see, according to Pender, 'that a male pregnancy of the type outlined in the *Timaeus* would not, on its own, result in the birth of a child'.[13] If male type pregnancy is the ejaculation of spiritual seed, the female type is the giving birth to the child – the 'many beautiful, even magnificent words and thoughts' (210d4–5) – which the lovers will join together in nurturing, 'with the result that such people enjoy a much greater partnership with each other than the one people have in their children and a firmer affection between them, insofar as their sharing is in children of a more beautiful and immortal kind' (209c6–7). Granted, Pender says, that this female type pregnancy is obscured – that 'the whole of the "female" experience of pregnancy and giving birth to a child has been suppressed', that 'all reference to the female role is avoided'[14] – it is a necessary part of the logical progression of the metaphor. For Pender, then, despite the extended metaphor of pregnancy, metaphorical female pregnancy is absent from the *Symposium*, although it must be assumed. This is a position that seems to rest, like Morrison's and Dover's on the literal interpretation of *kuein* in relation to the male. For all three commentators, the imagery of pregnancy in the *Symposium* is not, therefore, primarily – for Morrison and Dover, not at all – 'female'. Nevertheless, Morrison's explanation of the use of *kuein* and Dover's sexually neutralizing translations implicitly acknowledge the need to account for or deal with what most people will surely read as references to specifically female functions.[15]

If other commentators, in a number of different ways, have presumed or insisted on the 'femaleness' of the images of pregnancy and birth, this has tended to be in the interest of an explanation of the function of the metaphor, or a broader interpretation of its meaning, rather than an analysis of its precise form. Ficino is unusual in this respect for interpreting the image of pregnancy as applying to both body and soul:

> The seeds of all of the body's own things are implanted in it from the beginning. Hence at appropriate intervals of time the teeth come through, hair appears, a beard develops and the seeds of procreation begin to flow. If the body is fecund or fertile with seeds, the soul, which is more excellent than the body, is much more fertile, and it possesses the seeds of all its own things from the beginning.[16]

Luc Brisson similarly looks for the broad meaning of the metaphors, understanding the, to him clearly feminine, image of pregnancy in relation to the account of the soul in the *Phaedrus*. The being already pregnant of the male lover refers to the idea that the soul carries within it the knowledge of the forms that it was its privilege to contemplate before its descent (fall) into the body, knowledge only now available to the embodied human being through reminiscence. 'Giving birth' is 'the re-appropriation of the knowledge that was already present in the soul'.[17] Frisbee Sheffield also interprets the metaphors in relation to Plato's epistemology, and acknowledges the specificity of pregnancy, as opposed to a more general idea of fertility, in construing it in terms of 'potentiality':

> *kuein* specifically indicates the state of fecundity intermediate between fertility and birth. The import of the metaphor, then, is not just that human beings have the *ability* to create children and, on the psychic level, poems and laws, but that *the essential resources for life*, as it were,

are already there . . . To say that the lover is in a state intermediate between fertility and birth, and that he has no need to generate anything in the encounter with beauty, is to indicate that he has all the internal resources for knowledge already potentially there, and so needs rather to elicit the knowledge which he already carries.[18]

In these interpretations the metaphors are explained, glossed or construed in ways that surely do make sense and are compelling, but the images are thereby somehow evacuated of their rhetorical charge. The specificity of the image of pregnancy is acknowledged, but sex or gender is simply not an issue. A gendered metaphorical vocabulary is employed, but the images do not raise questions *about* sex or gender.

Plato dreams in female

In a very different vein, foregrounding the issue of sex, a number of Plato's other readers have insisted on the femaleness of the images of pregnancy and birth from various appreciative and critical feminist perspectives. Despite their being sometimes quite opposed to each other, these readings have in common the conclusion that the deployment of the metaphors of pregnancy and birth has far-reaching consequences for the interpretation of the dialogue and for, variously, Plato's view of human nature, his metaphysics and his conception of philosophy more generally. For these interpretations the issue of sex and/or gender is not just part of the form and content of the metaphors, to be overcome by their interpretative translation into a literal or philosophical register. Rather, the images raise issues about sex and/or gender itself, about the relation between sex and philosophy, or even about the sex of philosophy.

For Arlene Saxonhouse the figure of Diotima and her metaphors of pregnancy and birth stand in the *Symposium* as an important corrective to the overly masculine, 'abstract', rational conception of public life and the city in the *Republic*, a conception in which the distinctions between the public and the private, male and female, war and peace, have been erased, or rather, in which the private is subsumed in the public, the female in the male, the space of peace in the space of war. The erasure of the feminine or the female (terms which Saxonhouse uses interchangeably) is, simultaneously, the erasure of sexuality or eros and of creativity. In contrast, Saxonhouse argues, Diotima's speech offers a radically different vision:

She does not distinguish between males and females – indeed she presents the male as transformed into the female – as capable of becoming pregnant. The virility, the strength, the courage of the father pales before the capacity to be pregnant. It is the female Diotima holds as the model for all mankind – it is her body with its capacity for reproduction that we must simulate in our progress up the ladder of love soon to be described in her speech. The male activity of impregnation yields to the priority of the language of conception and birth.[19]

Saxonhouse claims that this bears witness to the necessarily 'hermaphroditic aspect of human nature', acknowledging that 'the feminine part of human nature puts limitations on the masculine', providing us with a model through which we may become 'complete individually through acknowledging the male and the female within us'.[20] Thus for Saxonhouse Diotima's speech, and the figure of Diotima herself, bear witness to a valorization of the female with, potentially, important consequences for the way we understand ourselves and organize our societies.

But perhaps the stronger strain of feminist interpretation of Diotima and her metaphors takes quite the opposite view. The strongest statement of this position is Adriana Cavarero's. According to Cavarero, Western metaphysics – and in particular, here, Platonic metaphysics – is founded on a disavowal of the mother, to the extent that the enduring existential-ontological obsession with which it deals concerns 'the fact that we must leave life through death, rather than the fact that we enter it though birth'[21] – hence the centrality, for Plato, of the desire for immortality. Western philosophy and the patriarchal social and symbolic order that depends on it exclude women, or the 'female element', 'female experience',[22] through the disavowal of the fundamental fact of birth – natality – or, more specifically, the fundamental fact that we are of woman born. This is because of both the unendurable (for the male) fact of the dependency of the male on the female and the 'blame' attached to birth – the index of sexual reproduction – for mortality.[23] The 'matricide' at the inauguration of Western philosophy is incessantly re-enacted in its history, according to Cavarero, in implicit and explicit fantasies of male self-birth.

In this Cavarero echoes the central claim in Luce Irigaray's critical exegesis of the allegory of the cave in the *Republic*. That cave – 'Plato's *Hystera*' – is, for Irigaray, an image or replica or re-presentation of 'another cave, the *hystera*, the mold which silently dictates all replicas, all possible forms, all possible relation of forms and between forms, of any replica'.[24] But in the inverted image of the cave, which is offered not just as itself an image but also as the scene of the production of images, the 'material elements' of the womb are 'turned into scenery . . . a theater of/for fantasies'.[25] The prisoner will be brought, by force, out of the cave, turning his back on the cave, to acknowledge 'a more distant, lofty, and noble origin', the 'unbegotten begetter', the Sun, the Father, the Idea of the Good:[26] 'The cave gives birth only to phantoms, fakes, or, at best, images. One must leave its circle in order to realize the factitious character of such a birth. Engendering the real is the father's task, engendering the fictive is the task of the mother – that "receptacle" for turning out more or less good copies of reality.'[27] In the allegory of the cave the empirical, maternal origin of the philosopher is repressed in his ascent. At the point in Irigaray's exegesis at which this becomes explicit her text interweaves the allegory of the cave in the *Republic* with aspects of the *Timaeus*, Socrates'/Diotima's speech in the *Symposium* and Socrates' second speech in the *Phaedrus*,[28] the common thread being the denial of mortal birth, the maternal realm, in the pursuit of the fiction of a 'simple, indivisible, ideal origin . . . Birth pushed further and further back into an infinity where all differences, and differings, fuse in a blind contemplation'.[29]

For Cavarero, Socrates' speech in the *Symposium* is a particularly egregious example of this symbolic matricide and of the fantasy of male self-birth. Far from valorizing 'the female' or proposing it as a model, as Saxonhouse claimed, the enactment of matricide is all the more daring and pernicious in its appropriation of female vocabulary[30] and is reinforced through the mimetic strategy of the character of Diotima such that, in Cavarero's view, the female is made to denounce itself:

> It is difficult to say that this discourse involves the simple deployment of a metaphor, because the metaphor ends up disempowering and negating the female experience – of motherhood as power – of which it is itself a metaphor . . . The result is an act of expropriation carried out through a woman's voice, namely the voice of someone against whom the expropriation is committed.[31]

The implication of Cavarero's position is also that the same complaint applies to the tradition of interpretation and scholarship that takes as its task the explanation of the philosophical meaning of Diotima's images without attention to their gender politics, such interpretations reiterating, rather than explaining or interpreting, the fundamental discursive gesture or ideological process in the use of the metaphors of pregnancy and birth in the *Symposium*.[32]

But if Cavarero sees nothing to celebrate in Plato's text, Irigaray's essay dedicated to Diotima's speech is much more ambivalent. Although Irigaray speaks of 'Diotima's teaching' and identifies a specific method – even a Diotimean philosophy – in the first half of Diotima's speech, still she, a woman, is strictly speaking absent from the dialogue. Nevertheless, the significance of what Socrates reports of her should not be underestimated. Diotima's non-Hegelian dialectical teaching is characterized by the preservation of the intermediary, permitting the productive communication between opposites rather than the domination of one term over the other or the sublation of both. This model of or for philosophizing allows Diotima to see the union of male and female as in itself potentially divine, 'fecund before all procreation', love realizing the 'immortality in the mortality between lovers'.[33] However, precisely with the introduction of the images of pregnancy and birth (or, for Irigaray, more generally, 'procreation') the method or way of the intermediary 'miscarries', and Diotima capitulates instead to 'metaphysics', to the schism between the physical and the spiritual, the mortal and the immortal. Love becomes a mere means to an end and immortality is 'put off until death'.[34]

At the beginning of her essay Irigaray claims that Plato borrows Diotima's wisdom and power.[35] In the absence of any fuller explanation from Irigaray, we may speculate that this means that Plato borrows Diotima's philosophical authority, from the first part of her speech, in order to legitimate the metaphysics of the second. In any case, the same appropriative gesture, elaborated by Cavarero, is identified in the use of the female character (although not in the images of pregnancy and birth associated with her). Defending Plato, Angela Hobbs takes issue with this idea of appropriation in the interpretation of the *Symposium*. Hobbs takes on Cavarero, in particular, in proposing an alternative interpretation of the pregnancy image. Hobbs argues, contra Morrison et al., that the use of 'kuousin' at 206c1 –'all human beings, Socrates, are pregnant [kuousin] both in body and in soul' – means that we *are* dealing with an image of a specifically female bodily function. Diotima could have used *tiktein* or *gennan* (which could apply to either sex) but she did not.[36] The *Timaeus* passage on which Morrison bases his own position only shows, according to Hobbs, that male arousal and orgasm can be thought of as analogous to pregnancy and birth.

Given this, is the femaleness of the image a contingent or an integral part of Plato's overall philosophical position and purpose in this dialogue?[37]

Hobbs' answer is that the use of the female imagery is both consistent with Plato's metaphysics and useful to his pedagogic purpose in the *Symposium*. The images, according to Hobbs, reveal something to us about Plato's 'attitude to gender', an attitude based on the metaphysical principle of the reality of the incorporeal, intelligible realm which is 'the ultimate context in which Plato's use of female imagery should be viewed'.[38] That is, gender or sex (Hobbs does not distinguish between them) is irrelevant in the transcendent realm of the Forms to which we should aspire,[39] but the use of these images has the virtue of suggesting 'to the more reflective and informed reader that it really is ultimately of little consequence whether the philosopher is male or female. Nor is it ultimately of much consequence whether a male or female philosopher is described in terms traditionally associated with the opposite gender.' At the same time, the use of the images acknowledges the importance of gender in the corporeal world of becoming such that they are 'an apt resource for rhetorical and pedagogic purposes'.[40] In response to Cavarero's claims Hobbs then concludes:

> The enjoyment of playing with, transgressing and utilizing concepts of gender is possible precisely because, finally, they are of no lasting importance. The *Symposium* is not so much a rejection of the female as gaily cavalier in its attitude towards the embodied. I submit, therefore, that Plato is chiefly concerned not with 'appropriating the feminine' but with liberating men and women alike from inessential bodily and cultural constraints.[41]

Although Hobbs succeeds in proposing an interpretation of the female imagery that renders its use consistent with Plato's broader philosophical commitments and educative goals, she misses the point of the feminist criticisms. For granted that 'the incorporeal, eternal realm of being manifest in the Forms' is the metaphysical context for the *Symposium*,[42] it does not follow that it should be the ultimate context of interpretation for those who do not subscribe to this metaphysics. Indeed, the feminist criticisms are partly *criticisms of* this metaphysics, and of the view, precisely, that gender is irrelevant. For mortal readers such as Cavarero the reality of the corporeal world of becoming – the only world there is – is the ultimate context of interpretation, and in this world, as Hobbs herself writes, the significance of gender cannot be denied. Hobbs interprets the *Symposium* in terms of what we might be able to say about Plato's conscious intentions and consequently thinks that Cavarero is concerned with the question of 'whether Plato is morally justified in describing male practices and institutions through the use of a female bodily function'.[43] For Cavarero, however, it is not a question of Plato's intentions. At issue is what the text 'performs', what it reveals about itself despite itself and about the socio-cultural and ideological function of philosophy and its meaning for the contemporary reader.

If, for ease of presentation, the literature discussed above has been divided, very broadly, into two camps – those who assert, and those who deny, the fundamentally female nature of the images – David Halperin's contribution to the debate could be read as revealing their speculative identity. Halperin begins his long essay on Diotima by arguing that she would represent, for Plato and his contemporaries, a recognizably 'feminine' perspective on eros, speaking in a recognizably female voice, 'drawing on a previously untapped source of "feminine" erotic and reproductive experience'.[44] Diotima's 'feminine' model of erotic desire is offered, according to Halperin, as an alternative to the rigidly hierarchical and one-sided form of the only acceptable model for the pederastic relation in classical Athens, in which the older, active, desiring lover secures his masculine position through penetration or other sexual action upon the young, passive, erotically indifferent and unaroused beloved, temporarily (until the first growth of beard) occupying the feminine position.[45] Diotima offers, instead, a model of reciprocal, creative eros, erasing the distinction between activity and passivity, or eliminating passivity altogether.[46]

But this is not, as Saxonhouse implies it is, Plato embracing his feminine side, for two reasons. First, this is a 'femininity' constructed by men, perhaps even, Halperin suggests, according to a male paradigm (for the inseparability of sexual pleasure and reproductive function that mark Diotima's images precisely as female projects on to the female what is in fact specific to male erotic experience).[47] Second, Diotima's function in the *Symposium* is to endow 'the pedagogic processes by which men recreate themselves culturally – by which they communicate the secrets of their wisdom and social identity, the "mysteries" of male authority, to one another across the generations – with the prestige of female procreativity'. Diotima ensures the success of 'the continual reproduction of [the] universalizing discourse [of Socratic philosophy] in the male culture of classical Athens'.[48] But, again, this is not straightforwardly the appropriation of the female, as Cavarero claims, for the female is in fact radically absent from the *Symposium*, according to Halperin. This is not about the female; it is about 'the male imaginary, the specular poetics of male identity and self-definition'. Diotima's 'femininity' is only illusory, 'a projection of male fantasy, a symbolic language employed by men in order to explain themselves and their desires to one another across the generations'. Accordingly Diotima is not a woman, but, rather, 'a "woman" '.[49]

The carnival

As this survey of the relevant literature has shown, there is a range of interpretation of Diotima and her images amongst which one finds no consensus and not a little contradiction. The broadest areas of disagreement concern not just details but some fundamental issues, basic to the ensuing interpretations of the philosophical significance of the images, both within the dialogue and beyond it. Are the images of pregnancy and birth specifically female? If so, what is the significance of this? Do the images valorize the female or, in appropriating it, deny it? Perfectly opposing answers to all of these questions have been given. And yet, despite differences and disagreements, there is a *common* interpretative strategy across these divergent readings, or a common foundational presupposition to them: the imperative to separate out what is proper to the male or masculine and what is proper to the female or the feminine. The presumption of sex difference itself grounds this imperative in a transcendental or a priori manner.

The common presumption of sex difference grounds the general form and aim of interpretations of Socrates' speech through an implicit articulation of its necessity, in two respects: sex is i) the non-metaphorical origin of the metaphorical terms; understood as ii) a biological necessity which is not itself amenable to interpretation or open to question. The aim of interpretation is then to convert the terms of the metaphors into a literal register, reassigning the elements to their proper place or apportioning out what belongs to the female and what to the male, explaining what the male borrows from the female, or how the properly female is travestied, appropriated or covered over. Furthermore this is the case even where interpretations stress the importance of the *confusion* of the categories of male and female as the central effect of the images.

Paul Plass, for example, for whom the images are decidedly female, argues that the use of the metaphor of pregnancy is to be understood both as a result of the structure of pederasty (where the younger man plays the 'feminine' role) and as a strategy to naturalize pederasty through the transferral on to it of the vocabulary of procreative heterosexuality. How else, he suggests, would homosexuals represent themselves, except in heterosexual terms? Thus although Plass refers to the 'confusion' and the 'pervasive blurring' of sexual roles in pederasty, his understanding of the metaphors is based on a clear distinction between what can be said to be feminine and what masculine, according to which homosexual 'blurring' is really the consequence of its being a poor copy of heterosexuality.[50] Even Halperin, whose interpretation questions what we mean when we speak of 'the female' and 'the male', has as his aim 'to establish and distinguish, or to salvage and preserve, what is authentically "feminine" from inauthentic male constructions of "the feminine" '. Halperin acknowledges that any attempt to do this risks falling into the same trap that it tries to identify: 'erasing female presence from the terms of its discourse, even as it adheres to an ostensibly feminist program, reproduc[ing] and exemplify[ing] the very strategies of appropriation – characteristic of male culture – that it purports to illuminate and to criticize'.[51] But this is a laudable expression of male feminist humility (which to future intellectual historians will date Halperin's essay very precisely in the early 1990s) rather than a positional statement on the nature of sex difference itself, and the 'genuinely feminine' remains the motivating term in Halperin's essay.

From the perspective of the imperative to separate out what is proper to the male or masculine and what is proper to the female or the feminine the structural and other shortcomings of the metaphors of pregnancy and birth are soon revealed. Extended metaphors always run the risk of becoming artificially stretched beyond their point of best functioning, and, as traditionally interpreted, this happens very quickly in Diotima's speech. In pursuing the metaphors their elements become more and more contrived and the structural equivalences – such as they are – quickly breakdown. Halperin, for example, takes issue with Vlastos' affirmation of the correctness of translating *kuein* as 'be pregnant', because pregnancy comes before intercourse in Diotima's account, calling this a 'crucial incoherence'.[52] Similarly, Pender distinguishes between a male type and a female type pregnancy precisely because there is no 'logical progression' to the account without it.[53]

However, the interpretative imperative to separate out what is proper to the male or masculine and what is proper to the female or the feminine does not do justice to the literary specificity and complexity of the images. This lies, precisely, in their *disregard* for propriety of reference in relation to the male and the female or the masculine and the feminine, obviating the need for any logical correlation with the sequence of physiological processes in human reproduction. This disregard is not their failing; it is their substance. To the extent that this is acknowledged by, for example, Hobbs and Plass, it is explained by its pedagogic or apologetic function in the dialogue. For Hobbs it is indicative of Plato's disdain for the reality of *all* things corporeal, his 'playfulness' with gender a consequence of a metaphysics that locates reality elsewhere than the corporeal world and according to which gender is of no significance. For Plass its function is the naturalization of pederasty. But these acknowledgements of the 'confusion of sexual roles'[54] are still based on a presumption of the clarity of the distinctions between male and female, masculine and feminine, as the literal basis for the images, and the possibility of assigning the parts of the images to their rightful or proper place.

But what if the constitutive confusions say something *about* sex difference and the distribution of 'proper' masculine and feminine identifications, rather than being grounded on the presumption of them? What, in the text itself, suggests that such an interpretation is warranted? Returning to an analysis of the metaphors of pregnancy and birth, we can identify certain aspects of their forms and presentation as a basis for their interpretation. First, pregnancy is posited as a universal state for all human beings, male *and* female. One begins by being pregnant, and the work of love is to bring the pregnancy to fruition, to bring to birth. The process of conception, of impregnating or becoming pregnant, is not part of the metaphorical constellation in the *Symposium*, except in so far as *kuein* implies, simultaneously, to have conceived (*to kuēma* is 'that which has been conceived', an embryo or foetus; *hē kuēsis*, is conception).[55]

Second, there are two kinds of pregnancy – physical (of the body) and spiritual (of the soul). The first introduction of the metaphor – 'All human beings, Socrates, are pregnant both in body and in soul' (*kuousin . . . ō Sōkrates, pantes anthrōpoi kai kata to sōma kai kata tēn psuchēn*) – suggests that, universally, all are pregnant in both respects. Later, however, in the explanation of this claim, Diotima separates those who are pregnant in their body (*hoi . . . enkumones . . . kata to sōmata ontes*) from those who are pregnant in their soul (*hoi de kata tēn psuchēn*), or at least those who are *more* pregnant in their soul than their body (*hoi en tais psuchais kuousin eti mallon e en tois sōmasin*). This complicates the metaphor. It means not that there is a metaphorical, spiritual kind of pregnancy, derived from the literal model of physical pregnancy, but that the physical pregnancy at issue here is also metaphorical. As 'those who are pregnant in their bodies' turn out to be men, directing their attention towards women to procreate human children, it seems that actual physical pregnancy is the model for a metaphorical *physical and spiritual* pregnancy for the male. But the furthest extension of the metaphor of procreation, including the renewal of each physical organism, its soul and its knowledge (207d–208b), as well as the first mention of the metaphor, suggests that there is a metaphorical physical pregnancy for women too. Diotima's pedagogic role in relation to Socrates means that there is at least one example of a woman's spiritual procreation; Alcestis is another (208d3).

Third, of the two kinds of pregnancy, the spiritual is, unsurprisingly, ostensibly the higher form. Although the extension of the metaphor of procreation implies that even animals partake of immortality through their offspring, from 208c an at-first-subtle shift decisively downgrades physical procreation, even suggesting that the immortality it achieves is dubious (those who are pregnant in body procreate physically to secure 'immortality, a memory of themselves, and happiness, *as they think* . . .' [*hōs oiontai*]).[56] Although animals are said to be prepared to die for the sake of their children, to secure their immortality that way, in the human example the mythical king Codrus of Athens dies for the sake of his children only because he thereby secures a *spiritual* procreation, the immortal memory of his own courage, immortal virtue and glorious reputation (208d4–e2). Everyone, according to Diotima, would thus prefer spiritual to human children, for no person ever achieved cultic status through the latter (209d1–2, e3–4).[57] In the final revelation Diotima claims that it is only in the contemplation of beauty in itself, in the Form of beauty, and the procreation of true virtue through philosophical discourse, that one may become beloved of the gods and immortal, to the extent that any mortal can. This being so, the climax of Socrates' speech achieves a kind of reversal in the form of the metaphor such that it moves from the spiritual to the physical. If what is real and true is the virtue brought to birth in beauty in itself, this – the apex of spiritual procreation – is the model for the achievement of immortality which physical procreation ressembles only metaphorically. This perhaps explains Diotima's otherwise odd claim that '[t]he intercourse of man and woman is in fact a kind of giving birth [*hē gar andros kai gunaikos sunousia tokos estin*]' (206c5–6), a line sometimes omitted as a 'meaningless intrusion'.[58]

Finally, we should note that Diotima's speech actually presents the extended discussion of pregnancy and birth as if it were a literal – or at least more literal – explanation of the definition of Eros as 'giving birth in the beautiful, in relation to both body and soul'. As Socrates cannot understand what this means, Diotima offers to tell him *saphesteron* – more clearly, more plainly: 'All human beings, Socrates, are pregnant both in body and soul . . .' For Morrison and others, as we have seen, both this and the idea that ejaculation is a giving birth *are* to be interpreted quite literally. But unless this also means that the seed or seeds in human ejaculate and the beautiful words and thoughts brought to birth by the advanced loving couple are similarly, quite literally, 'children', even Morrison et al. would have to concede that there is at least an entwining of the literal with the metaphorical in Diotima's speech.

Taken together, these four points mean that the metaphors do not work by simply moving from an obvious literal ground to a metaphorical image, from the female (literal pregnancy) to the male (metaphorical pregnancy), or from the physical to the spiritual, but by shifting around between and within the distinctions literal/metaphorical, male/female, physical/spiritual simultaneously, in different ways. Furthermore, the imagery of 'male' excitation and ejaculation is not a separate or even merely overlapping element in Diotima's speech – it is fully integrated into the explanation of the claim that all human beings are pregnant in body and soul, which is itself the beginning of the explanation for the definition of love as 'giving birth in the beautiful'. No doubt this purposeful confusion is partly explained by the fact that, at the simplest level, it is love between men, the education of boys into men and the spiritual life of men more generally that seems to concern Plato, given the identification of erotic maturity with 'the correct kind of boy-loving [*orthōs paiderastein*]' (211b6). But the text does not allow for the separation of one set of metaphors from the other, such that the imagery of 'male' sexual excitation and ejaculation could be interpreted as an accommodation to sexual normality, making the imagery of male pregnancy more palatable. To say that those who are pregnant 'desire' to give birth and procreate already suggests the mutual implication of the two sets of metaphors. With this desire the pregnant man 'goes round looking for the beautiful object in which he might procreate', a formulation that highlights that pregnancy *precedes* the sexual encounter. On approaching the beautiful he melts with joy, is full to bursting (*spargōnti*, both to be ripe – ready for birth – and swollen with passion) and is freed from the great pain (*ōdinos*, specifically labour or birthing pain). Ugliness, on the other hand, makes him contract, curl up, painfully retaining what he would like to release. As Dover points out, 'the vivid physical terms in which reaction to beauty and ugliness is expressed . . . describe equally the reactions of the male and of the female genitals to sexual stimulation or revulsion'. Indeed, Dover writes, 'melting' and 'relaxing' is 'more appropriate to the female', but with this he misses his own point. Plato's carnival of images pays little heed to received wisdom concerning the sequence of events in human sexual behaviour and human procreation. If pregnancy precedes intercourse then detumescence ('melting', 'relaxing') may as well precede ejaculation. Further, it is only our lack of intimacy with, and lack of tolerance for, the discourses of the experience of pregnancy and birth that motivate the presumption that their association with 'desire' and 'orgasm' in Diotima's speech must be metaphorical references to the male – as if pregnancy could not actually be a swelling with desire, and as if birth could not actually be orgasmic. In fact, this presumption is made against the explicit result of the entwining of the two sets of metaphors: an eroticization of pregnancy and birth, however the latter are understood.

The images of pregnancy and birth do not, however, work in isolation from other aspects of the dialogue. They function in the broader context of the whole of Diotima's and Socrates' speech(es) and of the dialogue as a whole. The dialogue simultaneously sets up and breaks down a series of general, abstract distinctions as well as a set of distinctions whose specific terms are shiftingly occupied by various of the characters. In the most general terms the dialogue raises questions about distinctions that usually serve to distinguish philosophical discourse from its others. The distinctions between truth and fiction (especially in the attempt to authenticate the speeches at the beginning of Apollodorus' narration) and between philosophy and myth (in Aristophanes' and Diotima's speeches especially) are seemingly purposefully muddied. The distinction between teacher and pupil is at once asserted and undone, not only in Socrates' successive and simultaneous occupation of both positions (in the pairs Socrates/Agathon, Diotima/Socrates, Socrates/Alcibiades) but also in the detail of Diotima's account of the nature of the erotic relation, which casts the beautiful beloved as the midwife of the ideas with which the older man is pregnant, as if the beloved is necessary to the intellectual development of the lover. The universality of the position of 'lover' (all human beings are pregnant, everyone is in love with the Good) and the reciprocity and mutual procreation and nurture of intellectual offspring similarly undoes the distinction between lover and beloved on which Diotima's speech is otherwise based, and, as Halperin has pointed out, effaces what was perhaps the most important distinction in codified pederastic relations in ancient Athens, that between activity and passivity.[59] This is most explicit in Alcibiades' speech at the end of the dialogue. The speech insists both that Socrates 'is in love with beautiful young men and is always around them, and overwhelmed' (216d2–3) – he is in love with Agathon, in particular – and that he has a 'mad attachment to being loved' by Alcibiades (213d7); the effects of loving and being loved are described in the same way. Alcibiades also describes the effect of Socrates' philosophizing on him in the same terms as the description of the madness of love in the *Phaedrus*: 'whether it's a woman listening or a grown man or a young lad, we're all over-whelmed and possessed [by Socrates' words] . . . whenever I hear them I'm in the same state as the Corybantes, only much worse – heart leaping, tears pouring out under the impact of this man's words' (215d5–e3). In a reversal of the usual roles ascribed to the older lover and his young beloved Alcibiades takes the initiative in his erotic relation with Socrates, sending his chaperone away, exer-cising with Socrates, and then, in a 'direct assault on the man', inviting Socrates to dine with him 'just as if I were a lover plotting to have his way with his beloved' (217c5–d2). Socrates resists Alcibi-ades even when he lies down with him under his cloak and embraces him (219b7–c2). Others – including the same Charmides who, in another dialogue, sets Socrates on fire when he (Socrates) 'saw what was inside his cloak'[60] – have similarly been 'deceived' by Socrates 'in the role of a lover, becoming more of a beloved himself instead of a lover' (222b3–4).

In this way important aspects of the dialogue as a whole, and of Socrates' speech in particular, partake of the logic of the neither/ nor or the intermediary, the in-between, that is the first emphatic characteristic of eros in Diotima's discourse. Seen in this broad context, in which any attempt to distinguish between Diotima and Socrates in 'Diotima's speech' now seems otiose, the blurring of what is proper to the male or masculine and what is proper to the female or feminine is intrinsic – *that is the point of the images* – and interpretative efforts aimed at distinguishing between them seem oddly misplaced.

The structure of the fantasy

How is it possible to understand the significance of these images in such a way as to preserve their constitutive blurring of what is proper to the male or masculine and what is proper to the female or feminine? How is it possible to explain that blurring itself without making it an item in an explanation that ultimately depends on an operation that separates them out? What kind of interpretation would make the images the proper object of interpretation, rather than treating them as a conduit to the main event: a biological theory of reproduction, a theory of love or eros, a fantasy of male self-birth, a metaphysics of transcendence, an ethics, and so on. How to look *at* the images rather than *through* them?

The formulation of the problem in this way echoes Laplanche and Pontalis' formulation of the problem faced by Freud in relation to the place of fantasy in psychoanalytical interpretation. Inheriting a word (*Phantasie*) used to refer to the imaginary inner, subjective world or the imaginings of poets and 'fantasists', in contrast with the external, objective world of reality – inheriting, indeed, the very distinction between illusion and reality – the most obvious inter- pretative strategy for Freud might have been to look in fantasy for the hidden or symbolized reality, disavowal of which explains the need for the fantasy in the first place. We might understand the default position in the interpretation of Diotima's images of preg- nancy and birth in the same way: the blurring of what is proper to the male or masculine and what is proper to the female or feminine is the illusion in a fantasy which hides the reality of the distinction between them. In the case of an interpretation like Cavarero's, it is this reality – the reality of sex difference and what is proper to the female – that is disavowed and that thus necessitates the imaginings.

However, for Freud, from early on, as Laplanche and Pontalis show, fantasy is not just manifest 'material to be analysed . . . it is also the result of analysis, an end-product, a latent content to be revealed behind the symptom'. Treated henceforth as an aspect of 'psychical reality', fantasies could thus 'acquire the consistency of an object, the specific object of psychoanalysis'.[61] Freud did not construct a metapsychological concept of fantasy. But Laplanche and Pontalis' excavation of Freud's discussions of fantasies gets them close to doing so. The first point in the 'Summary' of their essay 'Fantasy and the Origins of Sexuality' indicates this: 'The status of fantasy cannot be found within the framework of the opposition reality–illusion (imaginary). The notion of *psychical reality* introduces a third category, that of structure.'[62]

Two points are important here. First, 'psychical reality' does not mean simply that psychical phenomena are 'real' – that, broadly speaking, they exist in some sense (although of course they do). It is not the result of the broadening of a general concept of 'the real' or 'reality' to include psychical phenomena as well as other onto-logical items. 'Psychical reality', according to Laplanche and Pontalis, is not defined as 'constituting the *whole* of the subjective, like the psychological field, but as a heterogeneous nucleus within this field, a resistant element, alone truly real, in contrast with the major-ity of psychological phenomena', these latter being specified by Freud as 'transitional or intermediate thoughts'.[63] Thus the view of the computer keyboard that passes through the psyche as a mental representation is real, to the extent that it is not unreal, but 'psychi-cal reality' refers, specifically, to something else, to the *effective* reality of the unconscious – its wishes, its fantasies, its role in psychic life. This means that as a metapsychological concept, 'fantasy', 'the central domain'[64] of psychic reality, refers not just to this or that imaginative content in the individual psyche – it is not a descriptive, empirical category – but to a psychic operation that articulates, for the subject, something that bears on its being-subject. This is because the fantasy articulates – in the sense this time of forming a joint between – a 'pre-subjective structure' and the product of the individual imagination.[65] One *may*, Laplanche and Pontalis imply, understand this reference to the 'structure' in terms of the possibility of 'a structural type of explanation'; one may, then, understand the pre-subjective structure in terms of 'the "symbolic order" defined by Lévi-Strauss and Lacan in the ethnological and psychoanalytical fields respectively'.[66]

The specification of psychic reality and the metapsychological concept of fantasy, which may seem, especially in Laplanche and Pontalis' formulation of the former, to suggest the privilege of the deeply hidden, the seriously opaque, should not blind us to what is the second point: the realm of fantasy, strictly speaking, includes not only unconscious fantasies but also screen memories, conscious fantasies, day dreams and reveries.[67] As fantasies these phenomena are ontologically (if not always therapeutically) equivalent. This point bears particularly for Freud on the interpretation of dreams. Freud 'discovers the same relationship between the deepest unconscious fantasy and the daydream: the fantasy is present at both extremities of the process of dreaming'. There is both the 'fantasy which lies at the heart of the dream' and 'the fantasy which serves to make it acceptable to consciousness',[68] the secondary revision or elaboration that orders the elements of the dream into an (at least quasi-) coherent tale for the telling.

There is no reason, it seems to me, not to understand the images of pregnancy and birth in Diotima's speech as elements of a fantasy thus defined. A summary version of this fantasy might be: 'I, a man, am pregnant and give birth.'[69] The contribution of the individual imagination in this instance is the precise form and content of the fantasy – its characters, its setting, the framing discourse of the account of love – which collectively make up not just 'Diotima's speech in Plato's *Symposium*' but 'Plato's *Symposium*' as a whole. 'Plato's *Symposium*' is thus analogous to the dream. 'I, a man, am pregnant and give birth' is the fantasy that animates the dream, simultaneously part of its manifest content and the latent wish to which the dream gives expression.

In one sense, Irigaray already understands the second part of Diotima's speech, in terms of fantasy, primarily a fantasy of male self-birth. In Irigaray's (post-Lacanian) interpretation, the pre-subjective structure of the fantasy would be the structure of sexual difference itself and the sexuate genealogy of birth. The male subject produces itself in the fantasy as self-birthing in relation to this structure through its disavowal. But just as the focal imaginative elements of the fantasy – the female character of Diotima and her images of pregnancy and birth – disavow this structure (I, a man, can be pregnant; the generation of men does not require women) they simultaneously admit it (the fantasy requires the female character and her images of specifically female functions). However, this interpretation does not do what we called upon the theory of fantasy to do for us: it does not *preserve* the constitutive blurring of what is proper to the male or masculine and what is proper to the female or feminine. As before, the interpretation separates them out, again according to the distribution between what is real (sex difference and the attributes proper to its terms) and what is not. In this interpretation, the fantasy is wholly in the imaginary elements, while the structure – reality – subsists outside it. The structure is a set of external terms; the fantasy is an imagined identification/appropriation across them: I, a man, identify with/ appropriate what is female. This 'I, a man' is not in question.

But what if it were?

Many years after the publication of his essay, with Pontalis, on fantasy, Laplanche pointed out the frequency with which psycho-analytical case histories begin, as if unproblematically, 'A man, 30 years old . . .', or 'A woman, aged 25 . . .' We find this form of untroubled starting point, moreover, even when the case history concerns the problematization of this very 'fact'; in Freud's descrip-tion of the extraordinary psychic life of Senatspräsident Daniel Paul Schreber, for example, and in the 'attempts at interpretation' and the discussion of the mechanism of paranoia that follow it.[70] Schreber – otherwise perfectly rational and sane – inhabits a delu-sional universe in which he is chosen by God to redeem mankind, restoring it to a lost state of bliss. An essential condition for this mission is that Schreber be first transformed from a man into a woman, a process which may take centuries, although he 'has a feeling that enormous numbers of "female nerves" have already passed over into his body, and out of them a new race of men will proceed, through a process of direct impregnation by God'.[71] Freud's interpretation of Schreber's delusion of persecution uncovers a 'feminine (that is, a passive homosexual) wishful phantasy, which took as its object the figure of his doctor'. Unable to reconcile himself to 'playing the part of a female wanton towards his doctor'[72] Schre-ber wards off the fantasy through the paranoiac transformation of the proposition 'I (a man) *love him* (a man)', via its contradiction ('I do not *love* him – I *hate* him'), into the proposition '*He hates* (perse-cutes) *me*, which will justify me in hating him.'[73] As Laplanche points out, at no point is the meaning of the proposition 'I, a man' put into question, even though this is precisely *Schreber's* 'problematic'.[74]

In alighting on Schreber's case the generality of the point is in danger of being lost, but it is this: is it so certain that 'I, a man' is in any particular case a merely empirical statement of biological fact, outside the compass of the fantasy? What if this 'I, a man' were as much a part of the fantasy as his being pregnant and giving birth? This is not to say, in the case with which we are concerned, that perhaps Plato is not a man, and that he only imagines that he is. That would be to fall for the default interpretation of fantasy as the illusory opposite of reality. It is to suggest that the affirmation 'I, a man' partakes of the structure of fantasy to the extent that it is an element of psychical reality that locates the subject each time in relation to a position with which it is not identical. The subject fantasizes its 'being a man' in the sense that 'being-a-man' is a place for a subject in a fantasy that constitutes it as a subject, rather than a natural-ontological category. 'Being a man' is a problem for a subject to negotiate, not a fact about the kind of natural object that one is. In the fantasy, 'I, a man', the 'I' congeals (but for how long?) as man, it does not pre-exist it as male.

Like Schreber's delusion, the fantasy of the *Symposium* is particularly complicated with regard to the enunciation of this 'I, a man'. The generality of the discourse, the proximity of the fantasy to a mythic structure rather than a personal reverie, permits it to be summarized in less individual terms: 'a man is pregnant and gives birth'. The 'peculiar character' of the structure of such a fantasy is, as Laplanche says, 'that it is a scenario with multiple entries', in which nothing shows where the subject will be located.[75] In this form of fantasy (again, unlike personal reverie) the subject is

> caught up in the sequence of images . . . himself represented as participating in the scene although . . . he cannot be assigned any fixed place in it (hence the danger, in treatment, of interpretations which claim to do so). As a result, the subject, although always present in the fantasy, may be so in a desubjectivized form, that is to say, in the very syntax of the sequence in question.[76]

The syntax of the fantasy of Diotima and her images of pregnancy and birth is one in which the subject position is peculiarly labile, the multiplicity of entry points being particularly clear. In the fantasy 'a man is pregnant and gives birth' the site of identification is also internally layered. If 'to be' a man in this fantasy is to 'have' what is proper to the woman, if the identification *as* man is effected through the identification *as* woman, this does not reveal a fault in the process, but rather the fantasmatic structure of the process of sexed subjectivization itself. 'Man' does not borrow the images of femininity, 'man' is an image itself. Man imagines himself as 'man' and thereby *is* the man he imagines himself to be.

Looking through the images of pregnancy and birth, according to the distinction between illusion (fantasy) and reality, we see a man, Plato, manipulating (identifying with, appropriating) the images of femininity or the female, separating out what is proper to the male or the masculine and what is proper to the female or the feminine. Looking at the images as the operation of a fantasy that cannot be interpreted as lying on one side of the distinction between illusion and reality, we see the process of identifying as 'man'. This is a particular example of a general structure. Man is not the reality behind this fantasy; 'man' congeals in it. Ironically, this is only 'illusion' if the presumptions of a Platonic metaphysics hold sway.

5

Of Gods and Men: The Natural Beginning of Sex (Timaeus)

In the *Timaeus*, a late dialogue concerning the nature of the universe as a whole and all the things in it, there is what seems to be a brief account of the origin of sex in the modern, double sense of the word: the origin of the distinction between male and female human beings and of heterosexual sexual intercourse and sexual reproduction. The *Timaeus*, traditionally seen as the first part of an unfinished trilogy (including the incomplete *Critias* and the projected *Hermocrates*), seems to follow on from the *Republic*. The dialogue begins with a preliminary recapitulation of the conversation of the previous day in which Socrates, acting as host to Timaeus, Critias, Hermocrates and an unnamed fourth spoke about politics, and 'the kind of political structure cities should have and the kind of men that should make it up so as to be the best possible'.[1] As arranged, the friends have reconvened; Socrates reminds them of some of the main points from the previous day's discussion and encourages the others to follow now with their assigned subject – the ideal city of Socrates' speech 'in motion', competing with other cities for prizes and at war.

However, in the intervening hours Critias has remembered a story – emphatically, a *true* story – told him by another, older Critias, who in turn heard it from the famous Solon, who was told it by an old priest in Egypt. This is the story of the ancient city and people of Athens, 'the finest and best of all the races of humankind' (23b8–9) from whom Critias and his friends are descended, though before the priest's telling the history was unknown amongst the Greeks themselves. According to Solon's report, the greatest of the many magnificent accomplishments of these Athenians was their leadership in the Hellenic victory against the aggressive attempt of the 'marvellous royal power' of the Isle of Atlantis (25a6–7) to enslave them. Soon after, the Athenian force was wiped out by flood and the Isle of Atlantis 'sank below the sea and disappeared' (25d3–4). The city and the people of ancient Athens in this story are so exactly like the ideal city and its inhabitants described by Socrates the day before that Critias proposes to tell the story in detail, 'to translate the citizens and the city you described to us in mythical fashion yesterday to the realm of fact' (26c10–d1).

However, before Critias goes on to tell his story in detail (a telling which will in fact be postponed to the *Critias* dialogue) it is proposed that Timaeus, 'our expert in astronomy [who] has made it his main business to know the nature of the universe' (27a5–6), and who, in Socrates' judgement, 'has mastered the entire field of philosophy' (20a4–5), will speak, 'beginning with the origin of the world and concluding with the nature of human beings [*anthrōpōn phusin*]' (27a7–8). This, then, is the subject matter of the *Timaeus*. Hermocrates' speech (concerning the city at war) is never to be heard.

After the opening discussion of the *Timaeus*, Timaeus' discourse may be divided into a prologue and three parts. In the prologue (27c–29d), Timaeus lays down three basic principles: i) the distinction between '*that which always is* and has no becoming, and *that which becomes* but never is'; ii) the principle that 'everything that comes to be must of necessity come to be by the agency of some cause'; and iii) that the universe has not always been, but has come to be (27d–28b) and is the work of a divine 'demiurge' (*dēmiourgos*) or god, who fashioned the best possible world (of becoming) in the image of an eternal model (that which always is).

The first part of Timaeus' speech (29e–47e) is then an account of the bringing of order to disordered chaos by *nous*, the intellect or reason of the creator- or producer-god or demiurge (*dēmiourgos*): the construction of the world's body and the world's soul and their union; the creation of the planets, identified with the race of created gods, co-incident with the creation of time; the creation of individual souls and bodies and their union; and the creation of various human bodily parts. In the second part (48a–68d), Timaeus begins the account of the creation of the universe again, with an account of the role of necessity (non-divine causality), and replaces or supplements the dualistic distinction of his prologue, between being and becoming, with a tripartite ontology that introduces a 'third kind', 'the receptacle' of all becoming, something that receives all things without having any distinct characteristics of its own, as if mediating between that which is and that which comes to be. This is, famously, the *chōra*, which Zeyl translates as 'space'. Timaeus then explains the constitution of the four primary bodies (fire, air, water and earth); the kind and proportion of triangles that make up each of them; the sensible properties of the primary bodies and the corresponding physiology of sensation.

In the third part (68e–92c), Timaeus describes how reason and necessity work together in the formation of ensouled human bodies; the assignment of the different parts of the soul to different parts of the body; the formation of the different body parts and various physiological mechanisms; the diseases of the body and of the soul; the maintenance of the well-ordered body and soul; and, finally, the origin (or so it seems) of sex difference and the physiology of human sexual reproduction, as well as (very briefly) the generation of the other animals.

One of the most striking structural features of the *Timaeus* dialogue, and of Timaeus' discourse in particular, is its repeatedly beginning again. Each time the new beginning is motivated by the desire to get things in their proper order, to speak of that which comes before, before that which comes after.[2] Stated as a general principle, Timaeus claims that 'in every subject it is of the utmost importance to begin at the natural beginning' (29b2–3). And yet, as Timaeus readily admits, the subject matter itself – the universe, that which has become, generated as a copy or likeness of an immutable model – prohibits the achievement of a completely orderly account. As 'the accounts we give of things have the same character as the subjects they set forth . . . accounts of what is stable and fixed and transparent to understanding are themselves stable and unshifting', whereas accounts of what is only a likeness (*eikōn*) of an immutable model are themselves likely (*eikōs*). As being is to becoming, so truth is to convincingness (*pistin*) and we should not be surprised, Timaeus says, 'if it turns out repeatedly that we won't be able to produce accounts on a great many subjects – on gods or the coming to be of the universe – that are completely consistent and accurate' (29b–c).

Timaeus reminds his listeners again and again that his discourse is a 'likely account' (*eikōs logos*) or 'likely story' (*eikōs muthos*).[3] Further, in the first part of his speech, noting that he has described the coming to be of the world's body before the coming to be of the world's soul, despite the fact that the soul has 'priority and seniority' (34c6) over the body, Timaeus ascribes this (as we may ascribe other similar problems with the account) to 'a tendency to be casual and random in our speech, reflecting, no doubt, the whole realm of the casual and the random of which we are a part' (34c3–5). As well as these explicit interventions from Timaeus himself, the form of his speech in the dialogue invites questions about its status or nature, questions which have crystallized for some in the issue of whether the account of the creation of the universe is mythical and symbolic or literally meant.[4]

This, then, is the context of the apparent account of the origin of sex that appears in the final paragraphs of the dialogue. These paragraphs refer back – explicitly and implicitly – to two earlier passages in the *Timaeus*. There are thus three passages from which commentators have tried to construct a reading of Timaeus' account of the origin of sex, one in the first part of Timaeus' speech and two in the third. The first appears in a discussion of the work of the demiurge in preparing the materials, as it were, for the creation of mortal human beings by the created gods. Having created the heavens and the gods who inhabit them, the demiurge uses the same ingredients as were used to create the world soul (though no longer 'invariably and constantly pure') to create a mixture for mortal beings.

And when he had compounded it all, he divided the mixture into a number of souls equal to the number of the stars and assigned each soul to a star. He mounted each soul in a carriage, as it were, and showed it the nature of the universe. He described to them the laws that had been foreordained: They would all be assigned one and the same initial birth [*genesis prōtē*], so that none would be less well treated by him than any other. Then he would sow each of the souls into that instrument of time suitable to it, where they were to acquire the nature of being the most god-fearing of living things, and, since humans have a twofold nature [*diplēs de ousēs tēs anthrōpinēs phuseōs*], the superior kind [*to kreitton genos*] should be such as would from then on be called 'man' [*anēr*]. So, once the souls were of necessity planted in bodies, and these bodies had things coming to them and leaving them, the first innate capacity they would of necessity come to have would be sense perception, which arises out of forceful disturbances. This they would all have. The second would be love [*erōta*], mingled with pleasure and pain. And they would come to have fear and spiritedness as well, plus whatever goes with having these emotions, as well as their natural opposites. And if they could master these emotions, their lives would be just, whereas if they were mastered by them, they would be unjust. And if a person lived a good life throughout the due course of his time, he would at the end return to his dwelling place in his companion star, to live a life of happiness that agreed with his character. But if he failed in this, he would be born a second time, now as a woman [*eis gunaikos phusin en tē deutera genesei metabaloi*].[5] And if even then he still could not refrain from wickedness, he would be changed once again, this time into some wild animal that resembled the wicked character he had acquired. (41d11–42c4)

The second passage appears in the third part of Timaeus' speech. After discussing the construction of various parts of the human body (the skull, spine, teeth, tongue, skin and hair), Timaeus explains why the body is furnished with nails:

Sinew, skin, and bone were interwoven at the ends of our fingers and toes. The mixture of these three was dried out, resulting in the formation of a single stuff, a piece of hard skin, the same in every case. Now these were auxiliary causes in its formation – the pre-eminent cause of its production was the purpose that took account of future generations: our creators understood that one day women and the whole realm of wild beasts would one day come to be from men [*ex andrōn gunaikes kai talla thēria genēsointo*], and in particular knew that many of these offspring would need the use of nails and claws or hoofs for many purposes. This is why they took care to include nails formed in a rudimentary way in their design for humankind [*anthrōpois*], right at the start. (76d5–e8)

At the end of the dialogue, the explicit account of the origin of sex difference and sexual reproduction seems almost to be an afterthought. Having 'all but completed our initial assignment, that of tracing the history of the universe down to the emergence of humankind [*anthrōpinēs*]', Timaeus says he 'should go on to mention briefly how other living things came to be – a topic that won't require many words' (90e1–5):

Let us proceed, then, to a discussion of this subject in the following way. According to our likely account, all male-born humans [*tōn genomenōn andrōn*] who lived lives of cowardice or injustice were reborn in the second generation as women [*gunaikes metephuonto en tē deutera genesei*]. And this explains why at that time the gods fashioned the desire for sexual union [*tēs xunousias erōta*], by constructing one ensouled living thing in us as well as another one in women. This is how they made them in each case: There is [in a man][6] a passage by which fluids exit from the body, where it receives the liquid that has passed through the lungs down into the kidneys and on into the bladder and expels it under pressure of air. From this passage they bored a connecting one into the compacted marrow that runs from the head along the neck through the spine. This is in fact the marrow that we have previously called 'seed' [*sperma*]. Now because it has soul in it and had now found a vent [to the outside], this marrow instilled a life-giving desire for emission right at the place of venting, and so produced the love of procreation. This is why, of course, the male genitals [*tōn andrōn aidoiōn*] are unruly and self-willed, like an animal that will not be subject to reason and, driven crazy by its desires, seeks to overpower everything else. The very same causes operate in women [*tais gunaixin*]. A woman's womb or uterus, as it is called, is a living thing within her with a desire for childbearing. Now when this remains unfruitful for an unseasonably long period of time, it is extremely frustrated and travels everywhere up and down her body. It blocks up her respiratory passages, and by not allowing her to breathe it throws her into extreme emergencies, and visits all sorts of illnesses upon her until finally the woman's desire and the man's love bring them together, and, like plucking the fruit from a tree, they sow the seed into the ploughed field of her womb, living things too small to be visible and still without form. And when they have again given them distinct form, they nourish these living things so that they can mature inside the womb. Afterward, they bring them to birth, introducing them into the lights of day.

That is how women and females in general came to be [*Gunaikes men oun kai to thēlu pan houtō gegone*]. As for birds . . . (90e8–91d9)

Are we meant to take these passages seriously? What determines whether we take them seriously or not? If we are inclined to take them seriously, in some sense, and pursue an interpretation, is there a coherent position to be extracted – albeit maybe strange, offensive, wrong or comic? How do these passages relate to the overall aim and structure of the *Timaeus* dialogue? And, most importantly, what can they mean for us today?

This chapter will address these questions via a consideration of some of the ways in which these passages have been viewed and interpreted, focusing on two contentious questions in particular: according to Timaeus, were men created before women, or were men and women created simultaneously? And were there originally sexless human beings? To the extent that these passages have been taken seriously, commentators have found themselves either unable to produce a coherent account of Timaeus' position, or they have produced a coherent account through extremely selective and partial readings. This chapter aims to show how a coherent reading of the passages is possible. However, there is still more about 'sex' to be taken seriously in the *Timaeus*, when the three passages are read anew in the broader context of their framing in the dialogue. Like Timaeus' discourse, the chapter will thus have to begin again, suggesting that the metaphysical meaning and contemporary philosophical significance of this aspect of the *Timaeus* may be found in the impossibility of discovering any coherent answer to its own implicit question: what is the 'natural beginning' of sex?

First sex, second sex

First, however, should we be taking these passages seriously at all? The answer, of course, is that we should take them seriously if it can be shown that they deserve to be so taken. But as the seriousness (or otherwise) of these passages has been an issue in their reception and understanding, often causing them to be passed over, it is worth addressing it directly.

There are three giants in the modern, mainstream English-language scholarship on Plato's *Timaeus*: R. D. Archer-Hind (*The Timaeus of Plato*, 1888; translation and commentary), A. E. Taylor (*A Commentary on Plato's 'Timaeus'*, 1928) and F. M. Cornford (*Plato's Cosmology*, 1937; translation and commentary). Archer-Hind has very little to say about the three passages above. He dismisses the first as 'a piece of questionable metaphysic', hopelessly confused; he remarks that the second is 'a very singular declaration'; and he passes over the third with a two-line gloss.[7] According to Taylor, the passages on the distinction between the sexes and the production of animals are not to be taken seriously. They are 'unmistakeably playful . . . that Plato is mainly in fun is quite certain . . . we can be sure that Plato is not in earnest'; 'it is best not to be too serious . . . At any rate it is wholly wrong to suppose that Plato is in deadly earnest, and to raise the question whether there really is an "ontological significance" in difference of sex'. According to Taylor, Proclus' extended discussion of 42b just goes to show that he was a man 'among whose great gifts a sense of humour was not included'.[8] Even so, Taylor devotes seven pages to 90e1–91d6 (on sex difference and sexual reproduction, not the generation of animals), making his the longest modern English commentary on these passages. Cornford discusses the first passage over a few pages, taking issue with Taylor's interpretation, passing over the second in embarrassment. His remarks on the third passage amount to little more than a brief reiteration of those on the first.

It is perhaps Taylor's view of the *Timaeus* as a whole – that it does not contain any 'distinctively Platonic doctrines', but is rather an amalgamation of Empedoclean biology and Pythagorean mathematics – that allows him to comment on the passages in more detail than Cornford, for whom the *Timaeus* is properly Plato's own thought.[9] Taylor, that is, need not find these passages embarrassing, whereas they clearly are for Archer-Hind and Cornford.[10] Why not, then, dismiss them as comic interludes? For there is no doubt that there are laughs to be had from these passages, though feminists may be laughing for reasons other than those of Taylor. (According to Taylor, '[w]e must not moralize here on the "inadequate ideal of womanhood" in the ancient world. That women are more timid than men and less scrupulously fair in their dealings may or may not be true, but it is the average man's opinion all the world over as the modern novel and comic paper are enough to prove. As such, the assumption is good enough to build a humorous fairy-tale on.'[11]) As Sallis puts it: 'The story is that from men are born women and then animals!' Surely this is some kind of sex comedy.[12]

But granted that there is comedy, *why* is there, and why most particularly at the very end of the dialogue? Why is sex difference and (perhaps) sexual reproduction treated only in derisory terms, and why does the dialogue end mockingly? Immediately after the remarks on sex difference Timaeus explains how birds developed from innocent but simpleminded men who believed the truth about the heavens was available to sensuous perception. Land animals come from men with 'no tincture of philosophy', following the lead of the lower elements of the soul, dragging them down towards the ground. The most mindless (presumably reptiles and snakes) 'stretch out completely along the ground', and the most completely stupid and ignorant, furthest from the heavens, are the fish and shellfish (918–92c4). As the final section is avowedly about the emergence of 'other living things' (90e4), the account of 'human-kind' allegedly already complete, women, sex difference, sexual reproduction and the beasts seem all to be part of the same, hasty, comic denouement.

This form of ending is difficult to understand, given that the stated aim of Timaeus' speech is to furnish Critias with an account of the origin and nature of human beings. Critias says that he will follow Timaeus, (in Bury's translation) 'taking over from him mankind, as it were created by his speech [*anthrōpous tō logō gego-notas*], and taking over from you [Socrates] a select number of men superlatively well trained' (27a9). Critias refers to Socrates' summary of the previous day's description of 'the kind of political structure cities should have and the kind of men that should make it up so as to be the best possible' (17c2–4). This, as we have said, refers at least in part to the discussion of the *Republic*, but Socrates' summary in the *Timaeus* covers only a few of the main themes of the earlier dialogue, and misses out many of the most important (for example, the tripartite structure of the soul and the structure of justice in the soul and in the city). In fact, of the *Timaeus'* fifty-nine lines of Socrates' summary of the 'main points' (19a9) of the previous day's speech, thirty-one – just over half – concern the nature and education of female Guardians, the having of wives and children in common, the procreation of children (mating arrangements) and the distribution of children within classes and outside the city. Thus, both the beginning and the end of the *Timaeus* dialogue concern women and procreation. Unless we ignore Socrates' speech at the beginning of the *Timaeus*, then, we should have to say that the need for an account of the origin of male and female beings is noted before Timaeus' speech has even begun, and perhaps an account of Timaeus' account needs to begin here also. If the end (both the aim and the conclusion) of Timaeus' speech is to provide Critias with the human beings, both male and female, that Socrates' speech had (out of turn) turned into the best of their kind, it seems that he has sold his friends short on what Socrates believes to be some of the most important questions to do with human nature. It may even seem that Timaeus, with his crude, sexist co-categorization of women and beasts, is mocking Socrates and his female Guardians. With what human material does this leave Critias with which to begin his speech? Does not the apparently superfluous 'comic' ending in fact undermine the seriousness of the whole of Timaeus' discourse?

Of course it does not if we take it seriously, which does not mean that we must interpret the passages literally, as, arguably, Archer-Hind must have done in order to find them embarrassingly wrong.[13] It means looking for and seeking to understand a coherent position across the three relevant passages, in the context of the dialogue as a whole, and accounting for the comic ending in relation to this. To the extent that these passages have attracted serious comment, two interpretative issues stand out. Were human beings always sexed, or does sex only come about in the 'second generation', according to this account? And were men and women created simultaneously or were men created first? Proclus devoted considerable attention to these questions in his commentary on 41e–42d. The complexities of these passages are compounded, for Proclus, by his attempt to make them broadly consistent with what he takes to be Plato's position on women in the *Republic*, a position reiterated in Socrates' summary of the previous day's discussion at the beginning of the *Timaeus*. This is no mean feat, given the manifest contradiction between the apparently progressive position on women in the *Republic* and the denigration of women in Timaeus' comments.[14] In discussing this summary Proclus ascribes to Plato the view that men and women 'both have one human form' or are 'the same in species'. As things that are the same in species or form share the same perfections or virtues, 'the virtues of men and women are common' and they should thus both have the same employments. The female, however, 'is more imbecile in all things than the male', and 'whatever proceeds from the male, this the female also can produce [but] in a diminished degree'.[15]

This claim about identity of species is carried through into Proclus' discussion of 41e–42d. What, he asks, does Plato mean by the 'first generation' (*genesis prōtē*, Zeyl's 'initial birth')? According to Proclus, if the 'first law of Fate' described to the souls mounted in their carriages is that 'they would all be assigned one and the same initial birth' (41e4–5) this first birth could not refer, as Iamblichus claims it does, to the assignation of each soul to its star and its process through the heavens, being shown the nature of the universe. It refers to the first descent 'from the intelligible', the descent into wordly generation, since it is the peculiarity of these souls that they should 'associate with generation'.[16] This first descent is common to all souls, such that the same 'portion of generation' is initially allotted to all (if this were not the case, and some souls did not ever 'descend', their treatment by the demiurge would not be equal).[17]

For Proclus, the creation of the human species and its nature 'according to the demiurgic intellections' is effected before the first birth or descent of the souls, and the male and female elements of the human species are created co-originally: 'if the Demiurgus by connecting each soul with a vehicle, produces a certain animal [i.e. a certain species], it is entirely necessary that the difference of male and female in the soul should at the same time be apparent. For this is the division of animal.'[18] That is, if the human male and the human female are the same species (which they are), they must be created simultaneously, just as the male and female of each other animal species are. This means, for Proclus, that we must admit that there are male and female souls mounted in their heavenly carriages. Proclus maintained that the soul had several 'bodies', corresponding to the level of being of the soul as it descended. The first body-vehicle is the 'astral', 'luminous', 'aethereal', or 'solar-like' body, the soul's permanent body-vehicle. The second body is the 'spirituous' or 'pneumatic'; the third the fleshy or material body.[19] The first body seems to be identified with the 'carriage' or vehicle into which the demiurge mounted the souls, according to Timaeus at 41e2. However, 'masculine souls do not entirely proceed into the generation of men, nor feminine souls into the generation of women', which is evident, according to Proclus, when Timaeus says 'that every soul makes its first descent into men'.[20] (This also explains the possibility of female Guardians: male souls in women's bodies). Proclus is very clear that this is what the *Timaeus* says, even if he does not agree with it. The first generation or descent of the souls is generation or descent into men, and women only come afterwards, in the second generation (that is, first re-birth): 'But the Demiurgus leads the first descent of each soul into the generation of man. Hence it is necessary that the descent which makes man, should not have been effected through woman, nor proceed into generation through this, the female not yet existing.'[21] The first generation into men is our common human fate; for a second generation into woman a man has only himself to blame.

As Taylor says, Proclus' commentary points out ('laboriously', for Taylor) 'the difficulties into which we get if we take this account of the origin of the sexes seriously'.[22] Not least of these is the problem of just how women are 'generated' in the second generation. How can men be 'reborn' as women if there are as yet no women to bear them? And if we must therefore suppose a generation of souls as women direct from their stars, then it is not, after all, the case that all souls are first generated as men.[23] Thus, in relation to the crucial issue – were humans originally created male and female, or was the first generation a generation only of men? – Proclus has it both ways. According to Proclus it is clear that the *Timaeus* says that the first generation were only men. Trying to make sense of this he supplements the textual evidence with a Platonic metaphysics of sex difference in which male and female are co-originary, even if the first generation are only men. The cost is the impossibility of explaining – or even imagining – how the second generation (of women) then comes about. That is, the elaborate metaphysical apparatus brought in to explain sex difference finds that sex difference is precisely the thing that it cannot explain.

Timaeus 41–42 was also very important for the Medieval Christian commentators, read in conjunction with the two different versions of the creation of man in Genesis 1.26 and 2.7 (where man is both a spiritual being, made in the image of God and a corporeal being, made from the slime of the earth). Following Gregory of Nyssa's claim that humanity was originally sexless and perfect in nature John Scottus Eriugena developed a theory of human nature, in which, in the words of Dermot Moran, he

> understands humanity under two aspects: (1) perfect human nature as it might be thought of before the Fall and (2) present-day fallen human nature . . . Eriugena asserts that the Greeks maintain that there are two creations of man: an indivisible and universal humanity, very similar to the angelic nature and lacking sexual differentiation; and a secondary nature, 'which was added to the rational nature as a result of the foreknowledge of the Fall' and which is sexually differentiated.[24]

Like Proclus, Gregory of Nyssa and Eriugena see these passages as significant because they refer us to important metaphysical and theological issues. If Taylor, on the other hand, finds them mostly comic, this is partly because these issues seem simply not to arise for him.

Taylor's position is, however, ambiguous. Despite his contempt for Proclus' seriousness on this matter, Taylor obviously does take some of it seriously himself. His lengthy commentary explicates elements of the passages in relation to various cosmogonical texts and physiological theories of reproduction in an exercise of intellectual history that does attempt to extract an, albeit confused, 'embryology'[25] from Timaeus' comments, as if some of them, at least, may be understood literally. What, for Taylor, is *not* to be taken seriously is the possibility of there being any metaphysical meaning in all this.[26] Taylor's point is that there is no positive philosophical doctrine in these passages (Platonic or otherwise), which amounts to their being, for him, of no philosophical interest or significance. As Taylor was no anti-metaphysician – far from it – it is interesting that it is specifically sex difference that has no metaphysical or ontological significance for him here.

Proclus, on the other hand, takes these problems seriously because there *are*, for him, metaphysical issues concerning the

understanding of sex difference within a Platonic philosophy (principally concerning the relation between male and female and species
or form). And it is quite normal for the interpretation of metaphysical questions in Platonic philosophy to lead commentators into
difficulties. No one would expect anything else with, for example,
the attempts of commentators to get to grips with the second, tripartite ontology of the *Timaeus*, and especially the nature of the
chōra, which attracts a good deal of serious attention.

On Proclus' interpretation, then, Timaeus' position on sex difference is as follows: souls are created as male and female – thus the
division into male and female is real and intelligible, in the sense
those words have in Plato's philosophy. The form or species of the
human includes both male and female. On their first 'descent' –
which seems to mean their first incarnation – all are 'born' or generated as men, with women only appearing in the second generation,
which shows that female souls can be found in male bodies.[27] This
seems odd. However, according to Proclus it is 'not proper . . . to
be incredulous, if in total souls, the vehicles are connascently conjoined to them, but in partial souls, they are sometimes conjoined,
and sometimes not. For in the former the colligation is essential, but
in the latter, is the effect of deliberate choice.'[28] That is, the sex of
the total (untainted) soul is essentially attached to it or its first
vehicle, but sex is only contingently attached to partial souls (souls
limited by their being bonded to generation) and their second or
third vehicles. How the secondary generation of women is possible
is not and cannot be explained; but the reason for it is the general
superiority of the male in relation to the female, and in particular
that 'the male is more adapted than the female to the demiurgic
intellect and the most divine of principles, and is more allied to
immutable and undefiled souls'.[29]

Because Proclus takes these passages seriously he is at pains to
make his interpretation both internally consistent and consistent
with Platonic metaphysics. This also means taking other controversial elements of Plato's dialogues seriously as sources of authority
for confirmation of his interpretation; so, for example, he refers to
the myth of Er in the *Republic* and Aristophanes' speech in the *Symposium*.[30] Not taking the passages seriously Taylor offers, instead, a
broadbrush reading of the claims about the origin of sex in which
the implicit critical criteria are not elements of Platonic metaphysics, but modern natural-biological presumptions about sex. (Which
is not to say that modern presumptions about sex owe nothing to
Platonic metaphysics.) In so doing he refers to other controversial

elements of Plato's dialogues which are also, according to him, not to be taken seriously, for example, Aristophanes' speech in the *Symposium*.[31]

Commenting on 90e6–91d5 (most of the third of the long passages quoted above), under the sub heading '*Sex*', Taylor reads Timaeus' account as claiming that 'sex came in in the second generation, when the more cowardly and unfair were reborn as women'.[32] The bulk of his more general comments on this passage concern the question of its presumption of the inferiority of women. What the nature of the human beings of the first generation was before sex 'came in', is not explained. Concerning 91a1–4 in particular ('And this explains why, at that time, the gods fashioned the desire for sexual union, by constructing one ensouled living thing in us as well as another one in woman. This is how they made them in each case . . .'), Taylor explains that physiological modifications were required in the second generation of humans; modifications, it seems, which constitute males as males and females as females for the first time. He notes that the modifications that constitute the female are not described in detail, unlike those that constitute the male. Male and female having been created, the issue of sexual reproduction (the production of the third and all subsequent generations) now arises, and Taylor compares Timaeus' to other ancient accounts of the roles of male and female in sexual reproduction.[33] Contra Proclus, then, Taylor's interpretation seems to be that humans are *not* originally created as male and female, but that the distinction of sex – created at the same time as eros – belongs only to the second generation, in which male and female are created simultaneously. This leaves him unable to say anything about the nature of the first generation, but as, according to Taylor, we are now in the realm of myth and fantasy, we should not expect to be able to say anything more, beyond a reference to the influence of Empedocles' 'notion that the earliest living creatures were not as yet differentiated into male and female'.[34]

But Taylor's is not a good interpretation, over-determined as it is by his comparison of the account with Aristophanes' speech in the *Symposium*, and with the relation of both to Empedocles. According to Taylor, Timaeus postulates a first-generation human kind before sex 'came in'. If this were the case it would not also be true, as Taylor claims it is, that it is 'the same theory' as in Aristophanes' speech where, in fact, the original human creatures come in three kinds (male-male, female-female and male-female). In fact it is an extremely partial memory of Aristophanes' account, in which only the original 'bi-sexual' human being is mentioned, that mediates between Empedocles and Timaeus in Taylor's commentary. Putting Empedocles and this partial Aristophanes together, Taylor produces a version of Timaeus' account that is blind to much of what Timaeus actually says in these passages, most notably the insistent idea (the only thing common to all three passages) that *men came first* and *women come from men.*[35]

Cornford's general view of Taylor's commentary on the *Timaeus* is that there is no justification for the latter's presumption that the doctrines in it are not Plato's own. In relation to the passages under discussion, this means that Cornford denies the validity of Taylor's Empedoclean interpretation, and struggles to give a more properly Platonic reading, drawing heavily on Proclus. Cornford's interpretation of *Timaeus* 91–2 is dealt with in advance, in his comments on 42b, and is constituted against Taylor's interpretation. Cornford understands Taylor to be claiming that Timaeus postulates a first generation of originally 'sexless' humans, when there is in fact 'nowhere in the *Timaeus* any mention of sexless creatures'.[36] On the contrary, Cornford writes, Timaeus is quite clear at 90e that there were '*men*' in the first generation, not sexless creatures. Thus the very line that motivates Taylor's interpretation – 'all male-born humans [*tōn genomenōn andrōn*] who lived lives of cowardice or injustice were reborn in the second generation as women' (90e9–11) – is proof of Taylor's error, according to Cornford. This does not, however, mean that there were *only* men in the first generation: 'We need not understand that there were no women until the bad men of the first generation began to die and to be reincarnated in female form, but only that a bad man will be reborn as a woman, a bad woman presumably as a beast . . . all that is meant is that every soul that is at any time incarnated for the first time, is incarnated in male form.'[37]

Cornford's position thus amounts to a flat contradiction: the first generation is neither sexless nor exclusively male, but the first generation of all souls is nevertheless male. The line that supposedly clinches Cornford's interpretation – 'all male-born humans [*tōn genomenōn andrōn*] who lived lives of cowardice or injustice were reborn in the second generation as women' (90e9–11) – is the line that fatally undermines it. Proclus attempts to resolve this same contradiction with a metaphysics of sex difference according to which the idea or form of the human encompasses both male and female, even if the first sensuous incarnation of the soul – a copy of the form – is always male. But Cornford's insistence on the generic nature of all of the discussion of human physiology prior to *Timaeus* 91 effectively rules out the possibility of this interpretative strategy for him. According to Cornford, when Timaeus begins to speak of human beings he speaks in general terms applicable to both sexes: discussion of 'the physical differences of the sexes are postponed to a sort of appendix at the end because all that will be said in the interval applies equally to men and women'.[38] This is important, because if Cornford is right, Timaeus could then be understood to have provided Critias with an account of the origin and creation of human beings *before* the embarrassing, appended comedy of sex and his (Timaeus') lack of seriousness there need not interfere with the seriousness of his discourse as a whole.

Although Cornford's interpretation is explicitly counter to Taylor's, it suffers from the same basic problem, in relation to the same insistent point: it only works by failing to explain much of what Timaeus actually says in these passages, especially, once again, the repeated claim that men came first and women came from men. To the extent that Cornford deals with this problem he makes an implicit distinction between what is to be taken seriously and what is not. The passage on the provision of nails in men for the benefit of future descended generations of women and beasts is 'one of the places where the mythical machinery becomes embarrassing and entails the use of vague language'; the degeneration of male into female at *Timaeus* 91 is described as a 'mythical representation' of what could, it is implied, be represented non-mythically in less embarrassing form.[39] For the most part, however, Cornford deals with it by ignoring it. *Timaeus* 90e–91b attracts little comment relative to the general level of detail in Cornford's book. Timaeus' last word on the subject – '[t]hat is how women and females in general came to be' – attracts no comment from Cornford at all.

In a more recent analysis of Timaeus' comments on sex – one which does take them seriously, as part of a larger argument in the *Timaeus* – Catherine Joubard interprets the creation of sex in terms of its being a necessary condition for the cycle of retribution, subjection to which differentiates the 'divine' human soul from the world soul (for there to be retribution there must be generation, and for there to be generation there must be sexual differentiation).[40] Sex difference is introduced, according to Joubard, in the second generation, the first human generation being quite without sexual differentiation. How does this cohere with Timaeus' explicit claim that 'all male-born humans [*tōn genomenōn andrōn*] who lived lives of cowardice or injustice were reborn in the second generation as women'? According to Joubard, 'Plato uses the term *anēr* (90e) as a generic term for the species of the first generation. A sexually undetermined living being appears, a human being in relation to whom the question of sex is not pertinent, as if we are dealing with a sort of hybrid being, or with a Man with a capital "M" representing an original humanity.'[41]

I think Joubard is wrong. Plato's language furnishes him with the distinction between *anthrōpos* and *anēr*, and he is usually careful in his choice of the latter to designate man, specifically, rather than woman or generic humanity. Further, he is especially careful in his choice between *anthrōpos* and *anēr* when the discussion in any dialogue touches on the issue of the distinction between male and female or man and woman, as it does in the line at issue here. Despite its receiving Luc Brisson's blessing, Joubard's reading is not plausible as an explanation for Plato's use of *anēr* in this instance. This may be because Joubard is not, in fact, concerned with the problem of sex in her interpretation here, but with the distinction between the human and world soul and the necessary conditions for the cycle of retribution. Despite her willingness to read into the passages the idea of the initially unsexed human being, Joubard's interpretation imposes a commonsensical view of sex on to Timaeus' words. When sex comes on the scene it appears in just that form in which we might commonsensically expect it to appear, and the awkward problem of an exclusively male first generation, and of the derivation of women from men, is swept under the carpet. Joubard takes these passages on sex seriously, but at the expense of interpreting them in such a way that their philosophical point has nothing to do with sex.

It is interesting that the most explicit, manifest position that emerges from the three passages on sex and reproduction is precisely the one that neither Taylor nor Cornford ostensibly countenance as a plausible overall reading, although Archer-Hind glosses it dutifully: 'For in the first generation the gods made man, and in the second woman.'[42] Man first, woman second. Moreover, woman is *derived from* man. On the other hand, critical references to the *Timaeus* by feminist writers do tend to presume that this is the basic claim about sex, and 42b7–c1 and/or 90e9–11 (in which bad men are reborn as women) is often quoted as proof of Plato's general tendency to denigrate all things female and feminine.[43]

In fact, there is more in the *Timaeus* than just the three main passages on sex and reproduction to support this reading. In Timaeus' account the creation of the human body is presupposed before it becomes his explicit theme, but the dedicated discussion of its creation begins at 69c. There Timaeus describes how the gods, in imitation of the demiurge who had created the world soul and the round body of the world, encased the immortal human soul within a round mortal body (the human head), and created the mortal part of the soul comprising sensation, perception and passion. To protect the immortal part of the soul from the mortal, they constructed the lower part of the body (the trunk) to house the latter, further subdividing mortal soul into its superior and inferior parts, the superior housed (roughly speaking) in the chest, the inferior (again roughly) in the belly (69c7–70e10). After a discussion of the mediating role of the liver in relation to the immortal and mortal parts of the soul and its divinatory role (71b–72c), Timaeus describes 'how the rest of the body came to be' (72e2). The gods created the lower abdomen and the coils of intestines to store the food and allow time for nourishment to be drawn from it, saving us from the gluttony of insatiable appetite to which an only short passage of food through us would have led.

The discussion of the crucial formation of the 'marrow' (*muēlos*) then recapitulates, in greater detail, the initial description of the formation of the parts of the soul and their being housed in the body. The marrow is the starting point for the formation of 'flesh and bones and things of that nature' and is the substance within which 'life's chains' are bound for so long as the soul is bound to the body, 'giving roots for the mortal race'. The marrow is 'a "universal seed" contrived for every mortal kind [*panspermian panti thnētō genei mēchanōmenos*]'; the different types of soul (*tōn psuchōn genē*) are implanted in it, the marrow divided into forms appropriate to these different types. The portion of the marrow containing the immortal part of the soul and its divine seed is what is called the brain. The whole of the rest of the body is then constructed around the marrow containing the other, mortal parts of the soul, the whole of the marrow encased in a protective covering of bone (72e–73d). More details follow on bones, joints, sinew, flesh, sweat ('a warm moisture'), teeth, tongue, skin ('an outer layer . . . separated off from the flesh') and hair (73e–76d).

According to Taylor's interpretation of the passages on sex and reproduction, the formation described would be that of a body that is neither male nor female, in the sense that it is as yet unsexed. According to Cornford's interpretation it must be a generic body, the characteristics of which are shared by both male and female, as everything said before *Timaeus* 91 applies equally to men and women.[44] Neither of these, however, can account for Timaeus' next detail in the description of the formation of the body: the creation of the finger- and toenails, the reason for which is the gods' fore-knowledge that 'one day women and the whole realm of wild beasts would one day come to be from men [*ex andrōn*] and . . . that many of these offspring would need the use of nails and claws or hoofs' (76e1–4).

This suggests, very strongly, that Timaeus has in fact been describing the formation of the male body. And in all of Cornford's comments on this section he is compelled, explicitly or implicitly, to admit as much. He confesses himself drawn to Albert Rivaud's interpretation of the discussion of the formation of the marrow, in which the ' "universal seed" contrived for every mortal kind [*pan-spermian panti thnētō genei mēchanōmenos*]' refers to every species, every kind of animal, and in which the different types of soul (*tōn psuchōn genē*) implanted in the marrow refers not to the differ-ent kinds of the human soul (mortal and immortal) but the kinds of souls of different kinds of beasts. On this preformatist conception, the marrow of man (*anēr*) contains within it the seeds of all kinds of mortal creatures, making provision for 'what is mythically represented later (91) as a degeneration of the male human type into woman and the lower animals', or the develop-ment of women and beasts out of men at 76e.[45] Cornford says, further, that the 'seed' received into the brain marrow (73c1–2) is specified at 91b1 as 'semen',[46] that is, *male seed*, as the context there makes clear. (The identification of the 'seed' as *male* seed is also clear in the discussion of 'sexual overindulgence' as a disease of the soul at 86c–e.) Accordingly, the physiological discussion of *Timaeus* 73 does not, as Cornford previously claimed, apply equally to men and women.[47]

Commenting on 76d on nails specifically, Cornford reassures us for the second time that

> Women and beasts have not actually developed from men; nor had anyone ever believed that they did. But Plato, having included trans-migration in his mythical machinery, with the unusual and fantastic addition that men are imagined as existing at first alone, has to take this way of conveying that claws and hoofs in animals are more obvi-ously useful to them than nails are to human beings.[48]

Here, then, Cornford is quite clear that Timaeus says that men *do* come first and that women *are* derived from men, contradicting what he says elsewhere about the simultaneous creation of male and female. Strangely, these first creatures must be 'men' without male sexual organs, as the creation of the genitals is co-incident with the later creation of sexual desire and of women (91a–b). To account for this Cornford suggests an explanation for the late appearing of specifically sexual desire and the genitals with which it is associated by reverting to a form of the claim that everything beforehand is true for both men and women: 'The individual human being requires all the faculties and functions that have hitherto been described; but he could be imagined as complete without the organs of sex, which are added only for the sake of the species.'[49] In which case are not these imagined human beings the original, sexless creatures of Taylor's interpretation, against which Cornford else-where argues? Or can we imagine sexed creatures without sex organs?

According, then, to Cornford, were human beings always sexed, or does sex only come about in the 'second generation' in Timaeus' account? Taking all of Cornford's comments together we would have to say: humans are originally both male and female, they are originally only male, they are originally sexless, and they are originally sexed without sex.

Degenerative evolution and sexual reproduction

The laudable aim of the commentators on the *Timaeus* discussed here is to render Plato's (or Timaeus') account consistent: logically consistent, consistent with itself, consistent with other of Plato's dialogues and, for some, consistent with what we think we know about sex. For Proclus this means rendering the discussion of sex in the *Timaeus* consistent with what Plato says elsewhere about women and with elements of Platonic metaphysics more generally. Proclus finds in the *Timaeus* a metaphysics of sex through which he attempts to resolve the fundamental contradiction between the claim that human beings have always been both male and female and the claim that human beings were originally male. If he fails to resolve the contradiction, his commentary at least has the merit of noticing that sex is a metaphysical topic.

Taylor renders the discussion of sex consistent with other 'myths' in the Platonic corpus, extracting a literal, biological core that can be taken seriously as a reflection of elements of the physiological theories of the time. But his highly selective reading presents

Timaeus with a consistent position only by ignoring what does not fit in with it. To this extent Taylor is flippant with Timaeus' words, believing Timaeus flippant himself. There is no philosophical meaning in any of this for Taylor; there is no metaphysics of sex in the *Timaeus*. But Taylor renders Timaeus' account consistent with his own (Taylor's) commonsensical presuppositions about sex precisely by dismissing it as comic myth. As such, the discourse may with impunity speak nonsense.

Like Proclus, Cornford attempts to render the discussion of sex consistent with the relevant aspects of Platonic metaphysics more generally, consistent with itself and with commonsensical presumptions about sex. In so doing the text presents him with plenty of embarrassments – the elements that simply cannot be fitted in to the overarching presumption that human beings *must* originally be both male and female, that male *cannot* come before female. Cornford deals with some of these embarrassments by dismissing them as myth or passing over them without comment; where he tries to resolve the contradictions with which they present him, he intensifies them. Similarly, Joubard elides the contradictions in the text to produce a confident account of Timaeus' position in which an unproblematic division of sex appears, albeit in the second generation, but at the expense of an unconvincing interpretation of some of the most important lines.

Is there a way to understand these passages that is not unduly selective and that openly confronts their apparent contradictions and most difficult claims? Let us consider the three major passages again, through the questions that animate the main controversy in the modern commentaries: were men created before women, or simultaneously? And were there originally sexless human beings, according to Timaeus? The first 'foreordained law' in the first passage is that the newly individuated souls 'would all be assigned one and the same initial birth (*genesis prōtē*), so that none would be less well treated by him (the demiurge) than any other'. And yet in speaking of the first 'sowing' of the souls into suitable instruments of time (these instruments being the Earth, Moon and other planets, as becomes clear at 42d6–8), the 'twofold nature of human being' is already established, its twofoldness is specified as its division into superior and inferior kinds, and it is stated that the superior would 'from then on be called man [*anēr*]'. This suggests that some souls were, from the very beginning, superior to others, a superiority that is subsequently marked by their embodiment as men. Thus human beings come in two kinds, men and women, because some souls are superior to others, and the existence of the lower animals is explained by the existence of even more inferior souls.

Strictly speaking, this means that we could not say of any soul, at its initial birth, that it was the soul of either a man or a woman; indeed we could not even say it was, at its initial birth, either human or beast. These distinctions (man/woman, human/beast) are *consequent upon* the actual embodiment of the soul in the form that reflects its relative superiority or inferiority. But once embodied as human, the soul must be either man or woman, because our becoming-human (not returning to our star or becoming-beast) is the assumption of the embodied kind appropriate to our relatively superior or inferior soul.

But in speaking only of the second birth of men – those men who failed to live well enough to return to their star and were thus (in Bury's translation) 'changed into woman's nature at the second birth [*eis gunaikos phusin en tē deutera genesei*]' – the text *suggests* that the first generation was in fact a generation only of men. The third passage refers back to this claim and repeats it (again, in Bury's translation): 'all those creatures generated as men [*tōn genomenōn andrōn*] who proved themselves cowardly . . . were transformed, at their second incarnation, into women [*gunaikes metephuonto en tē deutera genesei*]'. This suggestion is made more concrete in the second passage, where the provision of nails is explained by the foresight of the creator-gods who 'understood that one day women and the whole realm of wild beasts would come to be from men', spring 'out of men' (Bury) (*ex andrōn gunaikes kai talla thēria genēsointo*). The lead into the third passage also seems to confirm this. The passage purportedly explains – Timaeus having 'all but completed' his account of the emergence of humankind (*anthrōpinēs*) – 'how other living things came to be' (90e). As the discussion to 91d7 concerns, according to Timaeus, 'how women and females in general came to be' (91d8), and the rest of the dialogue deals with birds and beasts, it must be that 'humankind' up to this point contains only men and the 'other living things' are women and beasts.

And yet – and this is the major puzzle and moment of contradiction – this third passage also claims that the advent of sexual desire and the transformation of the genitals into *sexual* organs comes about in the second generation, at the same time as the appearance of women. The passage suggests, that is, that sex comes about *in the second generation*, hence the interpretations that see the passage as being about the origin of sex. How can there have been men in the first generation if the origin of sex lies in the second?

This is an insuperable contradiction *if* the categories of 'man' and 'woman' are taken to be synonymous or effectively identical with those of 'male' and 'female', which is indeed how they are taken in Zeyl's translation of and the various modern commentaries on the *Timaeus*. The assumption that these terms are effectively synonymous in this context is, as I have argued, an assumption internal to the modern natural-biological conception of sex, where 'sex' functions conceptually (and also allegedly empirically) as the basis for the categories of 'man' and 'woman', in the sense that the sex categories of male and female are taken to determine, in the last instance, what a man or a woman *is*. When being a man or a woman is tied to one's being male or being female respectively, the conflation of the two sets of terms is easily explained. But this book has argued against the presumption of the modern natural-biological category of sex in the interpretation of Plato's dialogues. In Chapter 1, it was argued that Socrates' argument in *Republic* V makes more sense when we see in it a distinction between the natural-biological reproductive categories of male and female and the social and political categories of man and woman and do not presume that the former determine the latter, ontologically. This was not to deny the existence of the categories of male and female in the *Republic*, but to insist on their conceptual distinction from those of man and woman and the extensive non-identity of the groups that are their respective referents. If this distinction and non-identity is rendered obscure in the de facto foundational function of the modern natural-biological concept of sex with respect to the categories of men and women, the argument of Chapter 1 suggests that it may become visible in the interpretation of certain passages in Plato's dialogues, including now the three crucial passages from the *Timaeus*.

In the parts of the *Timaeus* that concern specifically human being, it is noticeable that the categories of sex ('male' and 'female') are absent until the end of the last of our three passages, when the origin of sexual desire and sexual reproduction is explicitly tackled. In fact, the mention of 'females' (*to thēlu*) at 91d8 is the first and only time the word is used in the dialogue in relation to human beings, and the word 'male' (*arren*) is never used of humans in Timaeus' discourse, not even where Zeyl's translation suggests it is ('all **male**-born humans [*tōn genomenōn* **andrōn**] who

lived lives of cowardice or injustice were reborn in the second generation as women').

We may hazard the following explanation for this. The categories
of 'man' and 'woman' are conceptually distinct from those of 'male'
and 'female' in Timaeus' discussion of human beings, and Timaeus
speaks as if men and women existed before their transformation
into males and females. Or, rather, *men* existed, and at the moment
of the second generation, when unjust or cowardly men were transformed into women, male and female were also created out of men
and women *in order that* men and women might reproduce themselves. This explains both Timaeus' introductory sentence in the last
passage and his summing up at the end of it. The account of the
emergence of humankind is the account of the emergence of men,
thus he is left with the task of explaining the existence of women.
The passage explains 'how women and females in general came to
be', which does not mean that 'women and females' are the same
thing, but that it explains two things: the emergence of women from
men and the creation of females (along with males) with the creation of sexual reproduction. It also explains something that Cornford finds puzzling. Why, he asks, are the sexual appetites not
mentioned in *Timaeus* 72–3 along with the nutritive appetites? He
postulates that it is because they belong to a different system of
organs, not dealt with until 90e. Cornford is puzzled because he
presupposes that sex was already there when there were men. If,
on the other hand, we distinguish between men and women and
males and females we would not expect to hear of the sexual appetites until there is sex difference and sexual reproduction, that is,
precisely from 90e.[50]

Of course, according to the modern conception of sex, men and
women cannot be conceived independently of their being-male and
being-female. But if, without the presumption of the modern conception of sex, they can be so conceived, what is it that makes men
'men' and women 'women'? It seems that Timaeus reduces the set
of behaviours and characteristics that constitute men as men and
women as women to one defining characteristic, or metonymically
substitutes one defining distinction for the whole collection of
defining characteristics: the being-superior or being-inferior of
souls. According to Morag Buchan, there is no female soul in the
Timaeus: 'souls do not polarize into male and female but into superior and inferior. The superior are deposited in male bodies.'[51] But
distinguishing between the categories of male and female and man
and woman we would rather say that 'man' and 'woman' *mean*

'superior' and 'inferior' before the distinction of sex is introduced to explain how these souls then reproduce themselves. If the distinction between men and women precedes that between males and females, where 'male' and 'female' are defined primarily by their roles in reproduction, Timaeus can say that women 'came out of men' because the transformation (*metabaloi, metephuonto*) of men into women, their 'rebirth' as such in the second generation, is not the outcome of sexual reproduction, which does not yet exist. It is an *evolution* (albeit a degenerative evolution) rather than a sexual generation, much like the 'evolution' of beasts and birds from women and men. Accordingly, there is no immanent conceptual contradiction in maintaining that men exist in the first generation though the origin of sex and sexual generation lies in the second. Moreover, in the context of Timaeus' discourse as a whole – concerning the creation of the world soul and world body by the demiurge, and his delegation of tasks to his creature-gods – this is no more odd than anything else.

In the *Timaeus* the categories of sex – male and female – are never explicitly discussed but are what is at issue in the passage beginning at 90e (as we have said, only the female is actually named). These categories are, at least so far as human beings are concerned, (in modern terminology) natural-biological categories that refer to function in sexual reproduction. The difference between man and woman, on the other hand, is not sexual, but *moral*. 'Man' and 'woman' in the *Timaeus* are moral categories, in so far as they refer to moral differences between souls. The degenerative evolution of man into woman – which is of course impossible to explain or even conceive in natural-biological terms[52] – is a claim of the same order as the claims that the demiurge assigned all souls 'one and the same initial birth' (41e5) in order that they be treated equally and that a person who lives a just life in the first generation will at the end of it 'return to his dwelling place in his companion star, to live a life of happiness that agree[s] with his character' (42b3–5). To the extent that Timaeus' discourse gives an explanation for certain phenomena, these are not restricted to the observable phenomena of the natural world but include the moral structure of the universe. In so doing it makes use of an ancient Greek commonplace – the moral inferiority of women – and justifies it cosmo-theologically. Our three passages thus explain two different but intimately related things: the moral differences between souls and the natural-biological phenomenon of sexual reproduction from a moral point of view, that is, in the service of the retributive cycle of the reincarnation of souls.[53]

And yet

Without the modern presumption of the effective identity of the categories of male and female and men and women one otherwise intractable problem in Timaeus' discussion of men and women and the origin of sex may be explained, but this is far from eliminating all of the contradictions and explanatory lacunae in his account, notably the problem of what it can mean to speak of a first generation of, exclusively, 'men' when that word has no meaning except in opposition to that of 'women', who do not yet exist. No doubt the mythical or quasi-mythical aspects of Timaeus' discourse (for example the role of the demiurge himself and his creature-gods) renders the aim of complete consistency otiose, as they are deployed, in part, to deal in general symbolic terms with things, the details of which are mysterious or unknown. Furthermore, we have been amply warned of the impossibility of any complete and consistent account, according to the principle that 'the accounts we give of things have the same character as the subjects they set forth', which means that accounts of what is only a likeness (*eikōn*) of an immutable model 'are themselves likely [*eikōs*]'. It may thus turn out, Timaeus says, that 'we won't be able to produce accounts on a great many subjects – on gods or the coming to be of the universe – that are completely consistent and accurate' (29b–c). Further, it will not always be possible to treat each phenomenon in good order, as when the account of the properties of bodies (in the most general sense) necessarily presupposes the existence of sense perception, and hence body and soul, before the coming to be of any of these latter have been discussed (61c7–d9).

And yet, Timaeus insists, 'in every subject it is of the utmost importance to begin at the natural beginning' (29b2–3). This principle, stated in the prologue to Timaeus' discourse determines, amongst other things, the priority of Timaeus' discourse over those of Critias and Hermocrates (thus the principle is not merely immanent to Timaeus' discourse), the way in which the first part of his speech begins, and also its beginning again in the second part. It is easy to say that this principle is contradicted by the methodological limitations of Timaeus' study, and that it is performatively contradicted by the series of new beginnings that structures the *Timaeus*. It is more interesting, however, to ask what the contradictory combination of the principle and the methodological limitations actually yields and how it is connected to the new beginnings. More specifically, what does the combination of the principle and the methodological limitations yield in Timaeus' discussion of the origin of male and female? Where or what is the 'natural beginning' of sex?

In fact we find, in keeping with the stated methodological limitations, that the categories of sex, 'male' and 'female', are presupposed almost from the very beginning of the *Timaeus*, taken for granted well before the explicit account of the creation of male and female human beings. This is not just to say that sexed men and women and their procreative capacities appear before the discussion of the origin of sex, in Socrates' opening speech in the *Timaeus*, reporting on the previous day's discussion of men and women and of the procreation of children (18b–19a), in Critias' speech, and in the discussion of 'sexual overindulgence' as a disease of the soul (86b–e). Male and female are presumed as cosmic procreative categories, providing the context within which any discussion of the origin of sexed men and women must take place.

First, the vocabulary of procreation permeates the whole of the account of the creation of the world soul and the world body, the planets and the gods in the first part of Timaeus' speech and the tripartite ontology of the second part.[54] In the first part Timaeus speaks of how the demiurge 'begat' or 'generated' (*egennēsato*) the world (34b10–11), and how the primary constituents (fire, earth, water and air) were used to 'beget' (*egennēthē*) the body of the world (32c2). The demiurge is called 'the father who had begotten the universe [*ho gennēsas patēr*]' (37c7) and refers to himself (when addressing his creature-gods) or is referred to as their father (41a8, 71d6, for example). His created Earth, 'our nurturer [*trophon*]' (40b9), is a goddess. Accepting the conventional account of how she and the other deities came to be, Timaeus describes how

> Earth and Heaven gave birth to Ocean and Tethys [*Gēs te kai Ouranou paides Ōkeanos te kai Tēthus egenesthēn*], who in turn gave birth to Phorkys, Cronus, and Rhea and all the gods in that generation. Cronus and Rhea gave birth to Zeus and Hera, as well as all those siblings who are called by names we know. These in turn gave birth to yet another generation. (40e6–41a3)

In the second part of Timaeus' speech, the 'third kind' is added to the distinction between the two kinds of the prologue, the distinction between '*that which always is* and has no becoming, and *that which becomes* but never is' (27d6–28a1). The third kind is first described as 'a receptacle [*hupodochēn*] of all becoming – its wet-nurse [*tithēnēn*], as it were' (49a7). The three kinds are then specified as 'that which comes to be, that in which it comes to be, and that after which the thing coming to be is modelled and which is the source of its coming to be'. It is quite appropriate, Timaeus says, 'to compare the receiving thing to a mother, the source to a father, and the nature between them to their offspring' (50d16). Thus the pro-creative categories of male and female are presupposed as cosmic or ontological principles before they are specifications of human beings, which is unsurprising, given the broad symmetry between the account of the creation of the universe and the creation of human beings. Where, then, is the 'natural beginning of sex'? Not in human being itself, but in the cosmo-ontological principle that conditions its possibility. It is interesting that this is explicitly the case in Proclus' interpretation of Timaeus on sex, where Proclus affirms 'in the intelligible, in the intellectual, and in the supermun-dane Gods, the harmonious conjunction of the male with the female'.[55] For Proclus it is because of the connascence of male and female in the universe and in the gods that we must affirm the con-nascence of male and female in the human.

But as Proclus' reference to 'the intelligible' indicates, the uni-verse itself is not 'original'. It 'take[s] its start from some origin [*ap' archēs tinos arxamenos*]' (Zeyl) or has 'begun from some beginning' (Bury) (28b8). The universe is a copy, 'modelled after that which is changeless and is grasped by a rational account' (29a10–11), it is an 'image of something' (29b2). It is immediately after this line that Timaeus says that 'in every subject it is of the utmost importance to begin at the natural beginning' (29b2–3). If the cosmo-ontological principle of the procreative male-female distinction is modelled, like everything else in the universe, after 'that which is changeless' must we look for the natural beginning of sex in the changeless intelligible realm, in the 'source' (*hothen*) (50d5) of becoming, the beginning from which the universe began? But the unchanging realm of that which always is, is itself called father or source, iden-tifying it with just one of the terms of sex, as if the other lay else-where. Does this mean that a meta-ontological male-female principle hovers above even this unchanging realm of that which always is? And how could any category of reproduction, the emblematic cat-egories of change, of becoming and passing away, be associated with the realm of the unchanging, the ungenerated and ungenerating?

What then, or where, is the natural beginning of sex? For an answer the *Timaeus* only leads us in circles. And perhaps, according to the principle of methodological limitations, this is exactly right. Timaeus stipulates that 'the accounts we give of things have the same character as the subjects they set forth' (29b5–6). When the subject is sex, the discourse cannot find its natural beginning. Sex itself leads us in circles. There is no natural beginning of sex.

Coda: The Idea of 'Sex'

In this book I have argued against the presumption that the modern natural-biological concept of sex is part of the conceptual apparatus of Plato's philosophy. I have tried to show, instead, how modern translations of and commentary on the relevant aspects of Plato's dialogues impose this modern concept upon them. This imposition has been invisible to the extent that the concept functions as if it were completely transparent, as unquestionable, rather than as a possible object of critical, philosophical reflection. The result of the book is twofold. First, reading the dialogues afresh, without the presumption of the modern natural-biological concept of sex, has allowed new interpretations of passages that have already been heavily commented upon. Second, the modern natural-biological concept of sex has come into view, both as a presupposition in translation and commentary and as an historically constituted concept whose meaning and function is rather more complicated than the popular view of it, as a natural given, allows.

The various interpretations of specific passages of Plato's dialogues have been worked out in the argument of each chapter and do not need to be reprised here. But to the extent that this book has been critically concerned with the peculiar function and seemingly self-legitimating status of the modern, natural-biological concept of sex, one task in particular remains at its end: that of a philosophical determination of this concept that might account for its nature and function.

If we had to furnish 'sex' with its metaphysical basis this would be classically Platonic, the Idea or Form of the categories of sex ('male' and 'female') determining its only imperfect copies, the imperfection of which explains anomalous bodies or genotypes, rather than letting them threaten the Idea. It is ironic, then, that it is in precisely the passages and themes in the three dialogues discussed in this book, where commentators have tended most readily to see the modern, natural-biological concept of sex, that an anti-'Platonic' metaphysics of sex may be seen to take form. In a general philosophical sense, Plato may have made the modern natural-biological concept of sex possible, but these texts also speak against it.[1]

However, it is not enough simply to point to the philosophical ground of the modern, natural-biological concept of sex in Platonic metaphysics, as if that afforded an adequate explanation of the meaning of 'sex' for us today. We still require a philosophical account of the nature of the concept in its contemporary operation, an account of the resilience of the concept and the mechanism through which it is effective.

The tentative conclusions about 'sex' drawn from the chapters of this book are, at first sight, varied. It was suggested, at the end of Chapter 1, that the apparent belief in contemporary societies in the givenness of sex and its naturally determining power in the development of men and women are contradicted by anxieties, first, about sex's ability to perform its natural determining function without help from a whole host of cultural practices (particularly, the identification of sex through sexually differentiated clothing, toys, books and activities for children), and, second, about the constant threats posed to the development of natural men and women by certain cultural phenomena (working mothers, homosexual parenting, gender theory, and so on). I claimed in Chapter 1 that Socrates' argument in Book V of the *Republic* makes best sense when the being of 'men' and 'women' is understood to be determined by the set of socially defined manly and womanly characteristics and behaviours, rather than by a modern, natural-biological concept of sex. This amounts to the claim that 'man' and 'woman' are kinds defined socio-politically and not naturally or biologically. The anxieties of contemporary societies seem to acknowledge this, whilst at the same time denying it with an ostentatious faith in the natural determining power of sex. This is the fetish character of sex; not of sexual practices, but of the concept of sex difference.[2]

The analyses of Chapter 2 (of Aristophanes' speech in the *Symposium*, of Freud's speculations on the origin of sex, and of the role of the modern natural-biological concept of sex in Lacan's psychoanalytical account of sexuation) suggest that the presumption of the resolutely non-mythic status of the modern natural-biological concept of sex is questionable. Although the empirical and conceptual inadequacy of the binary terms of sex ('male' and 'female') in relation to human sexual diversity (anatomically, genotypically, hormonally and existentially) does not in itself entitle us to say that sex *is* mythic, it does lead us to consider the status of the binary division. It was suggested here that, *qua* exclusive binary division, sex is presupposed in much the same way as Aristophanes' mythic principle of the division of all things into male and female is presupposed, as a structuring or organizing principle. The conclusion of Chapter 5 – the impossibility of locating the natural beginning of sex in the *Timaeus* – suggests a similar point. We cannot get behind 'sex', as it were, to see the neutral ground from which it springs, because for us, today, 'sex' is always already there, as a first principle of division.

In Chapter 4 the images of pregnancy and birth in Diotima's/ Socrates' speech are interpreted according to a notion of fantasy that is not opposed to reality, in which the being-a-man of the fantasist is not part of reality external to the fantasy, as opposed to the fictional transsexual identification internal to it, but is instead, itself, the psycho-existential achievement of the fantasy. A given entity, a man, does not borrow the images of femininity; a man is imagined as such and imaginarily realized in this fantasy (no mention of the phallus!). This is but one example of a psychic mechanism by which identification as or with the categories of man and woman – one's being-subject as man or woman – is effected and sustained. Being-a-man is a place for a subject in a fantasy that creates it as such, not a natural fact grounded on one's sex.

There are two common points in these suggestions. First, 'men' and 'women' are socio-political categories, not naturally determined groups, and one's being-a-man or being-a-woman is therefore a psycho-existential achievement, constantly needing to be reaffirmed. Second, 'sex', a particular and privileged, exclusively binary difference, is nevertheless presumed to be the natural basis for the (thus naturalized) categories of 'man' and 'woman' – presumed in the sense of functioning as a structuring principle of division; a given for thought, rather than an object of it. So far, however, that is merely to note the positing of 'sex' without being able to account philosophically either for the concept's status or its modes of operation. What philosophical determination of the nature of the concept of 'sex' would be able to account for these?

An object only in the idea

In his *Critique of Pure Reason*, Kant, having discussed the a priori contribution to experience of the faculties of sensibility and understanding and the legitimate employment of the concepts of the understanding (limited to the realm of possible experience), introduced what he called the 'ideas' of pure reason, or 'transcendental ideas'. Aware of the confusion likely to be caused by the use of a term so ubiquitous in philosophy, Kant drew attention to what he seemed to consider its 'original meaning' in Platonic metaphysics, noting particularly the necessary incongruence between the idea and any possible object of sensuous experience.[3] Plato erred, according to Kant ('since he may not have determined his concept sufficiently and hence sometimes spoke, or even thought, contrary to his own intention'),[4] in ascribing to the ideas a creative power and in indulging in 'ideal explanations of natural appearances, [neglecting] the physical investigation of them'. Nevertheless, in recognizing both the inherent tendency of reason to 'exalt' itself to cognitions beyond possible experience and the 'true causality' of reason, 'where ideas become efficient causes (of actions and their objects), namely in morality, but also in regard to nature itself', Plato anticipated Kant's concept of the idea of pure reason, or 'transcendental idea'.[5]

Reason (distinguished from the faculty of understanding), according to Kant, itself generates, a priori, certain concepts (that is, ideas) and principles which, according to the 'demand of [speculative] reason . . . to bring the understanding into thoroughgoing connection with itself',[6] guide the use of the understanding, pointing it towards the absolute totality of the series of conditioned appearances, its unconditioned ground. The idea of 'freedom' is, according to Kant, an idea in this sense. Since, in nature, the cause of every event must itself, *qua* event or happening, be caused (or have a cause), 'no absolute totality of conditions in causal relations is forthcoming', either in experience itself or in any possible extensive employment of the understanding's concept of causality. Reason therefore 'creates the idea of a spontaneity, which could start to act from itself, without needing to be preceded by any other cause that in turn determines it to action according to the law of causal connection' ('freedom in the cosmological sense'), in order that the absolute unity of the conditions of appearance may be thought (although not known), or in order that the understanding be directed towards a certain (ideal) goal.[7] So, the idea has no possible congruent object in experience, it does not determine any object for cognition (it has no 'objective validity', in Kant's specific sense of being valid for the determination of empirical objects of experience), but 'serve[s] the understanding as a canon for its extended and self-consistent use'.[8] This is what Kant calls the legitimate or proper 'regulative' use of the ideas of pure reason.

But the ideas of reason are also misused, or misapplied, in illegitimate 'constitutive' uses; that is, by mistaking their subjective necessity for objective validity, giving a purported objective reality to the object of the idea. This gives rise to what Kant calls 'dialectical' or 'transcendental' illusion, which is distinguished from both error and empirical and logical illusion in being 'natural', unavoidable and incorrigible – 'irremediably attached to human reason'. For even when the being-illusory of the transcendental illusion is revealed it does not cease to deceive us: 'They [dialectical illusions] are sophistries not of human beings but of pure reason itself, and even the wisest of all human beings cannot get free of them; perhaps after much effort he may guard himself from error, but he can never be wholly rid of the illusion, which ceaselessly teases and mocks him.'[9] The unavoidable tendency to understand the necessity of the 'constant logical subject of thinking' (my being the 'absolute subject of all my possible judgements') as 'a real subject of inherence',[10] that is, a substance in the ontological sense, is just such a dialectical illusion, according to Kant.

If the trick of all transcendental illusion rests in 'the taking of a subjective condition of thinking for the cognition of an object', its necessity is perhaps in reason's inability to think its idea 'in any other way than by giving its idea an object'. And in fact, Kant writes, the dialectical illusion of the substantiality of the soul, for example, expresses a proposition ('the soul is substance') that is perfectly valid *so long as we keep in mind* that nothing further can be deduced or inferred from this, 'that it signifies a substance only *in the idea* but not in reality'.[11] (We can, Kant says, have an only 'problematic' concept of the object of an idea.)[12] This 'object in the idea' is really only a 'schema for which no object is given': 'Thus they [the ideas of reason] should not be assumed in themselves, but their reality should hold only as that of a schema of the regulative principle for the systematic unity of all cognitions of nature; hence they should be grounded only as *analogues of real things*, but not as things in themselves.'[13]

The regulative principles of pure reason – 'which rest solely on reason's speculative interest'[14]– are called 'transcendental

principles' to the extent that they *must* be presupposed for a coherent use of the understanding. For example, 'we simply have to
presuppose the systematic unity of nature as objectively valid and
necessary' in order to determine within the 'manifoldness of individual things' in nature the identity of species, understood as determinations of genera, themselves understood as determinations of
families: 'a certain systematic unity of all possible empirical concepts must be sought insofar as they can be derived from higher
and more general ones'.[15] (The mistake is to suppose that this unity,
which is a mere idea, is to be encountered in nature itself.)

Kant's example here of the specifications of species, genera and
families pertains to the domain of what he elsewhere called the
'systematic description of nature',[16] distinguished from 'natural
history'. But as Robert Bernasconi has shown, the idea of reason
also has a role to play in natural history, specifically – and this is of
immense historical significance – in determining the concept
of race.[17] A science of natural history, according to Kant,
'would . . . concern itself with investigating the connection between
certain present properties of the things of nature and their causes
in an earlier time in accordance with causal laws that we do not
invent but rather derive from the forces of nature as they present
themselves to us',[18] a necessarily speculative undertaking based on
the assumption that nature is organized purposively.[19] Kant's
natural history of race therefore investigates the observable differences between groups of humans, the purposiveness in or of these
differences, and the (speculative) origin of these different natural
forms in preformed 'seeds'.[20] But as Bernasconi points out, the
concept of race is not derived, for Kant, from nature; rather it is
explicitly posited as a conceptual necessity for natural history. As
Kant writes:

> What is a *race*? The word certainly does not belong in a systematic
> description of nature, so presumably the thing itself is nowhere to be
> found in nature. However, the *concept* which this expression desig-
> nates is nevertheless well established in the reason of every observer
> of nature who presupposes a conjunction of causes placed originally
> in the line of descent of the genus itself in order to account for a self-
> transmitted peculiarity that appears in different interbreeding
> animals but which does not lie in the concept of their genus. The fact
> that the word race does not occur in the description of nature (but
> instead, in its place, the word *variety*) cannot keep an observer of
> nature from finding it necessary from the viewpoint of natural
> history.[21]

For Kant, as Bernasconi explains, 'in the present state of our knowledge the idea of race imposes itself', as a regulative idea.[22]

Clearly the idea of race provided an example, for Kant, of the legitimate, regulative employment of an idea of reason. In response, Bernasconi glosses Anthony K. Appiah's late twentieth-century objection to the continued use of the concept of race ('the residue of earlier views') in terms of its current illegitimacy, its no longer being compatible with scientific knowledge. If, on the other hand, as Bernasconi also points out, other critical race theorists have also argued that the concept of race cannot simply be done away with, this is more to do with the strategic, *political* necessity of the employment of a concept of race in combating actually existing racism and redressing the history of racial discrimination, than with any Kantian claim about the necessary imposition of the concept as a regulative idea of reason.[23]

What remains true is that the concept of race has no corresponding, scientifically identifiable, object in experience, although the lived experience of being-raced is undeniable. Does this mean that 'race' imposes itself as transcendental illusion? The pragmatic historical need for the concept of race (for Kant, in opposing the theory of polygenesis; for post-Kantian racists, in justifying slavery; for anti-racists, in explaining and opposing racism[24]) suggests that this is an illusion of a more historical kind, and one which progressive political movements could eventually dispel. This in turn suggests that the philosophical productivity of Kant's idea of transcendental illusion depends today precisely in its being historicized.[25]

But what of the modern, natural-biological concept of sex? What grounds are there for thinking that sex might be an idea of reason and – in a sense yet to be determined – a transcendental illusion?

The presumptions internal to the modern, natural-biological concept of sex, as stated in the Introduction, are that there simply is sex duality (the exclusive division into male and female) and that this duality is naturally determined. Further, in so far as 'sex' refers to a natural ground for human existence it is presumed to be something naturally determining. Wherever, or in whatever, the essence of sex has, historically, been thought to reside – gonadal tissue, or hormones, or chromosomal configuration[26] – the exclusive duality of its terms is empirically inadequate to the variety that it would allegedly encompass without remainder. The duality of sex is therefore not descriptive, but prescriptive – quite literally prescriptive in the case of the intersexed infant who will be made to conform, more or less successfully, to one or other of its terms. Taken together, the constitutive presumptions and the prescriptive function of the modern natural-biological concept of sex contradict each other. As previously stated, the concept has no purely descriptive function in relation to human existence, but the presumption in its use is precisely that it does.

These two contradictory elements in the concept of sex may perhaps be understood as the difference between its uses as an abstract and as a concrete noun: abstractly, the general term for the (presumed exclusive) duality of male and female; concretely, referring to particular instances of one of either of those two terms. The equivocation between these uses – a conceptual juddering so fast as to be invisible – accomplishes the same 'transcendental subreption' that Kant identified in the representation of a formal regulative principle as constitutive, the result of which is hypostatization. Or, just as, in the first paralogism of pure reason, the formal, transcendental unity of apperception (the purely logical subject of thought) is taken for the 'real subject of inherence'[27] (substance understood ontologically), so too the formal principle of the exclusive division into male and female (the prescriptive or, in Kant's terminology, regulative, principle) is taken for the cognition of an objectively real object (for Kant, an object given in intuition). The 'transcendental doctrine of the soul', or 'rational psychology', is the taking of the idea of the soul for a real object and the subsequent claims to be able to infer from this idea alone the essential attributes of the soul (its substantiality, simplicity and 'personality', that is, its being a 'person') and the (problematic) ideality of external objects.[28] In the same way, we may say, the 'transcendental doctrine of sex', taking the idea of sex for a real object, claims to be able to derive from the idea of sex alone the essential attributes of men and women. To this extent the ideas of 'race' and 'sex' are analogous, and analogous also in the fact that, just as some anti-racists retain the concept of race as an object only in the idea, so too many feminists feel that, politically, we cannnot do without 'sex'.

Is 'sex', then, a transcendental illusion? Sex is not a transcendental illusion to the extent that Kant's definition of the latter includes a reference to its ahistorical inevitability, 'irremediably attache[d] to human reason'. (It is our illusion; it was not Plato's.) But to the extent that we are also required to account for the actual effects of the concept of sex – its effective imbrication in, or its real existence as a structuring component of, human experience – there is, to use Kant's word, something 'unavoidable' about it.[29] The idea of sex, like all ideas of reason according to Kant, is 'merely a creature of reason'. But the ideas 'nonetheless have their reality and are by no means merely figments of the brain'; 'we will by no means regard them as superfluous and nugatory'.[30] Thus, we might say, sex is an objective historical illusion: an illusion that cannot be contrasted with reality because it *is* real to the extent that its effects are real. However, given as object only in the idea, 'sex' (like the transcendental idea of the soul, for Kant) 'leads no further',[31] or its leading further is precisely the form of its ideological function ('transcendental illusion' is today another way of saying 'ideology').

Perhaps it is now time to question the future of this illusion.

Notes

Introduction

1   See Stella Sandford, 'Contingent Ontologies: Sex, Gender and "Woman" in Simone de Beauvoir and Judith Butler', *Radical Philosophy*, 97, September/October 1999; Stella Sandford, *How to Read Beauvoir*, Granta, London, 2006, especially Chapter 7, 'Sex'.

2   Shulamith Firestone, *The Dialectic of Sex: The Case for Feminist Revolution*, Paladin, London, 1972 (1970), p. 24. On Firestone's concept of sex see Stella Sandford, 'The Dialectic of *The Dialectic of Sex*', in Mandy Merck and Stella Sandford, eds., *Further Adventures of 'The Dialectic of Sex'*, Palgrave, Basingstoke, 2010.

3   For recent debate on these questions see the articles by Alison Stone ('The Incomplete Materialism of French Materialist Feminism') and Stella Sandford ('Sexmat, Revisited') in *Radical Philosophy*, 145, September/October 2007.

4   Judith Butler, *Gender Trouble: Feminism and the Subversion of Identity*, Routledge, New York and London, 1990, p. viii.

5   Ibid., p. 7. See also, Butler's 'Variations on Sex and Gender: Beauvoir, Wittig, Foucault', in Seyla Benhabib and Drucilla Cornell, eds., *Feminism as Critique*, Polity, Oxford, 1987.

6   Suzanne J. Kessler, *Lessons From the Intersexed*, Rutgers University Press, New Brunswick, New Jersey and London, 1998, n. 2, p. 134. Here Kessler is referring to the terminological decision made in Suzanne J. Kessler and Wendy McKenna, *Gender: An Ethnomethodological Approach*, Chicago University Press, Chicago, 1985, carried through to the later *Lessons From the Intersexed*.

7   Butler, *Gender Trouble*, pp. ix, 17. See also p. 148: 'The task is not whether to repeat, but how to repeat or, indeed, to repeat and, through

a radical proliferation of gender, to displace the very gender norms that enable the repetition itself.'

8   There is nothing to say, even now, that the popular, hegemonic view of sex is shared by all peoples in all places.

9   A recent, popular textbook in the philosophy of biology illustrates this. Although many aspects of species distinctiveness – for example, 'absence of extreme sociality among the birds' – 'turn on small accidents of history . . . there are other patterns in life's richness that are not likely to be historical accidents. Sex – one, two, but no more – is a good candidate for such a pattern.' Kim Sterelny and Paul E. Griffiths, *Sex and Death: An Introduction to Philosophy of Biology*, University of Chicago Press, Chicago, 1999, p. 26.

10 See Thomas Laqueur, *Making Sex: Body and Gender From the Greeks to Freud*, Harvard University Press, Cambridge MA and London, 1990, especially Chapter 2, where Laqueur argues that for Galen and Aristotle and in the Hippocratic Treatises '[a]natomy in the context of sexual difference was a representational strategy that illuminated a more stable extracorporeal reality. There existed many genders, but only one adaptable sex' (p. 35). Laqueur is concerned with different 'biologies' and the relation between these biological theories and ways of understanding the nature of sexed bodies and aspects of sexual politics: 'My goal is to show how a biology of hierarchy in which there is only one sex [characteristic of the ancient Greeks], a biology of the incommensurability between two sexes, and the claim that there is no publicly relevant sexual difference at all, or no sex, have constrained the interpretation of bodies and the strategies of sexual politics for some two thousand years' (p. 23).

11 Gregory Vlastos, 'Was Plato a Feminist?', in Nancy Tuana, ed., *Feminist Interpretations of Plato*, Pennsylvania State University Press, Pennsylvania, 1994; Julia Annas, 'Plato's *Republic* and Feminism', in Julie K. Ward, ed., *Feminism and Ancient Philosophy*, Routledge, London and New York, 1996.

12 Susan Moller Okin's *Women in Western Political Thought*, Princeton University Press, Princeton NJ, 1992, is one of the best examples of the former; Angela Hobbs' 'Female Imagery in Plato' (in James Lesher et al., eds., *Plato's Symposium: Issues in Interpretation and Reception*, Harvard University Press, Cambridge MA and London, 2006) is a recent example of the latter. These are discussed in Chapters 1 and 4, respectively.

13 See, for example, Alison Stone, *An Introduction to Feminist Philosophy*, Polity, Cambridge, 2007, Chapter 4.

14 Both elements are to be found in Luce Irigaray, 'Sorcerer Love: A Reading of Plato's *Symposium*, Diotima's Speech', trans. Eleanor H. Kuykendall, in Tuana, ed., *Feminist Interpretations of Plato*. This is discussed at greater length in Chapter 4.

Chapter 1

1 See, for example, Moller Okin, *Women in Western Political Thought*.
2 For the purposes of this chapter, 'Plato' refers to the author of the *Republic*, 'Socrates' to a character in this dialogue.
3 See, for example, Vlastos, 'Was Plato a Feminist?'
4 See, for example, Annas, 'Plato's *Republic* and Feminism'.
5 See, for example, Arlene W. Saxonhouse, 'The Philosopher and the Female in the Political Thought of Plato', in Tuana, ed., *Feminist Interpretations of Plato*; and Saxonhouse, *Fear of Diversity: The Birth of Political Science in Ancient Greek Thought*, University of Chicago Press, Chicago and London, 1996.
6 Unless otherwise stated, quotations are from Plato's *Republic*, trans. Desmond Lee, Penguin, London, 1987. The translation of this passage (423e/424a) has been modified. Greek transliteration into Roman script has been kept as simple as possible throughout, using accents only where these change the meaning of words (for example, *tís*).
7 See James Adam, *The Republic of Plato*, Cambridge University Press, Cambridge, 1963, pp. 346, 354; R. G. Ussher's editor's introduction to Aristophanes, *Ecclesiazusae*, Clarendon Press, Oxford, 1973, pp. xv, xvi; Friedrich Schleiermacher, *Introductions to the Dialogues of Plato*, trans. William Dobson, Cambridge University Press, Cambridge, 1836, p. 377.
8 Lee's translation of this part of the passage is as follows: ' "We can, I think, only make satisfactory arrangements for the possession and treatment of women and children by men born [*phusi*] and educated [*paideutheisin*] as we have described, if we stick to the course on which we started; our object, you remember, was to make them [*tous andras*] like watchdogs guarding a flock." "Yes." "Let us, then, proceed to arrange for their birth [*genesin*] and upbringing [*trophēn*] accordingly. We can then see if it suits our purpose." ' Robin Waterfield's translation of Socrates' last remark, however, changes its grammatical subject: ' "So let's keep to the same path and have the women born and brought up in a closely similar way, and see whether or not it turns out right for us." ' (Plato, *Republic*, trans. Robin Waterfield, Oxford University Press, Oxford, 1993.) From the perspective of the discussion that follows on immediately, Waterfield's translation might make more sense, although Lee's – and Shorey's (Plato, *Republic*, trans. Paul Shorey, Loeb edition, Harvard University Press, Cambridge MA and London, 1937): 'Let us preserve the analogy, then, and assign them a generation and breeding answering to it' – is probably technically more accurate in linking 'their' and 'them' to the preceeding explicit subject, *tous andras*. The difference between the translations highlights the condensed nature of the argument.
9 Translation modified, emphasis added. Readers of some English translations may also not notice it, as Shorey and Lee, for example, do

not translate *nomimōn* explicitly. Shorey: 'about the honourable, the good and the just'. Lee: 'about what is fair and good and just'.

10 See F. M. Cornford, *From Religion to Philosophy: A Study in the Origins of Western Speculation*, Edward Arnold, London, 1912, pp. 73, 123.

11 Aristotle, *The Politics* and *The Constitution of Athens*, trans. Jonathan Barnes (revising Benjamin Jowett), Cambridge University Press, Cambridge, 1996, p. 39 (1264b, 4–7). I will return to Aristotle's objection, below.

12 Shorey: 'And we must throw open the debate to anyone who wishes either in jest or in earnest to raise the question whether female human nature is capable of sharing with the male all tasks or none at all . . .' See also Plato, *Republic 5*, trans. and ed. S. Halliwell, Aris & Phillips, Warminster, 1993: 'a chance to dispute whether the nature of the human female is able to share in *all* tasks with that of the male . . .' See also Halliwell's commentary on this phrase, p. 144.

13 See Platon, *La République*, trans. Georges Leroux, Flammarion, Paris, 2004, n. 18, p. 622.

14 So, Waterfield's translation: 'shouldn't we allow that there is room for doubting . . . whether women do have the natural ability to cooperate with men'.

15 This part of the argument is the basis of Julia Annas' riposte to those who would claim Plato as a 'feminist': 'it is hardly a feminist argument to claim that women do not have a special sphere because men can outdo them at absolutely everything'. Annas, 'Plato's *Republic* and Feminism', p. 5.

16 Ibid., p. 4. See also Julia Annas, *An Introduction to Plato's Republic*, Clarendon Press, Oxford, 1982, p. 182: 'the only natural differences between men and women are biological: the male begets, the female gives birth. And this is not a relevant difference for determining occupation, any more than baldness is relevant to whether someone should become a cobbler.'

17 Annas, 'Plato's *Republic* and Feminism', p. 3.

18 See, for example, Susan B. Levin, 'Women's Nature and Role in the Ideal *Polis*: *Republic* V Revisited', in Ward, ed., *Feminism and Ancient Philosophy*. Levin argues elsewhere ('Plato on Women's Nature: Reflections on the *Laws*', *Ancient Philosophy* Vol. 20, No. 1, 2000, especially p. 87) that the situation is quite otherwise in the *Laws*, where Plato proposes different upbringings for boys and girls because of the natural differences between men's and women's natures. The other major strand in feminist responses to the *Republic* – that associated with the so-called 'feminism of difference' – is discussed later in this Chapter and in Chapter 4.

19 Janet Farrell Smith, 'Plato, Irony, and Equality', in Tuana, ed., *Feminist Interpretations Of Plato*. Farrell Smith's argument draws on that of Gregory Vlastos in 'Was Plato a Feminist?', also in Tuana, ed., *Feminist Interpretations Of Plato*.

20   To the extent that some feminist Lacanian psychoanalytic theory does argue that the fact of 'sex difference' is psychically determining for men and women, it is both incoherent (it contradicts the role it otherwise assigns to the different, specifically psychoanalytic concept of 'sexual difference') and reactionary. This is discussed at length in Chapter 2.

21   Elizabeth V. Spelman, 'Hairy Cobblers and Philosopher-Queens', in Tuana (ed.), *Feminist Interpretations of Plato*, pp. 89, 94.

22   Vlastos, 'Was Plato a Feminist?', p. 15. See also G. E. R. Lloyd, *Science, Folklore and Ideology: Studies in the Life Sciences in Ancient Greece*, Cambridge University Press, Cambridge, 1883, p. 107: '[Plato] insists that difference in sex is just as irrelevant to the question of education as whether a person has hair or is bald. What matters is not sex, but what kind of psyche a person has.'

23   See *Sophist* 254b–e, where Fowler (Loeb edition, William Heinemann, London, 1921) also translates *genos* as 'classes or genera'.

24   Rachana Kamtekar, 'Race and Genos in Plato', in Julie K. Ward and Tommy L. Lott, eds., *Philosophers on Race*, Blackwell, Oxford, 2002, pp. 4–5.

25   Of course the same is true when *genos* is translated as 'species' or 'breed', for example, but the focus here is sex.

26   These are the definitions of the Collins English Dictionary. According to the entry for 'sex' in the Shorter Oxford English Dictionary (1977): '1. Either of the two divisions of organic beings distinguished as male and female respectively; the males or the female (esp. of the human race) viewed collectively.' '3. The distinction between male and female in general. In recent use: The sum of those differences in the structure and function of the reproductive organs on the ground of which beings are distinguished as male and female, and of the other physiological differences consequent on these.'

27   For example, in Book V of the *Republic*: 453a2, *'tou arrenos genous'*, 'of the male race'; 454d6–7, *'to tōn andrōn kai to tōn gunaikōn genos'*, 'the race of men and the race of women'; 455c5–6, *'to tōn andrōn genos . . . to tōn gunaikōn'*, 'the race of men . . . the [race] of women'; 455d1–2, *'to gunaikeion genos'*, 'the race of women', 'the womanish race'; 455d4–5, *'to genos tou genous'* (genitive of comparison), 'the race of [men] [in comparison with] the race [of women]'; 457b1 *'dia tēn tou genous astheneian'*, 'because of the weakness of the race [of women]'.

28   John J. Winkler (*The Constraints of Desire: The Anthropology of Sex and Gender in Ancient Greece*, Routledge, New York and London, 1990, p. 50) quotes P. Manuli making much the same point: 'the notion of sex never gets formalized as a functional identity of male and female but is expressed solely through the representation of asymmetry and of complementarity between male and female, indicated constantly by abstract adjectives (*to thēlu, to arren*), female being merely the opposite of the male. Sex as an abstract, homogenous, unified notion, something *common* to each of the two genders, has no place in this system.'

Winkler supplies the reference: P. Manuli, 'Donne mascoline, femmine sterili, vergini perpetue: La ginecologica greca tra Ippocrate e Sorano', in S. Campese, P. Manuli and G. Sissa, *Madre Meteria: Sociologica e biologica della donna greca*, Turin, 1983.

29 Bruno Snell, *The Discovery of the Mind: The Greek Origins of European Thought*, trans. T. G. Rosenmeyer, Harper & Row, New York, 1960, pp. 7, 6.

30 Ibid., p. 5.

31 Ibid., p. 8.

32 Bernard Williams, *Shame and Necessity*, University of California Press, Berkeley, 1993, p. 36, 40.

33 See this book's Introduction, pp. 3–4

34 Of course, as discussed in the Introduction to this book (pp. 2–3), there are critical discourses on 'sex' that dispute the legitimacy of this function, but they nevertheless agree that, in general terms, this *is* its function. See, for example, Butler, *Gender Trouble*; Anne Fausto-Sterling, *Sexing the Body: Gender Politics and the Constructions of Sexuality*, Basic Books, New York, 2000.

35 The issue of the priority of these three *genē* over the two *genē* of men and women, and the distribution of the two *genē* thoughout the three classes is discussed by Averroes in *Averroes' Commentary on Plato's Republic*, trans. and ed. E. I. J. Rosenthal, Cambridge University Press, Cambridge, 1956, pp. 164–6.

36 K. J. Dover, *Greek Popular Morality in the Time of Plato and Aristotle*, Basil Blackwell, Oxford, 1974, pp. 88, 90, 92.

37 See Winkler, *The Constraints of Desire*, p. 66.

38 Ibid., p. 65.

39 Despite the elasticity of the concept of 'nature' in the *Republic*, Plato is more circumspect with regard to the use of the word there – where it has important work to do in the detail of the philosophical arguments – than he is in the *Laws*, where its frequent use in a whole variety of contexts suggests that it is mobilized in its labile, everyday availability without special philosophical attention. Drinking wine reveals a man's nature (652a); the spontaneous and willing acceptance of the rule of law is natural (690b8); reason is by nature the ruling principle (689b); mathematics help the slow-witted progress beyond their nature (747b); and so on.

40 S. Halliwell also implicitly accepts the idea that women as a *genos* are, for Socrates interlocutors, constituted by a set of womanish characteristics in arguing that Socrates introduces a new definition: 'By attempting to reduce the impact of child-bearing . . . and by insisting on the capacity of women to participate alongside men in athletic, military and political activities, Plato constructs an ideal which ought to alter the intrinsic conception of women as a *genos*. Book 5 does not dispense with such a conception, but it implicitly reduces it to the single factor of reproductive function . . . The notion of women as

forming a *genos* definable by essential intellectual or psychological differences from men is therefore discarded.' Plato, *Republic 5*, trans. S. Halliwell, p. 15.

41 Chloë Taylor Merleau, 'Bodies, Genders and Causation in Aristotle's Biological and Political Theory', *Ancient Philosophy*, Vol. 23, No. 1, Spring 2003, p. 135.

42 Ibid., p. 148.

43 Ibid., p. 140. See also Laqueur, *Making Sex: Body and Gender from the Greeks to Freud*.

44 Taylor Merleau, 'Bodies, Genders and Causation in Aristotle's Biological and Political Theory', p. 147.

45 Translation modified.

46 Correctness, according to the Athenian in the *Laws* (668b), 'lies in the imitation and successful reproduction of the proportions and characteristics of the model'. Plato, *Laws*, trans. Trevor J. Saunders, Penguin, London, 1975. Unless otherwise stated all quotations from the *Laws* use this translation.

47 Moller Okin, *Women in Western Political Thought*, p. 65.

48 Glenn Morrow, *Plato's Cretan City: A Historical Interpretation of the Laws*, Princeton University Press, Princeton NJ, 1960; Natalie Harris Bluestone, *Women and the Ideal Society: Plato's 'Republic' and Modern Myths of Gender*, Berg, Oxford and Hamburg, 1987, p. 115.

49 Bluestone, *Women and the Ideal Society*, p. 115.

50 Bluestone regularly criticizes feminist writers on Plato for what she sees as their ahistorical approach to the texts (for example ibid. pp. 104, 127), but never considers the possibility that the concept of 'sex' central to her interpretation of the passage in question may be historically specific. Okin's interpretation is based in particular on Plato's verbal adjectives (*phateon, paradoteon*), the second denoting the handing down, the transmission, of legend or tradition. It appeals in general to the emphasis on education in the *Laws* and to Plato's attempts (most notably with the discussion of ambidexterity, [794d ff.]) to show that what we take to be natural in the division of labour between men and women is a matter of convention. To this extent I find her interpretation less 'ahistorical' than Bluestone's own.

Bluestone also mourns the passing of the age of nineteenth-century scholarship, the ideals of which are lost 'because of the structure of the university system, the end of elitism and the education of women'; having to deal with day-to-day reality, scholars have less time to devote to their work (ibid., p. 79). She does not stop to reflect that the rank sexism (or what she calls the 'anti-female bias') that she criticizes in the literature on Plato from 1870–1970 is the direct result of precisely that elitist nineteenth-century university system (which excluded women) or that having to deal with day-to-day realities might make one a *better* philosopher in many respects. Is there not a relationship between the sexist idiocies deforming the work of much of the earlier scholarship (many of which Bluestone cites disapprovingly) and their authors' freedom from the day to day realities which informed the work of feminists from the 1970s?

51 Winkler, *The Constraints of Desire*, pp. 45–6.

52 On *andreia* see Angela Hobbs, *Plato and the Hero: Courage, Manliness and the Impersonal Good*, Cambridge University Press, Cambridge, 2000. Hobbs reads Plato as contesting dominant definitions of *andreia* but nevertheless demonstrates the tension in the dialogues between the 'masculinity' of *andreia* and the idea that virtues are not gender-specific.

53 The passage reads: '*ho de ophlōn tēn dikēn pros tō apheisthai tōn andreiōn kindunōn kata phusin tēn hautou prosapotisatō misthon . . .*' Saunders translates: 'and in addition to being thus permitted, like the woman he is by nature, to avoid the risks that only men can run, the guilty man must also pay a sum of money . . .'

54 Quoted in Dover, *Greek Popular Morality in the Time of Plato and Aristotle*, p. 100.

55 Aristophanes, *Assemblywomen*, trans. and ed. Jeffrey Henderson, in *Three Plays*, Routledge, London and New York, 1996. The quotations are from lines 57 and 60–1 respectively.

56 Lauren K. Taaffe, *Aristophanes and Women*, Routledge, London and New York, 1993, p. 110.

57 Aristophanes, *Women at the Thesmophoria*, trans. Jeffrey Henderson, in *Three Plays*, lines 170–2.

58 Interestingly both Vlastos and Spelman come close to making the same point. According to Vlastos ('Was Plato a Feminist?', p. 18), when Plato denigrates all things 'womanish' 'he is speaking of women as they are under present, non-ideal, conditions . . . he is not saying that [these characteristics] are there as the permanently fixed, invariant, character of the female of the species, its nature: there is no reference to women's *phusis* in [the relevant passages in the *Republic*]'. What prevents Vlastos from going any further is his effective identification of the concepts of 'woman' and 'female'. Spelman similarly sees that the definition of 'woman' is a major issue in interpreting the *Republic*, but instead of distinguishing between 'woman' and 'female' she refers (as does Vlastos, implicitly) to the distinction between the body and the soul, such that the female philosopher-ruler could be said to have a manly soul in a female body. See Spelman, 'Hairy Cobblers and Philosopher-Queens', pp. 101–3.

59 In the brief *resumé* of the argument of the *Republic* in the *Timaeus* (Plato, *Timaeus*, trans. Donald J. Zeyl, Hackett, Indianapolis/Cambridge, 2000, 18c2–3), Socrates recalls their agreeing that 'their [women's] natures should be made to correspond with those of men'.

60 Saxonhouse, 'The Philosopher and the Female in the Political Thought of Plato', pp. 68, 70. See also Saxonhouse, *Fear of Diversity*, especially pp. 147–57.

61   Saxonhouse, 'The Philosopher and the Female in the Political Thought of Plato', pp. 72, 71.

62   John Hooper and Tania Branigan, 'Pope Warns Feminists', *Guardian*, 31 July 2004; http://www.guardian.co.uk/international/story/ 0,,1273102,00.html (accessed August 2004).

63   http://news.bbc.co.uk/1/hi/world/europe/7796663.stm . . . (accessed February 2009).

Chapter 2

1   Unless otherwise stated, the name 'Aristophanes' refers, in this chapter, to the character of Aristophanes in the *Symposium*, and not to the historical figure (although, of course, the two are related).

2   Strictly speaking *arren* and *thēlus* are adjectives, declining according to the gender of the subjects they qualify; *arren* and *thēlus* are the nominative masculine forms of the adjectives 'male' and 'female'; *to thēlu genos*, the race of women, which is often also translated as 'the female sex', is an example of the nominative neuter form of the adjective conforming with the neuter noun (*genos*).

3   Plato, *Symposium*, edited with an introduction, translation and commentary by C. J. Rowe, Aris & Phillips, Warminster, 1998. Unless otherwise stated all quotations from the *Symposium*, in this and subsequent chapters, use this translation.

4   Nicole Loraux, *Les enfants d'Athéna: Idées athéniennes sur la citoyenneté et la division des sexes*, Seuil, Paris, 1990, pp. 35, 50. This discussion of ancient Greek myths is heavily indebted to Loraux's book. See also Simon Hornblower and Anthony Spawforth, eds., *Oxford Classical Dictionary*, 3rd edition, Oxford University Press, Oxford, 1996, p. 224.

5   On the creation of Pandora see Hesiod, in *Hesiod and Theognis*, trans. Dorothea Wender, Penguin, London, 1973: *Theogony* 570ff., pp. 42–3; *Works and Days*, pp. 60–61.

6   Loraux, *Les enfants d'Athéna*, pp. 124–5.

7   Ibid., p. 128.

8   Ibid., p. 23.

9   Ibid., p. 80.

10 Indeed for a while, it seems, the reference to Rabelais was almost compulsory. See, for example, Alfred Fouillée, *La philosophie de Platon* (Tome première), Librarie Philosophique de Ladrange, Paris, 1869, p. 331; C. Huit, *Études sur le Banquet de Platon*, Paris, Ernest Thorin, 1889, pp. 50, 51; Theodor Gomperz, *Greek Thinkers: A History of Ancient Philosophy*, Vol. II, trans. G. G. Berry, John Murray, London, 1905, p. 386; J. A. Stewart, *The Myths of Plato*, Macmillan, London, 1905, p. 408; R. G. Bury, ed., *The Symposium of Plato*, Heffer & Sons, Cambridge, 1973, p. xxx. Rabelais himself parodied the *Symposium* in the prologue

to *Gargantua* (in Samuel Putnam, ed., *The Portable Rabelais*, New York, Viking, 1946, p. 47).

11 According to K. J. Dover: 'This is the only surviving passage from classical Attic literature which acknowledges the existence of female homosexuality.' Dover, *Plato: Symposium*, Cambridge University Press, Cambridge, 1980, p. 118. This claim is reiterated by Christopher Gill, *The Symposium*, trans. Christopher Gill, Penguin, London, 1999, n. 65, p. 72. Plato does, however, refer to the 'unnatural pleasure' of female to female intercourse at *Laws* 636c.

12 Dover, *Plato: Symposium*, p. 114. W. R. M. Lamb (Plato, *Symposium*, Loeb Edition, Harvard University Press, Cambridge MA and London, 1925) and Walter Hamilton (Plato, *Symposium*, Penguin, London, 1951) both translate *genos* as sex; Gill prefers 'gender'. See also Thomas Gould, *Platonic Love*, Routledge and Kegan Paul, London, 1963, p. 32: 'There were three sexes then . . .'. The translation of *genē* as 'sexes' is particularly insistent in M. C. Howatson's recent translation (Plato, *The Symposium*, edited by M. C. Howatson and Frisbee C. C. Sheffield, trans. M. C. Howatson, Cambridge University Press, Cambridge, 2008).

13 Monique Canto comes to the same conclusion from a different perspective and to a different end: 'The three kinds of beings who live in the prior condition of narcissistic love do not yet form three sexes. For they are three complete beings, who cannot love any but themselves and who bear towards themselves a love that the subsequent tradition would call divine love, to be understood reflexively, as the love that God directs toward his own perfection.' Monique Canto, 'The Politics of Women's Bodies: Reflections on Plato', trans. Arthur Goldhammer, in Tuana, ed., *Feminist Interpretations of Plato*, p. 63.

14 Dover, *Plato: Symposium*, p. 114.

15 Luc Brisson, *Sexual Ambivalence*, trans. Janet Lloyd, University of California Press, Berkeley, Los Angeles and London, 2002, p. 1. See also n. 1, p. 152. Hermaphroditus, for example, is simultaneously dual-sexed; Tiresias is successively dual-sexed.

16 Ibid., p. 72.

17 See Rowe's commentary to his translation of the *Symposium*, p. 154.

18 The same presumption pervades commentaries on the *Timaeus*; this is discussed in Chapter 5.

19 The distinction between 'sex' and 'sexual difference' is clarified below; see pp. 60–1.

20 Psychoanalysis as a theoretical discipline has crossed paths with ancient Greek literature in ways that have shaped some of its central terms and constructions decisively. Not only Oedipus but also Narcissus, Eros and Thanatos, for example, have lent their names to tendencies, complexes and drives that, in part, derive their theoretical authority from the ancient associations and suggest a continuity in the structure of the psyche across the centuries. The linguistic derivation

of important elements in the vocabulary of psychoanalytical theory – for example, psyche, phallus, hysteria, schizophrenia, paranoia – suggests, further, a conceptual dependence on the classical Greek that has been little investigated and even less criticized.

21 Freud, 'Three Essays on the Theory of Sexuality', in *On Sexuality*, trans. James Strachey, Pelican Freud Library Volume 7, Penguin, London, 1977, p. 43; Freud, 'Resistances to Psychoanalysis', in *Historical and Expository Works on Psychoanalysis*, trans. James Strachey, Pelican Freud Library Volume 15, Penguin, London, 1986, p. 269. The relation between Freud's 'sexuality' and Plato's 'Eros' is discussed in Chapter 3.

22 Freud, 'Beyond the Pleasure Principle', in *On Metapsychology, The Theory of Psychoanalysis*, trans. James Strachey, Pelican Freud Library Volume 11, Penguin, London, 1984, p. 306. Although Strachey's famous English translations of Freud's works always render *Trieb* as 'instinct', in common with many recent commentators on Freud I have changed this throughout to 'drive' (leaving 'instinct' to translate the German *Instinkt*), except in the title of the paper 'Instincts [*Triebe*] and Their Vicissitudes'. The significance of the distinction between drive and instinct is discussed in Chapter 3.

23 Freud, 'Beyond the Pleasure Principle', pp. 308–9.
24 Ibid., p. 310.
25 Ibid., p. 311.
26 Ibid., p. 312.
27 Ibid., p. 316.
28 Ibid., p. 329.
29 Ibid., p. 331.
30 Ibid., p. 332.
31 Ibid., p. 313.
32 'We describe as "traumatic" any excitations from the outside which are powerful enough to break through the protective shield [of the organism]. . . . Such an event as an external trauma is bound to provoke a disturbance on a large scale in the functioning of the organism's energy and to set in motion every possible defensive measure.' Ibid., p. 301.
33 Ibid., pp. 332, 334.
34 Freud, 'Three Essays on the Theory of Sexuality', p. 52.
35 Ibid., n. 2, pp. 54–5. Here Freud attributes the theory of bisexuality to Wilhelm Fliess.
36 Ibid., p. 55.
37 Freud, 'Femininity', in *New Introductory Essays*, trans. James Strachey, Pelican Freud Library Volume 2, Penguin, London, 1973, p. 114.
38 Freud, 'Three Essays on the Theory of Sexuality', p. 142. In a letter to Fleiss of 1901, Freud wrote that his forthcoming book on the theory of sexuality was to be called 'Bisexuality in Man'. In this letter Freud offers Fleiss co-authorship of the book, expecting Fleiss' contribution on the

anatomical and biological aspects. This book, which was never written under this title or in this form, became the 'Three Essays on the Theory of Sexuality'. Writing to Fleiss in 1906 Freud says that the 'Three Essays' will 'avoid the theme of bisexuality as much as possible', presumably because the origin of the theory had become a source of conflict between Freud and Fleiss, and was eventually the cause of their 'break'. See Frank J. Sulloway, *Freud: Biologist of the Mind. Beyond the Psychoanalytic Legend*, Burnett Books, London, 1979, pp. 183–7, 223–5.

39 Freud, 'Civilization and its Discontents', in *Civilization, Society and Religion*, trans. James Strachey, Pelican Freud Library Volume 12, Penguin, London, 1985, p. 295.

40 Ibid., n. 3, pp. 295–6. The passage continues: 'Sex [*Die Geschlechtichkeit*] is a biological fact which, although it is of extraordinary importance in mental life, is hard to grasp psychologically. We are accustomed to say that every human being displays both male [*männliche*] and female [*weibliche*] instinctual impulses, needs and attributes; but though anatomy, it is true, can point out the characteristic of maleness and femaleness [*den Charakter des Männlichen und Weiblichen*], psychology cannot. For psychology the contrast between the sexes fades into one between activity and passivity, in which we far too readily identify activity with maleness and passivity with femaleness, a view which is by no means universally confirmed in the animal kingdom. The theory of bisexuality is still surrounded by many obscurities and we cannot but feel it as a serious impediment in psychoanalysis that it has not yet found any link with the theory of the instincts.'

41 See Sulloway, *Freud: Biologist of the Mind*, p. 159–60.

42 See ibid., pp. 223–4. In a footnote to the first of the 'Three Essays on the Theory of Sexuality' (n. 2, p. 55), Freud says that the theory of bisexuality is erroneously thought, 'in lay circles', to originate in Weininger's 1903 *Sex and Character*, but Weininger simply made this theory 'the basis of a somewhat unbalanced book'. It may be that this lay association of the theory with Weininger's 'unbalanced' book also accounts for Freud's avoidance of the theme in the 'Three Essays'. See above, note 38.

43 Lesley Dean-Jones, *Women's Bodies in Classical Greek Science*, Clarendon Press, Oxford, 1994, pp. 43–4.

44 'The Seed', trans. I. M. Lonie, in G. E. R. Lloyd, ed., *Hippocratic Writings*, Penguin, London, 1983, p. 320–1. See also Iain M. Lonie, *The Hippocratic Treatises: 'On Generation', 'On the Nature of the Child', 'Diseases IV'* (translations and commentary), Walter de Gruyter, Berlin and New York, 1981, 'On Generation', paragraph 6, p. 3. 'The Seed' and 'On Generation' are different titles given to the same treatise.

45 See Lonie's commentary, *The Hippocratic Treatises*, p. 129. See also Lloyd, *Science, Folklore and Ideology*, p. 91, for a discussion of the three kinds of men and the three kinds of women said to be produced by the various combinations of male and female sperm from both male

and female in the Treatise 'On Regimen'. Lloyd discusses all the embryological treatises on pp. 88–94.

46 Lonie, *The Hippocratic Treatises*, p. 4 ('On Generation', paragraph 8).

47 Dean-Jones, *Women's Bodies in Classical Greek Science*, p. 168. Dean-Jones thinks that this is a problem for the theory of 'On Generation': 'Since the father has no female parts in his body and the mother has no male parts in hers, it is hard to see how they could provide weak and strong seed respectively.' But the assumption that 'the father has no female parts in his body and the mother has no male parts in hers' begs the question, since the treatise strongly suggests otherwise.

48 Freud, 'The Psychogenesis of a Case of Homosexuality in a Woman' (1920), in *Case Histories II*, trans. James Strachey, Pelican Freud Library Volume 9, Penguin, London, 1979, pp. 399–400.

49 Lacan, *Encore: The Seminar of Jacques Lacan, Book XX*, ed. Jacques-Alain Miller, trans. Bruce Fink, Norton, New York and London, 1999, p. 10. The English language distinction between sex and gender finds no direct translation in French, nor indeed many other European languages, some of which have adopted the English 'gender' to mark the conceptual distinction.

50 Ibid., p. 57.

51 Ibid., pp. 80, 61. The formulas appear on p. 78.

52 Ibid., pp. 79, 64. Slavoj Žižek (in 'Otto Weininger, or, "Woman Doesn't Exist" ', *New Formations, Lacan and Love*, 23, Summer 1994, p. 111) is surely right that 'the parallel between Lacan's "formulas of sexuation" and Kant's antinomies of pure reason is fully justified'.

53 Lacan, 'The Signification of the Phallus', in *Écrits*, trans. Bruce Fink, Norton, New York and London, 2006, p. 576.

54 Lacan, *Encore*, p. 80.

55 Ibid., p. 71.

56 Ibid., p. 80.

57 Ibid., p. 97.

58 Lacan, 'The Signification of the Phallus', p. 582.

59 Cf. Kirsten Campbell on 'the paradox of the classical account of sexuation': 'the phallus is a sexually neutral signifier which produces all subjects, but men and women become sexed subjects because of their different relation to the phallus'. Kirtsen Campbell, *Jacques Lacan and Feminist Epistemology*, Routledge, London and New York, 2004, p. 61.

60 See Philippe Van Haute, *Against Adaptation: Lacan's Subversion of the Subject*, trans. Paul Crowe and Miranda Vankerk, The Other Press, New York, 2002, pp. 27, 212, 215, 216: 'Anatomical constitution as such cannot give us an answer to the question of what it means to be a "man" or a "woman", and we cannot deduce from anatomical constitution itself which of its aspects will count as decisive for sexual difference. . . . the respective significations of "being male" and "being female" must . . . be understood in terms of a different relation to the symbolic phallus'. Any answer to the question of the relation between

sexual difference and anatomy 'necessarily implies the intervention of the symbolic system; for it is the symbolic system that established order by making distinctions, and only the symbolic can therefore make a given anatomical distinction . . . decisive in the determination of the psychic meaning of sexual difference'.

61 Lacan, *The Four Fundamental Concepts of Psychoanalysis*, trans. Alan Sheridan, Penguin, London, 1979, p. 198.

62 Ibid., pp. 204–5.

63 Ibid., p. 205, translation modified.

64 Ibid., p. 205. Lacan also speaks at length of Plato's *Symposium*, including Aristophanes' speech, in Seminar VIII, *Le Transfert*, Seuil, 2001, but to different ends.

65 Lacan, *The Four Fundamental Concepts of Psychoanalysis*, p. 199, translation modified.

66 Ibid., p. 188, translation modified. 'Que le sujet comme tel est dans l'incertitude pour la raison qu'il est divisé par l'effet de langage . . . Par l'effet de parole, le sujet se realise toujors plus dans l'Autre, mais il ne poursuit déjà plus là qu'une moitié de lui-même.' Lacan, *Le séminaire Livre XI, Les quatre concepts fondamentaux de la psychanalyse*, Seuil, Paris, 1973, p. 211.

67 See Lacan, *Encore*, p. 66, where Lacan rebuts the idea of eros as fusion with the imbrication of sex and death and the 'subtraction' of meiosis. Meiosis is the process of the division of diploid cells (having paired homologous chromosomes) into haploid cells (having one set of chromosomes).

68 Lacan, *The Four Fundamental Concepts of Psychoanalysis*, p. 205.

69 After the brief and enigmatic mention of meiosis in *Encore* Lacan refers back to it as a 'biological metaphor' (p. 67).

70 Lacan, *Encore*, p. 80.

71 Paul Verhaeghe, *Beyond Gender: From Subject to Drive*, The Other Press, New York, 2001, pp. 81, 82, 83.

72 Slavoj Žižek, *How to Read Lacan*, Granta, 2006, p. 65.

73 Lacan, *Le séminaire Livre V, Les formations de l'inconscient*, Seuil, Paris, 1998, p. 165.

74 A paralogism is a syllogism of fallacious form. For Immanuel Kant a 'transcendental paralogism' 'has a transcendental ground for inferring falsely due to its form'. Kant, *Critique of Pure Reason*, trans. Paul Guyer and Allen W. Wood, Cambridge University Press, Cambridge, 1998, A341/B399. The most famous paralogism is that which fallaciously infers the substantiality of the soul from the logical necessity of the grammatical subject. This – and the meaning of 'the paralogism of sex' – is explained in greater detail in the Coda to this book.

75 Lacan, *Encore*, p. 72.

76 Ibid., pp. 10, 33.

77 Cf. Campbell, *Jacques Lacan and Feminist Epistemology*, p. 63.

78 Lacan, *Les formations de l'inconscient*, p. 165.

79   Ibid., p. 166. See also pp. 207–12 on homosexuality. Some of the essays
      collected in *Psychoanalytical Notebooks: A Review of the London Society of
      the New Lacanian School*, No. 11, *Sexuation and Sexuality*, December
      2003, amply demonstrate the moralism of much contemporary
      Lacanianism.
80   Joan Copjec, 'Sex and the Euthanasia of Reason', in *Read My Desire:
      Lacan Against the Historicists*, MIT Press, Cambridge MA and London,
      1994, p. 202.
81   Ibid., p. 206.
82   Ibid., p. 216.
83   Ibid., p. 207.
84   Ibid., p. 11.
85   Ibid., pp. 209–10.
86   See, for example, Freud, 'Instincts [*Triebe*] and Their Vicissitudes', in
      On Metapsychology, trans. James Strachey, Pelican Freud Library
      Volume 11, Penguin, London, 1984. This is discussed in Chapter 3.
87   This may look like an echo of Žižek's position in *The Ticklish Subject*,
      but it is not. Žižek writes there that 'sexual difference is real precisely
      in the sense that it can never be properly symbolized, transposed/
      translated into a symbolic norm which fixes the subject's sexual iden-
      tity . . . the claim that sexual difference is "real" equals the claim that
      it is "impossible" – impossible to symbolize, to formulate as a sym-
      bolic norm'. In so far as sexual difference is impossible 'it is precisely
      not binary'. Slavoj Žižek, *The Ticklish Subject: The Absent Centre of Politi-
      cal Ontology*, Verso, London and New York, 2000, p. 273. The claim
      that *sexual difference* is real is not the claim that *sex* is real; Copjec does
      not make this distinction. Again, however, Žižek here avoids the ques-
      tion of the relation between the natural-biological concept of sex and
      sexual difference.
88   This time Copjec *does* echo Žižek, for whom 'the opposition of female
      and male . . . however symbolically mediated and culturally condi-
      tioned, remains an obvious biological fact'. What is the link between
      this 'obvious biological fact' and the 'logical antinomies' of sexuation?
      '[T]*here is no link.*' Žižek, 'Otto Weininger, Or, "Woman Doesn't
      Exist" ', p. 109.
89   For a detailed discussion of human anatomical and genotypical diver-
      sity, and of the politics of the presumption of the duality of sex, see
      Fausto-Sterling, *Sexing the Body: Gender Politics and the Construction of
      Sexuality*.

Chapter 3

1   Freud, 'Beyond The Pleasure Principle', p. 295.
2   Freud, 'Three Essays on the Theory of Sexuality', p. 43.
3   Freud, 'Resistances to Psychoanalysis', p. 269.

4 Freud, 'Group Psychology and the Analysis of the Ego', in *Civilization, Society and Religion*, trans. James Strachey, Pelican Freud Library Volume 12, Penguin, London, 1985, p. 119.

5 Where English usage allows I use the transliterated 'Eros' and 'eros' to refer to the god and the human passion respectively, but retain 'Love'/'love' in quotations where translators have used them. As there are no transliterated English equivalents for them, the verbal form (*eraō*) and the participle forms (*erōn* or *ho erōn*) are generally translated into English using forms of 'love' ('I love', 'loving' and 'lover' respectively). *Eraō* could be translated as 'I desire' but 'desire' is usually reserved for the Greek *epithumeō* and Plato sometimes uses the two verbs together (e.g. *Symposium* 200a6).

6 All proper names here – except that of Plato himself – refer to the characters in Plato's dialogues rather than the historical personages themselves (if such personages existed: whether 'Diotima' was, or is based on, any actual person is not known for sure and is the topic of some debate). For the purposes of this essay, anything said by Diotima is usually referred to as 'Socrates' speech', as he reports her words. The relation between the characters of Socrates and Diotima is discussed in Chapter 4.

7 I have included the quotation marks around reported speech within reported speech (which constitutes the vast majority of the dialogue) only where they are necessary to distinguish voices in quotations.

8 The detail that Diotima comes from Mantinea suggests *hē mantikē*, and Socrates introduces her with examples of her prophesying (201d1–5).

9 Rowe: 'the one who loves, loves beautiful things: why does he love them?'; Gill, p. 41: 'The lover of beautiful things has a desire – what is it that he desires?'; Hamilton, p. 84: 'What is the aim of the love which is felt by the lover of beauty?'

10 Rowe's translation sounds awkward but allows the point (established earlier in the dialogue) that love is necessarily love *of* to be reiterated in the English.

11 Translation modified.

12 As Rowe points out, in his commentary on the *Symposium* (p. 180).

13 'Thus beauty is both Fate and Eileithyia for coming-into-being' (206d1–2). Fate or the Fates and Eileithyia or the Eileithyiae are goddesses associated with childbirth. The point seems to be that beauty, like these goddesses, exerts its power at the time of birth.

14 Rowe's translation supplies 'a kind of' (see his commentary, p. 103). The imagery of pregnancy and birth is discussed in Chapter 4.

15 In other contexts in psychoanalytical theory 'love' and 'sexuality' are not identical concepts.

16 Freud, *Introductory Lectures on Psychoanalysis*, trans. James Strachey, Pelican Freud Library Volume 1, Penguin, London, 1991, p. 344.

17 Freud, 'Three Essays on the Theory of Sexuality', p. 45.

18   Freud, *Introductory Lectures on Psychoanalysis*, p. 361.
19   Freud, 'Group Psychology and the Analysis of the Ego', p. 119. Freud's sense of his proximity to Plato seems here to produce an almost mimetic homage. The second sentence in this quotation sounds (at least in English) like one of the textual voices of Plato.
20   Freud, 'Group Psychology and the Analysis of the Ego', p. 119.
21   Ibid., p. 120.
22   Freud, 'Three Essays on the Theory of Sexuality', p. 43.
23   According to Jean Laplanche, 'perhaps the most significant opposition in psychoanalytic theory'. Jean Laplanche, 'The So-Called "Death Drive": A Sexual Drive', trans. Luke Thurston, in Rob Weatherill, ed., *The Death Drive: New Life for a Dead Subject?*, Rebus Press, London, 1999, p. 42.
24   Freud, 'Instincts [*Triebe*] and Their Vicissitudes', pp. 114, 115. See also Freud, 'Three Essays on the Theory of Sexuality', pp. 82–3.
25   Freud, 'Instincts [*Triebe*] and Their Vicissitudes', p. 116.
26   Ibid., pp. 117–8.
27   Ibid., p. 123.
28   The 'Three Essays on the Theory of Sexuality' suggest that excitation is the aim. This is discussed below.
29   Freud, 'Instincts [*Triebe*] and Their Vicissitudes', pp. 118, 119.
30   Ibid., pp. 120, 122.
31   Jean Laplanche, *Life and Death in Psychoanalysis*, trans. Jeffrey Mehlman, John Hopkins University Press, Baltimore and London, 1976, p. 8.
32   Freud, 'Instincts [*Triebe*] and Their Vicissitudes', p. 123, translation modified.
33   Freud, 'Three Essays on the Theory of Sexuality', p. 98.
34   Freud, *Introductory Lectures on Psychoanalysis*, p. 367. Furthermore, as Freud points out (p. 366), if we insist on identifying some kind of 'sensual' infantile pleasure distinct from sexual pleasure, we will be left with the problem of accounting for the emergence of the latter, merely postponing the issue.
35   Freud, 'Three Essays on the Theory of Sexuality', pp. 59–60.
36   Ibid., n. 1.
37   Ibid., p. 61.
38   Or what we might now want to call the self-preservative instinct.
39   Freud, 'Three Essays on the Theory of Sexuality', pp. 82–3.
40   Ibid., p. 109. See also *Introductory Lectures on Psychoanalysis*, p. 352: 'perverse sexuality is nothing else than a magnified infantile sexuality split up into its separate impulses'.
41   Freud, 'Three Essays on the Theory of Sexuality', p. 45.
42   Freud, *Introductory Lectures on Psychoanalysis*, pp. 353, 365.
43   Freud, 'Instincts [*Triebe*] and Their Vicissitudes', p. 123.
44   Freud, ' "Civilized" Sexual Morality and Modern Nervous Illness' (1908), in *Civilization, Society and Religion*, trans. James Strachey, Pelican Freud Library Volume 12, Penguin, London, 1985, p. 39.

45 Freud, 'Leonardo da Vinci and a Memory of his Childhood', trans. James Strachey, in *Standard Edition*, Volume XI, Vintage, London, 2001, p. 78; *Introductory Lectures on Psychoanalysis*, pp. 47–8; 'Two Encyclopaedia Articles', in *Historical and Expository Works on Psychoanalysis*, p. 155.

46 Bury, ed., *The Symposium of Plato*, p. xxxvii.

47 Gerasimos Santas, *Plato and Freud: Two Theories of Love*, Basil Blackwell, Oxford, 1988, p. 172. F. M Cornford also denies that Plato's account of eros can be understood in terms of a theory of sublimation – indeed he says the two are diametrically opposed. Man's roots are in heaven, according to Cornford's interpretation, not the earth, so the soul 'does not rise from beneath but sinks from above when the spirit is ensnared in the flesh. So, when energy is withdrawn from the lower channels, it is gathered up into its original source. This is indeed a conversion or transfiguration, but not a sublimation of desire that has hitherto only existed in the lower forms. A force that was in origin spiritual, after an incidental and temporary decension, becomes purely spiritual again.' Cornford, 'The Doctrine of Eros in Plato's Symposium', in *The Unwritten Philosophy and Other Essays*, Cambridge University Press, Cambridge, 1950, pp. 78–9.

48 Freud, 'Three Essays on the Theory of Sexuality', p. 69.

49 Freud, ' "Civilised" Sexual Morality and Modern Nervous Illness', p. 41.

50 Freud, 'Three Essays on the Theory of Sexuality', p. 77, emphasis added.

51 Freud, ' "Civilized" Sexual Morality and Modern Nervous Illness', p. 39.

52 Note that the concept of 'force' [*Kraft*] from this earlier (1908) essay no longer has a place in the account of the drives in 'Instincts [*Triebe*] and Their Vicissitudes' (1915).

53 'Mastering [the sexual drive] by sublimation, by deflecting the sexual instinctual forces away from their sexual aim to higher cultural aims, can be achieved by a minority and then only intermittently, and least easily during the period of ardent and vigorous youth.' Freud, ' "Civilized" Sexual Morality and Modern Nervous Illness', p. 45.

54 Freud, 'Three Essays on the Theory of Sexuality', p. 43.

55 Lacan, *The Four Fundamental Concepts of Psychoanalysis*, p. 166. For Lacan it also raises, more seriously, the question of what is meant by 'satisfaction'.

56 Laplanche, *Life and Death in Psychoanalysis*, pp. 25, 27.

57 Laplanche, 'The So-Called "Death Drive": a Sexual Drive', p. 45.

58 Freud, 'Three Essays on the Theory of Sexuality', p. 138. These remarks were added to the 'Three Essays' in the third edition (1915). See also *Introductory Essays on Psychoanalysis*, p. 355.

59 Freud, 'Two Encyclopaedia Articles', p. 154.

60 Freud, *Introductory Lectures on Psychoanalysis*, p. 362.
61 Jean Laplanche points out this contradiction in 'Pulsion et instinct', in *Sexual: La sexualité élargie au sens freudienne*, PUF, Paris, 2007, pp. 13–15.
62 See Laplanche, *Life and Death in Psychoanalysis*, p. 14.
63 See Laplanche, 'The So-Called "Death Drive": A Sexual Drive', pp. 46–7.
64 Freud, 'Three Essays on the Theory of Sexuality', p. 46.
65 Freud, 'Beyond the Pleasure Principle', p. 312.
66 G. R. F. Ferrari, 'Platonic Love', in Richard Kraut, ed., *The Cambridge Companion to Plato*, Cambridge University Press, Cambridge, 1992, p. 269.
67 Irving Singer, *The Nature of Love*, Volume 1, Plato to Luther, University of Chicago Press, Chicago and London, 1984, p. 74.
68 Stanley Rosen, *Plato's 'Symposium'*, Yale University Press, New Haven and London, 1968, p. 256 ff.; Plato, *Symposium*, trans. Allan Bloom, University of Chicago Press, Chicago and London, 1993, pp. 107, 139, 140, 153.
69 A. W. Price, 'Plato and Freud', in Christopher Gill, ed., *The Person and The Human Mind: Issues in Ancient and Modern Philosophy*, Clarendon Press, Oxford, 1990.
70 See Rowe's commentary on Plato's *Symposium*, p. 180. In *Plato's 'Symposium': The Ethics of Desire*, Oxford University Press, Oxford, 2006, p. 78, Frisbee C. C. Sheffield explicitly follows Rowe on this. The presumption of the popular conception of sexuality in the interpretation of eros also explains Rowe's claim, in his commentary on the *Phaedrus*, that none of the banter between Socrates and Phaedrus there 'is obviously of an erotic kind'. Plato, *Phaedrus*, trans. C. J. Rowe, Aris & Phillips, Warminster, 2000, p. 167.
71 David M. Halperin, 'Platonic *Erōs* and What Men Call Love', *Ancient Philosophy*, Vol. V, No. 1, Spring 1985, p. 171.
72 Ibid., p. 174.
73 Ibid., pp. 186–7. See also p. 184.
74 Ibid., pp. 180, 188.
75 Ibid., p. 188.
76 Ibid., p. 163.
77 Ibid., pp. 163, 174.

Chapter 4

1 See, for example, Bury's commentary in his edition of Plato, *The Symposium*, p. 89; Dover's commentary in his edition of Plato, *Symposium*, pp. 133–4.
2 Plato, *The Symposium*, trans. Gill, p. 34. See also Rowe's commentary, p. 169.
3 Or through 'procreation' (Hamilton); 'reproduction' (Gill).

4   All bodies and souls thus have the status of the in-between previously preserved for the daimon.

5   M. F. Burnyeat, 'Socratic Midwifery, Platonic Inspiration', *Bulletin of the Institute of Classical Studies*, 24, 1977, p. 8.

6   As Hamilton translates: 'The function [of love] is that of procreation in what is beautiful, and such a procreation can be either physical or spiritual.'

7   H. G. Liddell and R. Scott, *A Greek/English Lexicon*, revised by H. S. Jones, Clarendon Press, Oxford, 1996. In fact Liddell and Scott identify a causal sense of a form of the verb, *kuō*, 'of the male, *impregnate*', but only in the aorist tense, which is not that used by Plato here. (*Kuein* is the infinitive form, but ancient Greek verbs are often discussed and are listed in lexicons using the first person present [here, *kuō, kueō*] as this better indicates how they will decline.)

8   J. S. Morrison, 'Four Notes on Plato's *Symposium*', *Classical Quarterly*, Vol. 14, No. 1, 1964, p. 54.

9   Ibid., pp. 54–5. Agreeing, Rowe (Plato, *Symposium*, p. 183) adds that this explains the claim that '[t]he intercourse of man and woman is in fact a kind of giving birth [*hē gar andros kai gunaikos sunousia tokos estin*]' (206c5–6): 'Diotima appears to mean that intercourse literally *is* giving birth.'

10 Morrison, 'Four Notes on Plato's *Symposium*', p. 55.

11 Dover, *Plato: Symposium*, pp. 147, 151. See also Michael C. Stokes, *Plato's Socratic Conversations: Drama and Dialectic in Three Dialogues*, Athlone, London, 1986, pp. 161–3.

12 A. W. Price, *Love and Friendship in Plato and Aristotle*, Clarendon Press, Oxford, 1989, pp. 16–17.

13 E. E. Pender, 'Spiritual Pregnancy in Plato's *Symposium*', *Classical Quarterly*, Vol. 42, No. 1, 1992, p. 73. Although Pender says Dover and Stokes are right to accept Morrison's main thesis (thus, Pender agrees with Morrison too) she speaks of the male type pregnancy as 'analogous to the build-up to physical ejaculation' (p. 72) or as 'simply a metaphor for ejaculation' (p. 79). But Morrison's thesis is not that there is an analogy or a metaphor – ejaculation *literally is* birth on Morrison's reading. The essays by Morrison, Pender, Plass (discussed later) and Burnyeat, and the relevant sections of Dover and Stokes, discussed above, are almost always cited as canonical in references to the topic of male or spiritual pregnancy in the literature on the *Symposium*.

14 Pender, 'Spiritual Pregnancy in Plato's *Symposium*', p. 79.

15 See also Diskin Clay, 'Platonic Studies and the Study of Plato', *Arion*, Vol. 2, No. 1 (1975), pp. 174–5; Léon Robin, *La théorie platonicienne de l'amour*, F. Alcan, Paris, 1933, pp. 16–17.

16 Marsilio Ficino, *Commentary on Plato's Symposium on Love*, trans. Seers Jayne, Spring Publications, Dallas, Texas, 1985, p. 132. In his commentary on the *Phaedrus*, Ficino applies the metaphor to Plato himself: 'Our Plato was pregnant with the madness of the poetic Muse, whom

he followed from a tender age or rather from his Apollonian generation. In his radiance, Plato gave birth to his first child, and it was itself
almost entirely poetical and radiant.' Michael B. Allen, trans. and ed.,
Marsilio Ficino and the Phaedran Charioteer, University of California
Press, Berkeley, Los Angeles and London, 1981, p. 72.

17 Luc Brisson, 'Paiderastia, Philosophia', in Lesher et al., eds., *Plato's
Symposium: Issues in Interpretation and Reception*, pp. 248–9. The model
of female conception and the delivering of the embryo is, Brisson
argues here, one of two sexual models of education in the *Symposium*
(linked to the themes of reminiscence and maieutics), the other being
the model of 'the transmission of seminal liquid', associated with the
hierarchical model of education, 'transmission of a knowledge from
master to disciple' (pp. 250–1).

18 Frisbee C. C. Sheffield, 'Psychic Pregnancy and Platonic Epistemology', *Oxford Studies in Ancient Philosophy*, Vol. XX, Summer 2001,
pp. 15–16. See also Sheffield, *Plato's 'Symposium': The Ethics of Desire*,
p. 88.

19 Arlene W. Saxonhouse, 'Eros and the Female in Greek Political
Thought: An Interpretation of Plato's *Symposium*', *Political Theory*, Vol.
12, No. 1, February 1984, p. 21. See also, for a more qualified version
of the claim, Wendy Brown, ' "Supposing Truth Were a Woman":
Plato's Subversion of Masculine Discourse', *Political Theory*, Vol. 16,
No. 4, November 1988, reprinted in Tuana, ed., *Feminist Interpretations
of Plato*; and for a reading of Diotima as a spokesperson of an earlier,
pre-Socratic metaphysics cannibalized by Plato see Andrea Nye, 'The
Hidden Host: Irigaray and Diotima at Plato's Symposium', in Nancy
Fraser and Sandra Lee Bartky, eds., *Revaluing French Feminism*, Indiana
University Press, Bloomington, 1992. For Saxonhouse's criticism of
what she sees as the 'desexing' of women in the *Republic* see her 'The
Philosopher and the Female in the Political Thought of Plato'. (This is
briefly discussed in Chapter 1, pp. 38–9.)

20 Saxonhouse, 'Eros and the Female in Greek Political Thought: An
Interpretation of Plato's *Symposium*', pp. 23, 25.

21 Adriana Cavarero, *In Spite of Plato*, trans. Serena Anderlini-D'Onofrio
and Áine O'Healy, Polity Press, Cambridge, 1995, pp. 105–6.

22 Ibid., p. 92.

23 On the latter see ibid., n. 4, p. 127. See also Page DuBois, 'The Platonic
Appropriation of Reproduction' in Tuana, ed., *Feminist Interpretations
of Plato*.

24 Luce Irigaray, 'Plato's *Hystera*', in *Speculum of the Other Woman*, trans.
Gillian C. Gill, Cornell University Press, Ithaca, New York, 1985, p. 246.

25 Ibid., p. 265.

26 Ibid., p. 294. The identification of the Sun/Good with the father is not
explained, exactly. Recall, however, that Aristophanes identifies the
Sun with the masculine principle in his speech in the *Symposium*
(190b2).

27 Irigaray, 'Plato's *Hystera*', p. 300. The 'receptacle' here refers to the 'third kind' of the *Timaeus*; see Chapter 5, pp. 129–30.
28 Amongst others things; for example, Lacan.
29 Irigaray, 'Plato's *Hystera*', p. 275.
30 Cavarero, *In Spite of Plato*, p. 94.
31 Ibid., p. 101. According to Vigdis Songe-Møller, the specifically female function of pregnancy and birth is 'made over in its entirety to man' in Diotima's speech meaning that 'sexual difference is eliminated'. Songe-Møller, *Philosophy Without Women: The Birth of Sexism in Western Thought*, Trans. Peter Cripps, Continuum, London and New York, 2002, p. 108. See also pp. 107, 110. See also Page du Bois, 'The Platonic Appropriation of Reproduction', in Tuana, ed., *Feminist Interpretations of Plato*.
32 In this respect, note, Pender should be classed with the feminist interpretations, rather than with Morrison et al.
33 Irigaray, 'Sorcerer Love', p. 187. See also pp. 181–2, 185–6. For other enthusiastic readings of Diotima's philosophy see Anne-Marie Bowery, 'Diotima Tells a Story: A Narrative Analysis of Plato's *Symposium*', in Ward, ed., *Feminism and Ancient Philosophy*; Susan Hawthorne, 'Diotima Speaks Through the Body', in Bat-Ami Bar On, *Engendering Origins: Critical Feminist Readings in Plato and Aristotle*, State University of New York Press, Albany NY, 1994.
34 Irigaray, 'Sorcerer Love', pp. 188, 190, 194.
35 Ibid., p. 181.
36 Cf. Burnyeat, 'Socratic Midwifery, Platonic Inspiration', n. 5, p. 14: 'The vocabulary allows no backing away from the implications of the metaphor'. See also Gregory Vlastos, *Platonic Studies*, Princeton University Press, Princeton NJ, 1981, p. 424: 'The primary sense of *kuō is* pregnancy, not just "fecundity or ripeness"; of this there can be no doubt.'
37 Hobbs, 'Female Imagery in Plato', pp. 261–4.
38 Ibid., p. 271.
39 See also James M. Rhodes, *Eros, Wisdom and Silence: Plato's Erotic Dialogues*, University of Missouri Press, Columbia and London, 2003, p. 334: 'all [men and women] are metaphysically androgynous in their pursuit of the good'.
40 Hobbs, 'Female Imagery in Plato', pp. 269, 257.
41 Ibid., p. 271.
42 Ibid.
43 Ibid., p. 255.
44 Halperin, 'Why is Diotima a Woman? Platonic Eros and the Figuration of Gender', in David M. Halperin, John J. Winkler and Froma I. Zeitlin, eds., *Before Sexuality: The Construction of Erotic Experience in the Ancient World*, Princeton University Press, Princeton NJ, 1990, p. 262. See also pp. 263, 279, 281. Halperin writes 'feminine' in inverted commas throughout; we shall see why.

45   See David M. Halperin, *One Hundred Years of Homosexuality and Other Essays on Greek Love*, Routledge, New York and London, 1990, p. 33. Of course not all sexual relations between men, of whatever age, actually conformed to this model. The point here is merely that this was the socially sanctioned form.

46   Halperin, 'Why is Diotima a Woman?', pp. 265, 269, 275, 277.

47   Ibid., p. 285: 'men have initially constructed "femininity" according to a male paradigm while creating a social and political ideal of "masculinity" defined by their own putative ability to isolate what only women can actually isolate – namely sexual pleasure and reproduction, recreative and procreative sex'. Halperin's point is somewhat confused here. Of course *anyone* can have purely recreative sex, especially when they are on their own, and men together or women together can *only* have recreative sex. But his point is that only women can procreate without sexual pleasure, at least before the advent of modern reproductive technologies.

48   Ibid., p. 288.

49   Ibid., pp. 289, 292, 295.

50   Paul C. Plass, 'Plato's "Pregnant" Lover', *Symbolae Oslenses*, Vol. LIII, 1978, pp. 48, 50, 51. Plass argus explicitly against Morrison's interpretation, on the basis of the usual use of *kuein* and the fact that Plato does not use the verb in the *Timaeus* passage cited by Morrison. He speculates – on the basis of an implicit endorsement of some dubious and certainly homophobic anthropology from the 1940s and 1950s – on the existence of an ancient Greek homosexual argot: '[T]he use of heterosexual terminology may arise directly from the situation itself, since in homosexual relationships one partner frequently assumes a feminine role . . . The distinctive vocabulary which they [homosexuals in ancient Greece] would develop would naturally consist in large measure of words ordinarily used of heterosexual relationships transferred to pederasty' (pp. 49–50).

51   Halperin, 'Why is Diotima a Woman?', pp. 296, 259.

52   Because of this, according to Halperin (ibid., n. 85, p. 280), in certain passages *kuein* 'cannot mean "be pregnant" in any simple or straightforward sense'.

53   Pender, 'Spiritual Pregnancy in Plato's *Symposium*', p. 86.

54   Plass, 'Plato's Pregnant Lover', p. 50.

55   Compare 203c2, where, in the story of the birth of Eros, poverty *ekuēse ton Erōta*, 'became pregnant with Eros' (Rowe), 'conceived Love' (Hamilton), 'conceived' (Dover). In his 'Socratic Midwifery, Platonic Inspiration', Burnyeat notes the 'strange reversal' in the *Symposium*, according to which pregnancy precedes intercourse (p. 8), and also the absence of any account, metaphorical or otherwise, of the process of conception (pp. 12–13).

56   208e5, emphasis added.

57 To the extent that the Christ child is human, Marianism is, of course, a prominent later refutation of this claim.
58 See Bury's edition of the *Symposium*, p. 111.
59 Halperin, 'Why is Diotima a Woman', p. 269. Halperin makes his claim here in relation to Socrates' second speech in the *Phaedrus*, not in relation to the *Symposium*, but the point holds.
60 Plato, *Charmides*, trans. Donald Watt, *Early Socratic Dialogues*, Penguin, London, 1987, 155d3–4.
61 Jean Laplanche and Jean-Bertrand Pontalis, 'Fantasy and the Origins of Sexuality' [no translator given], in Victor Burgin, James Donald and Cora Caplan, eds., *Formations of Fantasy*, Methuen, London and New York, 1986, p. 14, 15.
62 Ibid., p. 27.
63 Ibid., p. 8. The second quotation is a citation from Freud. See also Jean Laplanche and Jean-Bertrand Pontalis, *The Language of Psychoanalysis*, trans. Donald Nicholson-Smith, Karnac Books, London, 1988, p. 315.
64 Laplanche and Pontalis, 'Fantasy and the Origins of Sexuality', p. 8.
65 This is a concept of fantasy constructed *out of* Laplanche and Pontalis' essay; it is not to be found in this exact, explicit form there. On the relationship between structure and imagination see ibid., p. 14.
66 Ibid., pp. 16, 17.
67 See ibid., pp. 20–1. Indeed 'Freud always held the model fantasy to be the reverie, that form of novelette, both stereotyped and infinitely variable, which the subject composes and relates to himself in a waking state' (p. 22).
68 Ibid., p. 21.
69 Cf. ibid., p. 22: ' "A father seduces a daughter" might perhaps be the summarized version of the seduction fantasy.'
70 Laplanche, 'Le genre, le sexe, le sexual' (2003), in *Sexual: La sexualité élargie au sens freudien*, p. 163. Freud's 'attempts at interpretation' are based on Schreber's own memoirs and the medico-legal reports connected to his case for release from psychiatric incarceration – he was not a patient of Freud's. See Freud, 'Psychoanalytic Notes on an Autobiographical Account of a Case of Paranoia (Dementia Paranoides)', in *Case Histories II*, trans. James Strachey, Pelican Freud Library Volume 9, Penguin, London, 1979. (Hereafter 'Psychoanalytic Notes'.)
71 Freud, 'Psychoanalytic Notes', p. 147.
72 Ibid., pp. 182, 183.
73 Ibid., p. 201. Schreber's case first took the form of a delusion of sexual transformation in relation to the conviction that he was being persecuted by his doctor, Flechsig. It was, according to Schreber, Flechsig who instigated his 'emasculation', for the purposes of sexual abuse. When Schreber became reconciled to his transformation into a woman (as part of his divine mission) the delusion of persecution receded. See Freud, 'Psychoanalytic Notes', especially pp. 143, 148–51, 171.

74   Laplanche, 'Le genre, le sexe, le sexual', p. 163.
75   Laplanche and Pontalis, 'Fantasy and the Origins of Sexuality', p. 22.
76   Ibid., p. 26.

Chapter 5

1   Plato, *Timaeus*, trans. Donald J. Zeyl, Hackett, Indianapolis/Cambridge, 2000, 17c2–4. Unless otherwise stated, all quotations from the *Timaeus* refer to this edition.
2   No reader can fail to notice this, and all commentators remark on it. However, the most insistent discussion of this aspect of the dialogue and its philosophical significance is in John Sallis' *Chorology: On Beginning in Plato's 'Timaeus'* (Indiana University Press, Bloomington and Indianapolis, 1999). This chapter was partly inspired by Sallis' book.
3   Twenty-seven times, according to Thomas H. Tobin (Timaios of Locri, *On the Nature of the World and the Soul*, trans. Thomas H. Tobin, Scholars Press, Chico, California, 1985, p. 8).
4   On this debate see Zeyl's introduction to *Timaeus*, pp. xx–xxv.
5   In Bury's more literal translation, 'changed into woman's nature at the second birth'. Plato, *Timaeus*, trans. R. G. Bury, Loeb Classical Library, Harvard University Press, Cambridge MA and London, 1929.
6   These words are Zeyl's addition to his translation. Bury does not specify in his translation to whom the 'passage' belonged. Lee's somewhat free translation reads 'what we drink makes its way through the lung . . .' perhaps echoing the 'us' in the previous sentence. Plato, *Timaeus*, trans. Desmond Lee, Penguin, London, 1965.
7   R. D. Archer-Hind, *The 'Timaeus' of Plato*, Macmillan, London and New York, n.d. (first published 1888), pp. 144, 283, 338. With regard to the second passage Archer-Hind mentions only that nails are formed for the later use of lower animals, not mentioning women specifically. Glossing 90e–92c: 'For in the first generation the gods made men, and in the second women: and they caused love to arise between men and women and a desire of continuing their race.'
8   A. E. Taylor, *A Commentary on Plato's 'Timaeus'*, Clarendon Press, Oxford, 1928, pp. 635, 636.
9   See Cornford contra Taylor in F. M. Cornford, *Plato's Cosmology: The 'Timaeus' of Plato*, Hackett, Indianapolis/Cambridge, 1997, pp. vi–ix.
10 On the formation of nails for the use of future women and beasts Cornford writes: 'this is one of the places where the mythical machinery becomes embarrassing and entails the use of rather vague language' (ibid., p. 295). The Platonist Timaois of Locri, whose *On the Nature of the World and the Soul*, dating from the late first-century BCE or early first-century CE, reprises much of the *Timaeus*, does not carry over a discussion of any of the three passages we are discussing here. However, in the context of a discussion of punishment he writes:

'Unusual punishments must surely be noted, in that the souls of the cowardly are clothed in female bodies which are given over to lust', and details the degeneration of murderers, debauchers, the foolish and so on into the bodies of lower animals. This is determined by 'Nemesis, together with the avenging and chthonic daimons'. Timaios of Locri, *On the Nature of the World and the Soul*, pp. 71–3. On Timaios of Locri and the relation of his *On the Nature of the World and the Soul* to Plato's *Timaeus* see Tobin's introduction. Albinus (a first century Platonist) also glosses this passage in his *Didaskalikos* but does not attempt to explain it. See Albinus, *The Platonic Doctrines of Albinus*, trans. Jeremiah Ready, Phanes Press, Grand Rapids MI, 1991, p. 50.

11 Taylor, *A Commentary on Plato's 'Timaeus'*, p. 635.

12 Sallis, *Chorology*, pp. 136, 137.

13 Concerning 42b: 'here, it must be confessed, we have a piece of questionable metaphysic. For the distinction of sex cannot possibly stand on the same logical footing as the generic differences between various animals; and in the other forms of animal life the distinction is ignored. It is somewhat curious that Plato, who in his views about women's position was immeasurably in advance of his age, has here yielded to Athenian prejudice so far as to introduce a discordant element into his theory.' Archer-Hind, *The 'Timaeus' of Plato*, p. 144.

14 A contradiction noted by, for example, Archer-Hind, ibid., p. 144; Taylor, *A Commentary on Plato's 'Timaeus'*, p. 636.

15 Proclus, *Commentary on the Timaeus of Plato*, trans. Thomas Taylor, The Prometheus Trust, Somerset, 1998, Vol. I, pp. 51, 53.

16 Proclus, *Commentary on the Timaeus of Plato*, Vol. II, pp. 975–6.

17 Ibid., p. 977.

18 Ibid., p. 980. See also p. 989: 'For that the male and female not only subsist in mortal natures, but also in the impartible lives themselves of souls, may be inferred by again recollecting what was before asserted, viz. that these sexual differences are both in the natures prior, and posterior to partial souls.'

19 See Lucas Siorvanes, *Proclus: Neo-Platonic Philosophy and Science*, Edinburgh University Press, Edinburgh, 1996, pp. 131–3.

20 Proclus, *Commentary on the Timaeus of Plato*, Vol. II, p. 980.

21 Ibid., p. 979. See also pp. 978, 988.

22 Taylor, *A Commentary on Plato's 'Timaeus'*, p. 636.

23 In fact, Proclus argues (*Commentary on the Timaeus of Plato*, Vol. II, p. 978), that unless we deny that women may lead apocatastatic lives (lives of virtue that would return their souls directly to their former dwelling in the star, without having to pass through a rebirth as a man), it makes no sense to say that souls could not be generated as women. That is, if they can ascend directly from woman to star, why may they not also descend directly from star to woman? Taylor also points out that some men must be too good to be reborn as women but not good enough to 'depart to their star', or there would be no

men with which the second generation of women could mate to per-
petuate the species, a necessity that Timaeus seemingly overlooks. See
Taylor, *A Commentary on Plato's 'Timaeus'*, pp. 260–1; Proclus, *Commentary on the Timaeus of Plato*, Vol. II, p. 989–90.

24   Dermot Moran, *The Philosophy of John Scottus Eriugena: A Study of Idealism in the Middle Ages*, Cambridge University Press, Cambridge, 1989,
p. 156. See also pp. 155, 162, 174–5, 184. I am grateful to Dermot Moran
for bringing the Medieval commentators to my attention.

25   Taylor, *A Commentary on Plato's 'Timaeus'*, p. 639.

26   Taylor compares *Timaeus* 90e1–92c3 to Aristophanes' speech in Plato's
Symposium. As only 'earnest-minded dullards have found a profound
"metaphysic of sexual love" in this Rabelaisian jest [Aristophanes'
speech]' one may presume that only they, too, will find a metaphysical
meaning in Timaeus' comments here. (Taylor, *A Commentary on Plato's
'Timaeus'*, p. 635.)

27   Proclus, *Commentary on the Timaeus of Plato*, Vol. II, p. 989.

28   Ibid., p. 989.

29   Ibid., p. 978.

30   See, for example ibid., pp. 975, 989.

31   Taylor, *A Commentary on Plato's 'Timaeus'*, p. 635.

32   Ibid., p. 635.

33   Ibid., pp. 637–9.

34   Ibid., p. 635.

35   This shows, incidentally, that Taylor and Sallis are not laughing at the
same thing in Timaeus' sex comedy. The humour for Taylor is in the
idea of the generation before sex being modified to produce men and
women (what he thinks of as the Aristophanesian element). For Sallis
the humour is in the ridiculous idea of the derivation of women from
men.

36   Cornford, *Plato's Cosmology*, n. 1, p. 145.

37   Ibid., p. 145.

38   Ibid., n. 1, p. 145. See also pp. 142, 291.

39   Ibid., pp. 295, 294.

40   Catherine Joubard, *Le corps humain dans la philosophie platonicienne*,
Vrin, Paris, 1991, pp. 140, 142.

41   Ibid., p. 141: 'Platon utilise le terme *anēr* (90e) comme terme génerique
de l'espèce de la première generation. Un vivant sans aucune déter-
mination de sexe apparaît: c'est une entité humaine au sujet de laquelle
une question de cet ordre n'est pas pertinente, comme s'il s'agissait
d'une sorte d'être hybride ou d'un Homme avec un "H" majuscule
représentant d'une humanité originelle'. Joubard seems to develop
this position on the basis of a hint from Luc Brisson. In *Le même et
l'autre dans la structure ontologique du Timée de Platon*, Editions Klincksteck, Paris, 1974, p. 456, Brisson says that despite the mention of 'men'
at 90e6–7 this does not mean that humans of the first generation were
male (*'avaient un sexe masculin'*). The male sex was formed, according

to Brisson, at the same time as the female and the usage of the word 'man' must be understood as a way of avoiding the word *gunē*, excluded as inappropriate vocabulary from the first generation. But why is it so excluded? And why not *anēr*? In his preface to Joubard's book Brisson presents Joubard's interpretation approvingly as follows (Joubard, *Le corps humain dans la philosophie platonicienne*, p. 15): 'At the time of the first incarnation the human soul finds itself in a sexually undifferentiated body, despite the fact that Plato describes this body as "male", because the body is not yet endowed with a sexual organ.' ('Lors de la toute première incarnation, l'âme humaine se retrouve dans un corps qui est sexuellement indifférencié, même si Platon le qualifie de "mâle", car ce corps n'est pas encore doté d'organe sexuel.')

42 Archer-Hind, *The 'Timaeus' of Plato*, p. 338, glossing 90e–92c.
43 There is no substantial feminist analysis of these passages of which I am aware. But for examples of critical mention see Saxonhouse, 'The Philosopher and the Female', p. 75; Page du Bois, 'The Platonic Appropriation of Reproduction', p. 142 (where 901a–d is cited as evidence of 'Plato's misogyny'); Julia Annas, 'Plato's Republic and Feminism', p. 11 (where evil men's rebirth as women is cited as an example of Plato's 'conventional contempt for women'); Eva Cantarella, *Bisexuality in the Ancient World*, trans. Cormac Ó Cuilleanáin, Yale University Press, New Haven and London, 2002, p. 580, where the rebirth of bad men as women is cited as evidence of Plato's profound conviction of the inferiority of women.

Feminist comment on the *Timaeus* has tended to focus instead on the notion of *chōra*. The tripartite ontology of the second part of Timaeus' speech, in which *chōra* is introduced, is an answer to a problem, fundamental to Timaeus' discourse and to Platonic metaphysics more generally: the problem of explaining the relation between that which always is and has no becoming and that which becomes but never is, or of explaining the generation of the world of becoming from the intelligible, unchanging source. *Chōra* is a name for the 'third kind' – that *in which* what comes to be comes to be (50d2) – standing as some sort of mediatrix between being and becoming. But far from solving the problem the introduction of the third introduces another, the problem of *chōra* itself. Timaeus begins to speak of the third kind by explaining how difficult it is to speak of it. It is a thing that does not itself have any qualities or determinations; it is 'totally devoid of any characteristics' (50e6). This must be the case if it is to perform its role: 'Its nature is to be available for anything to make its impression upon, and it is modified, shaped, and reshaped by the things that enter it. These are the things that make it appear different at different times' (50c3–6). And yet it is itself, and is not identical with these things: 'We must always refer to it by the same term, for it does not depart from its own character in any way' (50b9–10). This 'receiving thing', upon which other things imprint themselves, may not 'show its own face' in any of its receptions or imprimaturs (50e). Difficult, if not impossible to characterise, because characterless, Timaeus nevertheless suggests that 'If we speak of it as an invisible and characterless sort of thing, one that receives all things and shares in a most perplexing way in what is intelligible, a thing extremely difficult to comprehend, we shall not be misled' (51a9–b2).

Small wonder that the notion of *chōra* – space, place, room, land, country, and yet none of these things, exactly – caught Derrida's attention, as the 'abyssal chasm' at the heart of the *Timaeus* (Jacques Derrida, *Khôra*, Éditions Galilée, Paris, 1993, p. 46). What little feminist literature there is on the *Timaeus* also takes the notion of *chōra* – mother, wet nurse, nurturer, receptacle, the 'female' kind, most closely associated with procreation in Timaeus' discourse – as its theme, sometimes reclaiming *chōra* enthusiastically, sometimes criticizing the degradation of the female in its identification with *chōra*. For an example of the former see Emanuela Bianchi, for whom *chōra* is 'fecund and generative philosophical terrain in which a feminist rethinking of corporeality, spatiality, figurality, temporality and life may take (its) place'. Bianchi, 'Receptacle/*Chôra*: Figuring the Errant Feminine in Plato's *Timaeus*', *Hypatia*, Vol. 21, No. 4, Fall 2006. David Farrell Krell, on the other hand, is altogether less celebratory. For Krell the introduction of the female *chōra* is the attempt to resolve 'the fundamental ontological problem in *Timaeus*, the generation of the visible world (*genesis*) from Being (*to on*)'. If the father is the only parent of becoming, it would need to be explained how the world of becoming is 'other than a perfect image of its father . . . Timaeus can account for the slippage between paradigm and copy, which prevents *that which* is generated from perfectly matching that *of which* it is a copy, only by blaming that *in which* the copy is generated'. Farrell Krell, 'Female Parts in the *Timaeus*', *Arion*, Vol. 2, No. 3, 1975, pp. 400, 414. Kristin Sampson makes a similar argument (in 'A Difference of Origin', in Ellen Mortensen, ed., *Sex, Breath, and Force: Sexual Difference in a Post-feminist Era*, Lexington Books, Rowman & Littlefield, Lanham MD, 2006, pp. 19, 21, 22), but also has hopes for the 'plural-parent structure' (rather than the one-parent, patrogenic structure) that is at least signalled in the *Timaeus* (p. 27).

44 Cornford, *Plato's Cosmology*, p. 145.
45 Ibid., pp. 294–5.
46 Ibid., n. 1, p. 295.
47 Interestingly, *Timaeus* 73, together with *Timaeus* 91, suggests an Aristotelian type theory of reproduction (in which only the male contributes seed, and the seed comes from the brain), rather than that typical of the Hippocratic treatises (in which both male and female contribute seed and the seed comes from all of the parts of the body). Timaeus' view of the ontological inferiority of the female and its derivation from the male also shares more with Aristotle than with the Plato of the

Republic. Farrell Krell remarks on the apparent Aristotelian influence in 'Female Parts in the Timaeus', especially p. 414.

48 Cornford, *Plato's Cosmology*, n. 2, p. 310. See also p. 295: The development of women and beasts from men 'never actually happened'.

49 Ibid., p. 356.

50 Cornford, *Plato's Cosmology*, pp. 291–2.

51 Morag Buchan, *Women in Plato's Political Theory*, Macmillan, Hampshire, 1999, p. 46.

52 So Proclus, for example, cannot explain how women come about in the second generation, having already postulated sex difference (and hence, sexual reproduction) in the first. But sex categories are ultimately cosmological and metaphysical for Proclus.

53 Carlos Steel argues that 'the *Timaeus* is not primarily a dialogue about physics or biology, but an attempt to explain from a moral perspective the constitution of the world and the creation of the human animal in it. The foreordained laws described to the souls mounted in their carriages 'are not cosmological laws but the moral laws that establish a correspondence ("retribution") between the diverse grades of moral behaviour and the (happy or unhappy) conditions of life'. Carlos Steel, 'The Moral Purpose of the Human Body: A Reading of *Timaeus* 69–72', *Phronesis*, Vol. XLVI, No. 2, May 2001, pp. 123, 124. The claim that 'man' and 'woman' are moral categories might seem to conform to Steel's reading. But by 'moral perspective' Steel means 'A teleological explanation of biological processes from the viewpoint of the "best" [which] must show how these processes are organised in such a way that they make it possible for the human being to attain a good life' (p. 109), whereas this chapter's claim that 'man' and 'woman' are moral categories means that they are differentiated only according to a moral criterion or through a moral judgement.

54 On the discourses of procreation and production in the *Timaeus* see Sallis, *Chorology*, pp. 52, 57–63, 77–8, 85–8.

55 Proclus, *Commentary on the Timaeus of Plato*, Vol. I, p. 52.

Coda

1 Cf. Sallis, *Chorology*, n. 24, p. 66: Cornford's translation of *ousia* as 'existence' 'is a prime instance of imposing back upon the Platonic texts a language and a conceptuality that first became possible on the basis of what was achieved in and through those texts'. Perhaps the same is true when we translate *genos* as 'sex'.

2 'Fetish character' in the sense that Marx writes of the fetish character of the commodity. Karl Marx, *Capital*, Volume 1, trans. Ben Fowkes, Penguin, London, 1990, Book I, Part One, Chapter 1.4, 'The Fetishism of the Commodity and its Secret'.

3   Immanuel Kant, *Critique of Pure Reason*, trans. Paul Guyer and Allen Wood, Cambridge University Press, Cambridge, 1998, A319/B376, A313–14/B370–1.

4   Ibid., A314/B370.

5   Ibid., A569/B597, A472/B500, A314/B371, A317/B374.

6   Ibid., A305/B362.

7   Ibid., A533/B561, A644/B672.

8   Ibid., A329/B285.

9   Ibid., A293–8/B249–355, A339/B397.

10 Ibid., A350. This is the first of the 'paralogisms of pure reason'.

11 Ibid., A396, A681/B709, A351, emphasis added.

12 Ibid., A339/B397.

13 Ibid., A670/B698, A674/B702, emphasis added.

14 Ibid., A666/B694.

15 Ibid., A652/B680.

16 Immanuel Kant, 'On the Use of Teleological Principles in Philosophy', in Robert Bernasconi, ed., *Race*, Blackwell, Malden MA/Oxford UK, 2001, pp. 40, 39.

17 Robert Bernasconi, 'Who Invented the Concept of Race?', in Bernasconi, ed., *Race*. Bernasconi's essay on race has provided me with a model for part of the present discussion of sex.

18 Kant, 'On the Use of Teleological Principles in Philosophy', p. 39.

19 Bernasconi, 'Who Invented the Concept of Race?', p. 23. According to Kant 'natural history can only offer us fragments or shaky hypotheses'. 'On the Use of Teleological Principles in Philosophy', p. 39.

20 Bernasconi, 'Who Invented the Concept of Race?', pp. 23–4, 26–8.

21 Kant, 'On the Use of Teleological Principles in Philosophy', p. 40.

22 Bernasconi, 'Who Invented the Concept of Race?', p. 29.

23 Ibid., p. 30; Anthony K. Appiah and Amy Gutman, *Color Conscious: The Political Morality of Race*, Princeton University Press, Princeton NJ, 1996. For the opposing view see Lucius Outlaw, *On Race and Philosophy*, Routledge, New York, 1996.

24 For a wider variety of approaches to the concept of race see also Peter Osborne and Stella Sandford, eds., *Philosophies of Race and Ethnicity*, Continuum, London and New York, 2002.

25 An example of the reception of Kant in just this way is to be found in Michel Foucault's conception of the 'historical *a priori*': 'This a priori is what, in a given period, delimits in the totality of experience a field of knowledge, defines the mode of being of the objects that appear in that field, provides man's everyday perception with theoretical powers, and defines the conditions in which he can sustain a discourse about things that is recognized to be true.' Foucault, *The Order of Things: An Archaeology of the Human Sciences*, (no translator given), Tavistock Publications, London, 1970, p. 158.

26 For an account of the historical attempts to locate sex in these various locations or entities see Fausto-Sterling, *Sexing the Body*, especially Chapters 6 and 7.
27 Kant, *Critique of Pure Reason*, A619/B647, A350.
28 In the (A) edition of the *Critique of Pure Reason* these are the conclusions of the four paralogisms of pure reason, constituting the 'topics of the rational doctrine of the soul, from which everything else that it may contain has to be derived' (A344/B402). In fact the second (B) edition is concerned almost exclusively with the first paralogism (of substantiality). More generally, in the section on the 'The system of the transcendental ideas' in the *Critique of Pure Reason* Kant writes that pure reason provides the ideas for a 'transcendental doctrine of the soul' (rational psychology), a 'transcendental science of the world' (rational cosmology) and a 'transcendental cognition of God' (transcendental theology) (A334–5/B391–2).
29 Ibid., A298/B354.
30 Ibid., A479/B507, A314/B371, A329/B385.
31 Ibid., A350–1: 'one can quite well allow the proposition **The soul is substance** to be valid, if only one admits that this concept of ours leads no further, that it cannot teach us any of the usual conclusions of the rationalistic doctrine of the soul, such as, e.g., the everlasting duration of the soul through all alterations, even the human being's death, thus that it signifies a substance only in the idea but not in reality.'

Bibliography

Adam, James, *The Republic of Plato*, Cambridge University Press, Cambridge, 1963.

Albinus, *The Platonic Doctrines of Albinus*, trans. Jeremiah Ready, Phanes Press, Grand Rapids MI, 1991.

Allen, Michael B., trans. and ed., *Marsilio Ficino and the Phaedran Charioteer*, University of California Press, Berkeley, Los Angeles, London, 1981.

Annas, Julia, *An Introduction to Plato's Republic*, Clarendon Press, Oxford, 1982.

Annas, Julia, 'Plato's *Republic* and Feminism', in Julie K. Ward, ed., *Feminism and Ancient Philosophy*, Routledge, London and New York, 1996.

Appiah, Anthony K. and Amy Gutman, *Color Conscious: The Political Morality of Race*, Princeton University Press, Princeton NJ, 1996.

Archer-Hind, R. D., *The 'Timaeus' of Plato* [1888], Macmillan, London and New York, n.d.

Aristophanes, *Ecclesiazusae*, ed. R. G. Ussher, Clarendon Press, Oxford, 1973.

Aristophanes, *Assemblywomen*, trans. and ed. Jeffrey Henderson, in *Three Plays*, Routledge, London and New York, 1996.

Aristophanes, *Women at the Thesmophoria*, trans. Jeffrey Henderson, in *Three Plays*, Routledge, London and New York, 1996.

Aristotle, *The Politics* and *The Constitution of Athens*, trans. Jonathan Barnes (revising Benjamin Jowett), Cambridge University Press, Cambridge, 1996.

Averroes, *Averroes' Commentary on Plato's Republic*, trans. and ed. E. I. J. Rosenthal, Cambridge University Press, Cambridge, 1956.

Bernasconi, Robert, 'Who Invented the Concept of Race?', in Bernasconi, ed., *Race*, Blackwell, Malden MA/Oxford UK, 2001.

Bianchi, Emanuela, 'Receptacle/*Chôra*: Figuring the Errant Feminine in Plato's *Timaeus*', *Hypatia*, Vol. 21, No. 4, Fall 2006.

Bowery, Anne-Marie, 'Diotima tells a Story: A Narrative Analysis of Plato's *Symposium*', in Ward, ed., *Feminism and Ancient Philosophy*.

Brisson, Luc, *Le même et l'autre dans la structure ontologique du Timée de Platon*, Editions Klincksteck, Paris, 1974.

Brisson, Luc, *Sexual Ambivalence*, trans. Janet Lloyd, University of California Press, Berkeley/Los Angeles/London, 2002.

Brisson, Luc, 'Paiderastia, Philosophia', in Lesher et al., eds., *Plato's Symposium: Issues in Interpretation and Reception*.

Brown, Wendy ' "Supposing Truth Were a Woman": Plato's Subversion of Masculine Discourse', in Tuana, ed., *Feminist Interpretations of Plato*.

Buchan, Morag, *Women in Plato's Political Theory*, Macmillan, Hampshire, 1999.

Burnyeat, M. F., 'Socratic Midwifery, Platonic Inspiration', *Bulletin of the Institute of Classical Studies*, Vol. 24, 1977.

Bury, R. G., ed., *The Symposium of Plato*, Heffer and Sons, Cambridge, 1973.

Butler, Judith, 'Variations on Sex and Gender: Beauvoir, Wittig, Foucault', in Seyla Benhabib and Drucilla Cornell, eds., *Feminism as Critique*, Polity, Oxford, 1987.

Butler, Judith, *Gender Trouble: Feminism and the Subversion of Identity*, Routledge, New York and London, 1990.

Campbell, Kirsten, *Jacques Lacan and Feminist Epistemology*, Routledge, London and New York, 2004.

Cantarella, Eva, *Bisexuality in the Ancient World*, trans. Cormac Ó Cuilleanáin, Yale University Press, New Haven and London, 2002.

Canto, Monique, 'The Politics of Women's Bodies: Reflections on Plato', trans. Arthur Goldhammer, in Tuana, ed., *Feminist Interpretations of Plato*.

Cavarero, Adriana, *In Spite of Plato*, trans. Serena Anderlini-D'Onofrio and Áine O'Healy, Polity Press, Cambridge, 1995.

Clay, Diskin, 'Platonic Studies and the Study of Plato', *Arion*, Vol. 2, No. 1, 1975.

Copjec, Joan, 'Sex and the Euthanasia of Reason', in *Read My Desire: Lacan Against the Historicists*, MIT Press, Cambridge MA and London, 1994.

Cornford, F. M., *From Religion to Philosophy: A Study in the Origins of Western Speculation*, Edward Arnold, London, 1912.

Cornford, F. M., 'The Doctrine of Eros in Plato's Symposium', in *The Unwritten Philosophy and Other Essays*, Cambridge University Press, Cambridge, 1950.

Cornford, F. M., *Plato's Cosmology: The 'Timaeus' of Plato*, Hackett, Indianapolis/Cambridge, 1997.

Dean-Jones, Lesley, *Women's Bodies in Classical Greek Science*, Clarendon Press, Oxford, 1994.

Derrida, Jacques, *Khôra*, Éditions Galilée, Paris, 1993.

Dover, K. J., *Greek Popular Morality in the Time of Plato and Aristotle*, Basil Blackwell, Oxford, 1974.

Dover, K. J., *Plato: Symposium*, Cambridge University Press, Cambridge, 1980.

DuBois, Page, 'The Appropriation of Reproduction', in Tuana, ed., *Feminist Interpretations of Plato*.

Farrell Krell, David, 'Female Parts in the *Timaeus*', *Arion* (second series), Vol. 2, No. 3, 1975.

Farrell Smith, Janet, 'Plato, Irony, and Equality', in Tuana, ed., *Feminist Interpretations Of Plato*.

Fausto-Sterling, Anne, *Sexing the Body: Gender Politics and the Constructions of Sexuality*, Basic Books, New York, 2000.

Ferrari, G. R. F., 'Platonic Love', in Richard Kraut, ed., *The Cambridge Companion to Plato*, Cambridge University Press, Cambridge, 1992.

Ficino, Marsilio, *Commentary on Plato's Symposium on Love*, trans. Seers Jayne, Spring Publications, Dallas, Texas, 1985.

Foucault, Michel, *The Order of Things: An Archaeology of the Human Sciences* (no translator given), Tavistock Publications, London, 1970.

Fouillée, Alfred, *La philosophie de Platon* (Tome première), Librarie Philosophique de Ladrange, Paris, 1869.

Freud, Sigmund, 'Femininity', in *New Introductory Lectures on Psychoanalysis*, trans. James Strachey, Pelican Freud Library Volume 2, Penguin, London, 1973.

Freud, Sigmund, 'Three Essays on the Theory of Sexuality', in *On Sexuality*, trans. James Strachey, Pelican Freud Library Volume 7, Penguin, London, 1977.

Freud, Sigmund, 'Psychoanalytic Notes on an Autobiographical Account of a Case of Paranoia (Dementia Paranoides)', in *Case Histories II*, trans. James Strachey, Pelican Freud Library Volume 9, Penguin, London, 1979.

Freud, Sigmund, 'The Psychogenesis of a Case of Homosexuality in a Woman' (1920), in *Case Histories II*, trans. James Strachey, Pelican Freud Library Volume 9, Penguin, London, 1979.

Freud, Sigmund, 'Beyond the Pleasure Principle', in *On Metapsychology: The Theory of Psychoanalysis*, trans. James Strachey, Pelican Freud Library Volume 11, Penguin, London, 1984.

Freud, Sigmund, 'Instincts and Their Vicissitudes', in *On Metapsychology: The Theory of Psychoanalysis*, trans. James Strachey, Pelican Freud Library Volume 12, Penguin, London, 1984.

Freud, Sigmund, 'Civilization and its Discontents', in *Civilization, Society and Religion*, trans. James Strachey, Pelican Freud Library Volume 12, Penguin, London, 1985.

Freud, Sigmund, ' "Civilized" Sexual Morality and Modern Nervous Illness', in *Civilization, Society and Religion*, trans. James Strachey, Pelican Freud Library Volume 12, Penguin, London, 1985.

Freud, Sigmund, 'Group Psychology and the Analysis of the Ego', in *Civilization, Society and Religion*, trans. James Strachey, Pelican Freud Library Volume 12, Penguin, London, 1985.

Freud, Sigmund, 'Resistances to Psychoanalysis', in *Historical and Expository Works on Psychoanalysis*, trans. James Strachey, Pelican Freud Library Volume 15, Penguin, London, 1986.

Freud, Sigmund, 'Two Encyclopaedia Articles', in *Historical and Expository Works on Psychoanalysis*, trans. James Strachey, Pelican Freud Library Volume 15, Penguin, London, 1986.

Freud, Sigmund, *Introductory Lectures on Psychoanalysis*, trans. James Strachey, Pelican Freud Library Volume 1, Penguin, London, 1991.

Freud, Sigmund, 'Leonardo da Vinci and a Memory of his Childhood', trans. James Strachey, in *Standard Edition*, Volume XI, Vintage, London, 2001.

Gomperz, Theodor, *Greek Thinkers: A History of Ancient Philosophy*, Vol. II, trans. G. G. Berry, John Murray, London, 1905.

Gould, Thomas, *Platonic Love*, Routledge and Kegan Paul, London, 1963.

Halperin, David M., 'Platonic *Erōs* and What Men Call Love', *Ancient Philosophy*, Vol. V, No. 1, Spring 1985.

Halperin, David, *One Hundred Years of Homosexuality and Other Essays on Greek Love*, Routledge, New York and London, 1990.

Halperin, David M., 'Why is Diotima a Woman? Platonic Eros and the Figuration of Gender', in David M. Halperin, John J. Winkler and Froma I. Zeitlin, eds., *Before Sexuality: The Construction of Erotic Experience in the Ancient World*, Princeton University Press, Princeton NJ, 1990.

Harris Bluestone, Natalie, *Women and the Ideal Society: Plato's 'Republic' and Modern Myths of Gender*, Berg, Oxford and Hamburg, 1987.

Hawthorne, Susan, 'Diotima Speaks Through the Body', in Bat-Ami Bar On, ed., *Engendering Origins: Critical Feminist Readings in Plato and Aristotle*, State University of New York Press, Albany NY, 1994.

Hobbs, Angela, *Plato and the Hero: Courage, Manliness and the Impersonal Good*, Cambridge University Press, Cambridge, 2000.

Hobbs, Angela, 'Female Imagery in Plato', in Lesher et al., eds., *Plato's Symposium: Issues in Interpretation and Reception*.

Hornblower, Simon and Anthony Spawforth, eds., *Oxford Classical Dictionary*, 3rd edition, Oxford University Press, Oxford, 1996.

Huit, C., *Études sur le Banquet de Platon*, Ernest Thorin, Paris, 1889.

Irigaray, Luce, 'Sorcerer Love: A Reading of Plato's *Symposium*, Diotima's Speech', trans. Eleanor H. Kuykendall, in Tuana, ed., *Feminist Interpretations of Plato*.

Irigaray, Luce, 'Plato's *Hystera*', in *Speculum of the Other Woman*, trans. Gillian C. Gill, Cornell University Press, Ithaca, New York, 1985.

Joubard, Catherine, *Le corps humain dans la philosophie platonicienne*, Vrin, Paris, 1991.

Just, Roger, *Women in Athenian Law and Life*, Routledge, London and New York, 1989.

Kamtekar, Rachana, 'Race and Genos in Plato', in Julie K. Ward and Tommy L. Lott, eds., *Philosophers on Race*, Blackwell, Oxford, 2002.

Kant, Immanuel, *Critique of Pure Reason*, trans. Paul Guyer and Allen Wood, Cambridge University Press, Cambridge, 1998.

Kant, Immanuel, 'On the Use of Teleological Principles in Philosophy', in Robert Bernasconi, ed., *Race*, Blackwell, Malden MA/Oxford UK, 2001.

Kessler, Suzanne J., *Lessons From the Intersexed*, Rutgers University Press, New Brunswick, New Jersey and London, 1998.

Kessler, Suzanne J. and Wendy McKenna, *Gender: An Ethnomethodological Approach*, Chicago University Press, Chicago, 1985.

Lacan, Jacques, *Le séminaire Livre XI, Les quatre concepts fondamentaux de la psychanalyse*, Seuil, Paris, 1973.

Lacan, Jacques, *The Four Fundamental Concepts of Psychoanalysis*, trans. Alan Sheridan, Penguin, London, 1979.

Lacan, Jacques, *Le séminaire Livre V, Les formations de l'inconscient*, Seuil, Paris, 1998.

Lacan, Jacques, *Encore: The Seminar of Jacques Lacan, Book XX*, edited by Jacques-Alain Miller, trans. Bruce Fink, Norton, New York and London, 1999.

Lacan, Jacques, *Le séminaire Livre VIII, Le Transfert*, Seuil, Paris, 2001.

Lacan, Jacques, 'The Signification of the Phallus', in *Écrits*, trans. Bruce Fink, Norton, New York and London, 2006.

Laplanche, Jean, *Life and Death in Psychoanalysis*, trans. Jeffrey Mehlman, John Hopkins University Press, Baltimore and London, 1976.

Laplanche, Jean, 'The So-Called "Death Drive": A Sexual Drive', trans. Luke Thurston, in Rob Weatherill, ed., *The Death Drive: New Life for a Dead Subject?*, Rebus Press, London, 1999.

Laplanche, Jean, 'Le genre, le sexe, le sexual', in *Sexual: La sexualité élargie au sens freudien*, Quadrige/PUF, Paris, 2007.

Laplanche, Jean, and Jean-Bertrand Pontalis, 'Fantasy and the Origins of Sexuality' (no translator given), in Victor Burgin, James Donald and Cora Caplan, eds., *Formations of Fantasy*, Methuen, London and New York, 1986.

Laplanche, Jean, and Jean-Bertrand Pontalis, *The Language of Psychoanalysis*, trans. Donald Nicholson-Smith, Karnac Books, London, 1988.

Laqueur, Thomas, *Making Sex: Body and Gender from the Greeks to Freud*, Harvard University Press, Cambridge MA and London, 1992.

Lesher, James, Debra Nails and Frisbee Sheffield, eds., *Plato's Symposium: Issues in Interpretation and Reception*, Harvard University Press, Cambridge MA and London, 2006.

Levin, Susan B., 'Women's Nature and Role in the Ideal *Polis: Republic* V Revisited', in Ward, ed., *Feminism and Ancient Philosophy*.

Levin, Susan B., 'Plato on Women's Nature: Reflections on the *Laws*', *Ancient Philosophy*, Vol. 20, No. 1, 2000.

Liddell, H. G., and Scott, R., *A Greek/English Lexicon*, revised by H. S. Jones, Clarendon Press, Oxford, 1996.

Lloyd, G. E. R, *Science, Folklore and Ideology: Studies in the Life Sciences in Ancient Greece*, Cambridge University Press, Cambridge, 1983.

Lonie, Iain M., *The Hippocratic Treatises: 'On Generation', 'On the Nature of the Child', 'Diseases IV'*, (translations and commentary), Walter de Gruyter, Berlin/New York, 1981.

Loraux, Nicole, *Les enfants d'Athéna*, Seuil, Paris, 1990.

Marx, Karl, *Capital*, Volume 1, trans. Ben Fowkes, Penguin, London, 1990.

Moller Okin, Susan, *Women in Western Political Thought*, Princeton University Press, Princeton NJ, 1992.

Moran, Dermot, *The Philosophy of John Scottus Eriugena: A Study of Idealism in the Middle Ages*, Cambridge University Press, Cambridge, 1989.

Morrison, J. S., 'Four Notes on Plato's *Symposium*', *Classical Quarterly*, Vol. 14, No. 1, 1964.

Morrow, Glenn, *Plato's Cretan City: A Historical Interpretation of the Laws*, Princeton University Press, Princeton NJ, 1960.

Nye, Andrea, 'The Hidden Host: Irigaray and Diotima at Plato's Symposium', in *Revaluing French Feminism*, Nancy Fraser and Sandra Lee Bartky, eds., Indiana University Press, Bloomington, 1992.

Osborne, Peter, and Stella Sandford, eds., *Philosophies of Race and Ethnicity*, Continuum, London and New York, 2002.

Outlaw, Lucius, *On Race and Philosophy*, Routledge, New York, 1996.

Pender, E. E., 'Spiritual Pregnancy in Plato's *Symposium*', *Classical Quarterly*, Vol. 42, No. 1, 1992.

Plass, Paul C., 'Plato's "Pregnant" Lover', *Symbolae Oslenses*, Vol. LIII, 1978.

Plato, *Sophist*, trans. H. N. Fowler, Loeb edition, William Heinemann, London, 1921.

Plato, *Symposium*, trans. W. R. M. Lamb, Loeb edition, Harvard University Press, Cambridge MA and London, 1925.

Plato, *Timaeus*, trans. R. G. Bury, Loeb edition, Harvard University Press, Cambridge MA, and London, 1929.

Plato, *Republic*, trans. Paul Shorey, Loeb edition, Harvard University Press, Cambridge MA and London, 1937.

Plato, *Symposium*, trans. Walter Hamilton, Penguin, London, 1951.

Plato, *Timaeus*, trans. Desmond Lee, Penguin, London, 1965.

Plato, *Laws*, trans. Trevor J. Saunders, Penguin, London, 1975.

Plato, *Charmides*, trans. Donald Watt, in *Early Socratic Dialogues*, Penguin, London, 1987.

Plato, *Republic*, trans. Desmond Lee, Penguin, London, 1987.

Plato, *Republic*, trans. Robin Waterfield, Oxford University Press, Oxford, 1993.

Plato, *Republic 5*, trans. and ed. S. Halliwell, Aris & Phillips, Warminster, 1993.

Plato, *Symposium*, trans. Allan Bloom, University of Chicago Press, Chicago and London, 1993.

Plato, *Symposium*, edited with an introduction, translation and commentary by C. J. Rowe, Aris & Phillips, Warminster, 1998.

Plato, *Symposium*, trans. Christopher Gill, Penguin, London, 1999.

Plato, *Phaedrus*, trans. C. J. Rowe, Aris & Phillips, Warminster, 2000.

Plato, *Timaeus*, trans. Donald J. Zeyl, Hackett, Indianapolis/Cambridge, 2000.

Platon, *La République*, trans. Georges Leroux, Flammarion, Paris, 2004.

204 *Bibliography*

Plato, *The Symposium*, eds. M. C. Howatson and Frisbee C. C. Sheffield, trans. M. C. Howatson, Cambridge University Press, Cambridge, 2008.

Price, A. W., *Love and Friendship in Plato and Aristotle*, Clarendon Press, Oxford, 1989.

Price, A. W., 'Plato and Freud', in Christopher Gill, ed., *The Person and The Human Mind: Issues in Ancient and Modern Philosophy*, Clarendon Press, Oxford, 1990.

Proclus, *Commentary on the Timaeus of Plato*, trans. Thomas Taylor, The Prometheus Trust, Somerset, 1998.

Psychoanalytical Notebooks: A Review of the London Society of the New Lacanian School, No. 11, *Sexuation and Sexuality*, December 2003.

Putnam, Samuel, ed., *The Portable Rabelais*, New York, Viking, 1946.

Rhodes, James M., *Eros, Wisdom and Silence: Plato's Erotic Dialogues*, University of Missouri Press, Columbia and London, 2003.

Robin, Léon, *La théorie platonicienne de l'amour*, F. Alcan, Paris, 1933.

Rosen, Stanley, *Plato's 'Symposium'*, Yale University Press, New Haven and London, 1968.

Sallis, John, *Chorology: On Beginning in Plato's 'Timaeus'*, Indiana University Press, Bloomington and Indianapolis, 1999.

Sampson, Kristin, 'A Difference of Origin', in Ellen Mortensen, ed., *Sex, Breath, and Force: Sexual Difference in a Post-feminist Era*, Lexington Books, Rowman & Littlefield, Lanham MD, 2006.

Sandford, Stella, 'Contingent Ontologies: Sex, Gender and "Woman" in Simone de Beauvoir and Judith Butler', *Radical Philosophy*, 97, September/October 1999.

Sandford, Stella, *How to Read Beauvoir*, Granta, London, 2006.

Sandford, Stella, 'Sexmat, Revisited', *Radical Philosophy*, 145, September/October 2007.

Sandford, Stella, 'The Dialectic of *The Dialectic of Sex*', in Mandy Merck and Stella Sandford, eds., *Further Adventures of 'The Dialectic of Sex'*, Palgrave, Basingstoke, 2010.

Santas, Gerasimos, *Plato and Freud: Two Theories of Love*, Basil Blackwell, Oxford, 1988.

Saxonhouse, Arlene W., 'Eros and the Female in Greek Political Thought: An Interpretation of Plato's *Symposium*', *Political Theory*, Vol. 12, No. 1, February 1984.

Saxonhouse, Arlene W., 'The Philosopher and the Female in the Political Thought of Plato', in Tuana, ed., *Feminist Interpretations of Plato*.

Saxonhouse, Arlene W., *Fear of Diversity: The Birth of Political Science in Ancient Greek Thought*, University of Chicago Press, Chicago and London, 1996.

Schleiermacher, Friedrich, *Introductions to the Dialogues of Plato*, trans. William Dobson, Cambridge University Press, Cambridge, 1836.

Sheffield, Frisbee C. C., 'Psychic Pregnancy and Platonic Epistemology', *Oxford Studies in Ancient Philosophy*, Vol. XX, Summer 2001.

Sheffield, Frisbee C. C., *Plato's 'Symposium': The Ethics of Desire*, Oxford University Press, Oxford, 2006.

Singer, Irving, *The Nature of Love*, Volume 1, Plato to Luther, University of Chicago Press, Chicago and London, 1984.

Siorvanes, Lucas, *Proclus: Neo-Platonic Philosophy and Science*, Edinburgh University Press, Edinburgh, 1996.

Snell, Bruno, *The Discovery of the Mind: The Greek Origins of European Thought*, trans. T. G. Rosenmeyer, Harper & Row, New York, 1960.

Songe-Møller, Vigdis, *Philosophy Without Women: The Birth of Sexism in Western Thought*, trans. Peter Cripps, Continuum, London and New York, 2002.

Spelman, Elizabeth V., 'Hairy Cobblers and Philosopher-Queens', in Tuana, ed., *Feminist Interpretations of Plato*.

Steel, Carlos, 'The Moral Purpose of the Human Body: A Reading of *Timaeus* 69–72', *Phronesis*, Vol. XLVI, No. 2, May 2001.

Sterelny, Kim and Paul E. Griffiths, *Sex and Death: An Introduction to Philosophy of Biology*, University of Chicago Press, Chicago, 1999.

Stewart, J. A., *The Myths of Plato*, Macmillan, London, 1905.

Stokes, Michael C., *Plato's Socratic Conversations: Drama and Dialectic in Three Dialogues*, Athlone, London, 1986.

Stone, Alison, 'The Incomplete Materialism of French Materialist Feminism', *Radical Philosophy*, 145, September/October 2007.

Stone, Alison, *An Introduction to Feminist Philosophy*, Polity, Cambridge, 2007.

Sulloway, Frank J., *Freud: Biologist of the Mind. Beyond the Psychoanalytic Legend*, Burnett Books, London, 1979.

Taaffe, Lauren K., *Aristophanes and Women*, Routledge, London and New York, 1993.

Taylor, A. E., *A Commentary on Plato's 'Timaeus'*, Clarendon Press, Oxford, 1928.

Taylor Merleau, Chloë, 'Bodies, Genders and Causation in Aristotle's Biological and Political Theory', *Ancient Philosophy*, Vol. 23, No. 1, Spring 2003.

Timaios of Locri, *On the Nature of the World and the Soul*, trans. Thomas H. Tobin, Scholars Press, Chico, California, 1985.

Tuana, Nancy, ed., *Feminist Interpretations of Plato*, Pennsylvania State University Press, Pennsylvania, 1994.

Van Haute, Philippe, *Against Adaptation: Lacan's Subversion of the Subject*, trans. Paul Crowe and Miranda Vankerk, The Other Press, New York, 2002.

Verhaeghe, Paul, *Beyond Gender: From Subject to Drive*, The Other Press, New York, 2001.

Vlastos, Gregory, *Platonic Studies*, Princeton University Press, Princeton NJ, 1981.

Vlastos, Gregory, 'Was Plato a Feminist?', in Tuana, ed., *Feminist Interpretations of Plato*.

Ward, Julie K., ed., *Feminism and Ancient Philosophy*, Routledge, New York and London, 1996.

Williams, Bernard, *Shame and Necessity*, University of California Press, Berkeley, 1993.

Wilson Nightingale, Andrea, *Genres in Dialogue: Plato and the Construct of Philosophy*, Cambridge University Press, Cambridge, 1995.

Winkler, John J., *The Constraints of Desire: The Anthropology of Sex and Gender in Ancient Greece*, Routledge, London and New York, 1990.

Žižek, Slavoj, 'Otto Weininger, or, "Woman Doesn't Exist" ', *New Formations, Lacan and Love*, Vol. 23, Summer 1994.

Žižek, Slavoj, *The Ticklish Subject: The Absent Centre of Political Ontology*, Verso, London and New York, 2000.

Žižek, Slavoj, *How to Read Lacan*, Granta, London, 2006.

Index